Neenah and Menasha

Twin Cities of the Fox Valley

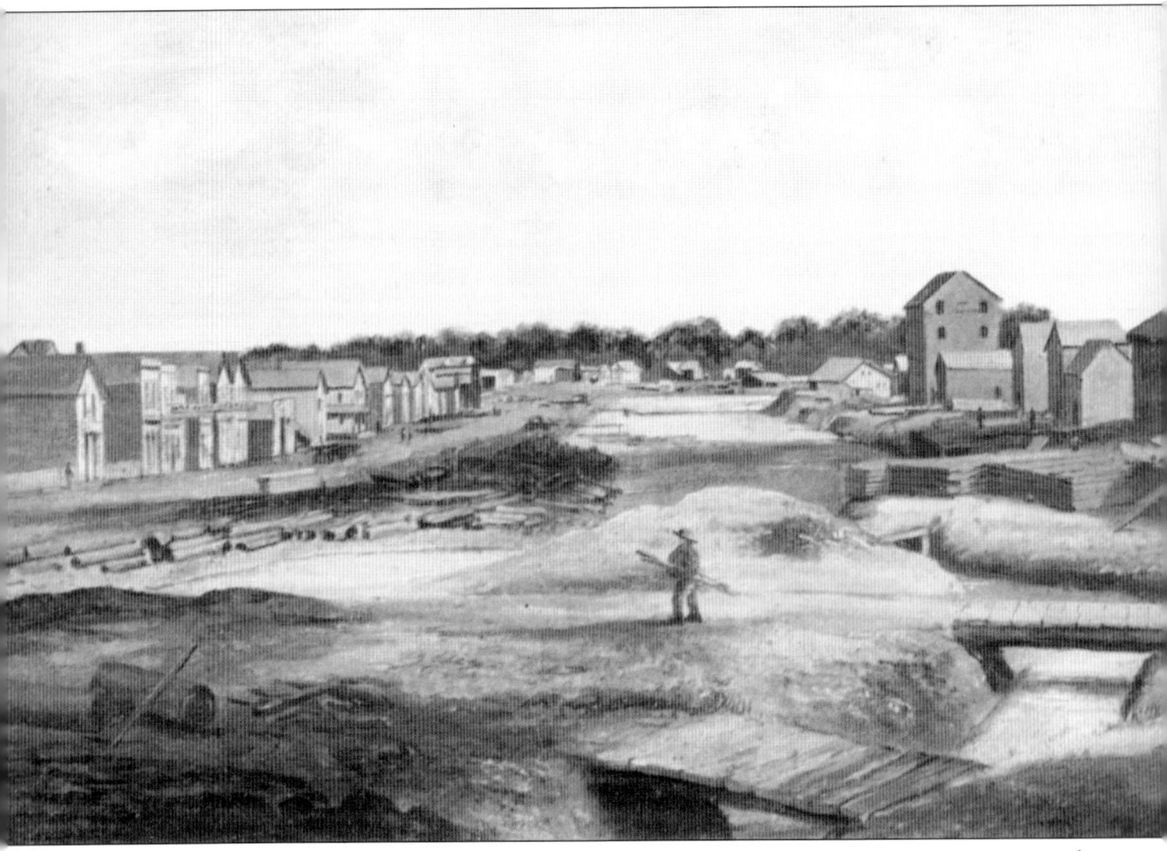

This 1856 painting by Samuel Brookes and Thomas Stevenson shows Water Street in Menasha and is titled *Fox River and Doty Island*. The then village of Menasha and site of the present-day marina are on the left, and the Menasha Wooden Ware is on the right. The Fox River is featured prominently with logs floating downstream, raw material for the wood products factories. Doty Island is to the right. This is one of a series of paintings commissioned by Morgan L. Martin, a Wisconsin legislator, in 1855–1856 to document the improvements in the Fox River–Wisconsin River waterway. Prints of this work were for sale when the 1986 marina opened in downtown Menasha. (Author's collection.)

On the Front Cover: This postcard shows downtown Menasha on a sunny day around 1958. Seen from the vantage point of the city square, this thriving hub of city commerce boasted two banks, four pharmacies, and an assortment of clothing, shoe, and appliance stores. The Hotel Menasha was on the corner of Main and Mill Streets in the heart of downtown. (Author's collection.)

On the Back Cover: Highlighting the boat landing at Neenah's Riverside Park, this postcard dates from 1914 to 1918. Excursion steamers plied their trade along the Fox River and Lake Winnebago, taking their passengers across the lake to the village of Clifton (better known today as High Cliff) and Stockbridge or down to Oshkosh or Fond du Lac. (Author's collection.)

POSTCARD HISTORY SERIES

Neenah and Menasha

Twin Cities of the Fox Valley

David Galassie

ARCADIA PUBLISHING

ISBN 978-1-4671-2826-1

Published by Arcadia Publishing
Charleston, South Carolina

Printed in the United States of America

Library of Congress Control Number: 2017963156

For all general information contact Arcadia Publishing at:
Telephone 843-853-2070
Fax 843-853-0044
E-mail sales@arcadiapublishing.com
For customer service and orders:
Toll-Free 1-888-313-2665

Visit us on the Internet at www.arcadiapublishing.com

To Teresa, as always, a source of inspiration and
a constant supporter of my efforts.

Contents

ACKNOWLEDGMENTS

Thank you to my wife, Teresa, for indulging my passion for the Fox Valley and especially Menasha.

A special thank-you to Steve Krueger, a fellow author at Arcadia and Menasha historian. His wisdom and knowledge of Menasha history aided me tremendously.

Thanks to the Neenah and Menasha Historical Societies for their continued commitment to preserving the Twin Cities' history and their tireless enthusiasm in sharing Neenah and Menasha's unique stories with others

I am indebted to the great editors at Arcadia Publishing, particularly Jeff Ruetsche, Midwest editor, who enthused over my proposal to create a postcard history of the Twin Cities, and to Stacia Bannerman, who nurtured it to fruition. Your generous help throughout this process helped to realize this dream.

Responsibility for the final text, including any factual errors or omissions, rests solely with the author.

Unless otherwise noted, all images appear courtesy of the author.

INTRODUCTION

It used to be that the stereotypical response to announcing a vacation was "Send me a postcard!" This usually meant requisite visits to hotel gift shops and souvenir stands while on those trips to satisfy our friends and, also, vain attempts to supplement woefully inadequate snapshots and home movies taken by a shaky hand using the latest Kodak Instamatic camera. I can still hear my mother saying, "Why don't we pick out some nice postcards in case the photos don't turn out?" Many times, she was dead right, because unlike some families who owned expensive 35-millimeter cameras using Kodachrome slide film, or who took Super 8 home movies, we were relegated to using an old square-format c. 1950 Kodak Brownie. This camera had no zoom lens, no ability to set exposure times, and no ability to open or close the lens aperture to adjust the light. The best we could do was hold the thing waist high, ensure the sun was at our backs, press the button, and hope for the best! I absolutely hated that camera. But for all its inefficiencies, it led me to a great appreciation of the picture postcard.

Several years ago, I wrote *Menasha*, part of this publisher's Images of America series. I tried to tell the story of Menasha from its beginnings as a village in the 1840s to today, presenting its history in an array of photographs, maps, drawings, and in many cases, postcards. In doing my research, I found a vast collection of photographic evidence of the city's history, courtesy of the Menasha Public Library and Menasha Historical Society, and eagerly showcased it in the book. But what really captivated my interest was discovering a remarkable number of picture postcards on the market that illustrated Menasha's history. I quickly became an avid collector, as the postcards supplemented my enjoyment and understanding of the time period and helped to illustrate those eras in ways I could not often find in the history books. My enjoyment was not limited to admiring the images and photographs that showcased street scenes and long-gone businesses and modes of transportation but also involved delving into the written messages on the backs, which often gave information the pictures themselves could not provide. Heartfelt communications from mothers to their children or husbands to their wives that commented on important family matters or mundane details like the weather were all in evidence. Sadly, this book cannot allow me to showcase those homespun missives, so the postcards' imagery will have to suffice to advance the narrative.

For those who may not know the story of the Twin Cities, Neenah and Menasha grew out of a mission to the Native Americans on Doty Island in the 1830s. The federal government established a settlement in an area of present-day Neenah near what is now East Wisconsin Avenue. In time, the mission failed, and the government entered into a treaty in which the Menominee sold their rights to the land. Various alliances between the Reed brothers, Harrison (Neenah) and Curtis (Menasha), and Gov. James D. Doty led to the founding of two separate villages, largely over the building of a canal to harness the waterpower of the Fox River. As it turned out, canals were built on both sides of the Fox, and this harnessing of the waterpower led to industrial development for both villages, initially in flour and sawmills. Later, after the flour trade died out, these entrepreneurs turned their attention to papermaking, which become the longest-lasting legacy of both cities.

So, why tell the story of a couple of paper mill towns via postcards? Well, postcards were, essentially, the text messages of the past—simple cards with handwritten messages, sent for a penny via the US Postal Service, no envelope required, no stationery to fuss with. Simply write on the card, address it, and mail it off. Sometime later, around 1871, an enterprising individual in Europe thought up the innovative idea to pair the postcard with a photograph or other image to the backs of those cards. And with that breakthrough, they became the Instagram of their time. As with many revolutionary ideas, Europe was at the forefront of picture postcards; it took the United States another 20 years to finally get into the swing of things. But in the late 19th and early 20th centuries, postcards' popularity in the United States far eclipsed anyone's expectations, and sending and collecting postcards became a craze for many years, until World War I's mail restrictions to and from Europe brought things to a standstill. After the war, telephones became increasingly prevalent in households and evolved into a more convenient means to stay in touch. Still, postcards endured, especially as souvenirs of big events such as world's fairs and as an advertising medium for hotels and restaurants and roadside attractions. Postcards' durability and physical beauty provide a concrete and tangible record of the social norms, historical structures, and events of their time period in ways a text or an online image cannot. Like a book, you can hold it in your hand.

One of the most indispensable types of postcards to students of history are those known as real-photo postcards, or RPPCs. An RPPC is especially valuable in that it documents an actual scene from the past, whereas a printed card is often an interpretation of how that particular scene appeared and may contain errors or exaggerations. Because of this difference, you will often in this book see many examples of the same building or park or street scene with minor variances, depending upon the composer's point of view. The advantage of the RPPC is clear: it is what is advertised by its name, a real photograph. Real-photo postcards were first produced using the Kodak postcard camera in the early 1900s. The camera would take a picture and then provide a postcard-size negative, complete with a divided back and a place for postage. And with that, you could document your hometown, school, business, or even your home and send it anywhere. This book will feature a significant number of RPPCs, invaluable photographic records of days gone by.

But other types of postcards will be in evidence too, as postcards themselves evolved over time. From the earliest postcards, which contained messages on the front with the image, to the fancy rag-content cards that had a linen-like texture, to the latest chrome postcards with their glossy, colorful photographs, all of these types will represent Neenah or Menasha at some time in this narrative. I have made an effort to provide a broad swath across the Twin Cities, showcasing the obvious landmarks and, hopefully, some not too obvious ones. If I have failed to deliver your favorite, it is simply that some postcards are much rarer than others, and often quite difficult to obtain. My intention is to not shortchange any business, landmark, or other entity. I hope you enjoy.

One

Parks and Recreation

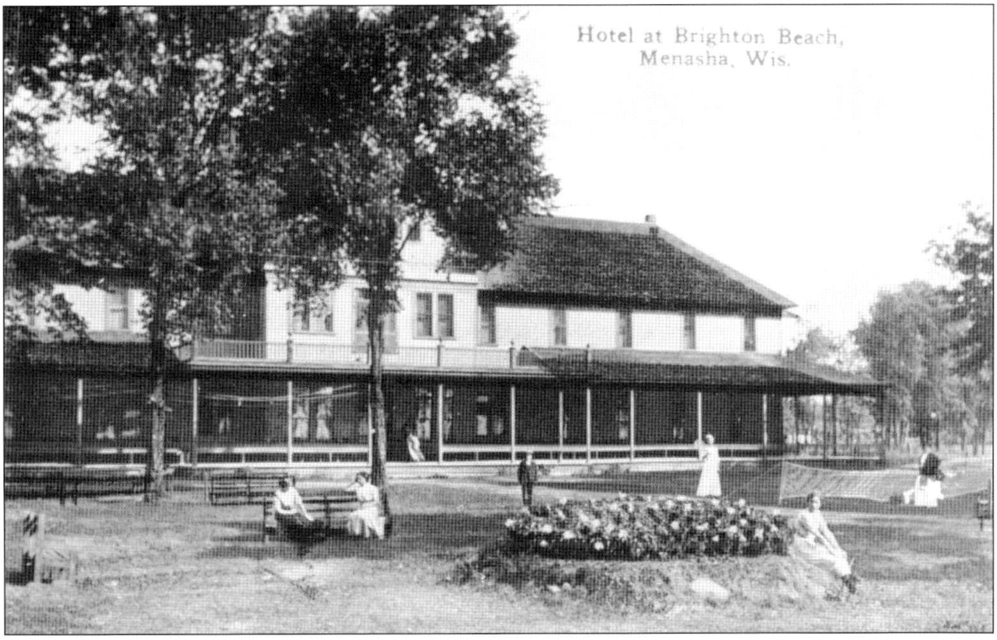

Brighton Beach was located at the end of Menasha's Third Street. This recreation area was developed around 1887 by Curtis Reed. In 1889, a two-story hotel was built, and the resort area then became an even more popular destination for picnics, band concerts, and other outdoor activities, appealing to both local residents and out-of-towners.

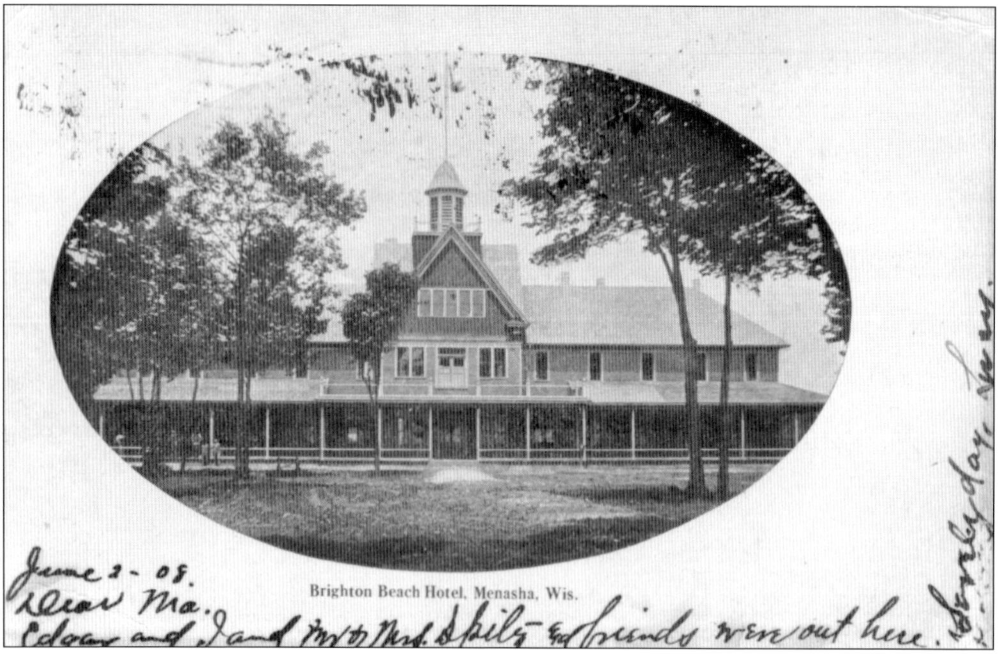

In spite of two renovations, the Brighton Beach property was sold off around 1927 and the hotel torn down after years of trying to compete with Waverly Beach's amusements, which even included a roller coaster at one time. A private home was constructed on the grounds, and in later years, the property was sold to a religious order of sisters for use as a retirement facility. The postcard above is from 1908 and features an actual photograph of the hotel. Notice the proper dresses the ladies are wearing in the postcard below, the only concessions to summer being the wearing of white and perhaps a parasol that one cannot detect in the illustration. There is no revealing swimwear here!

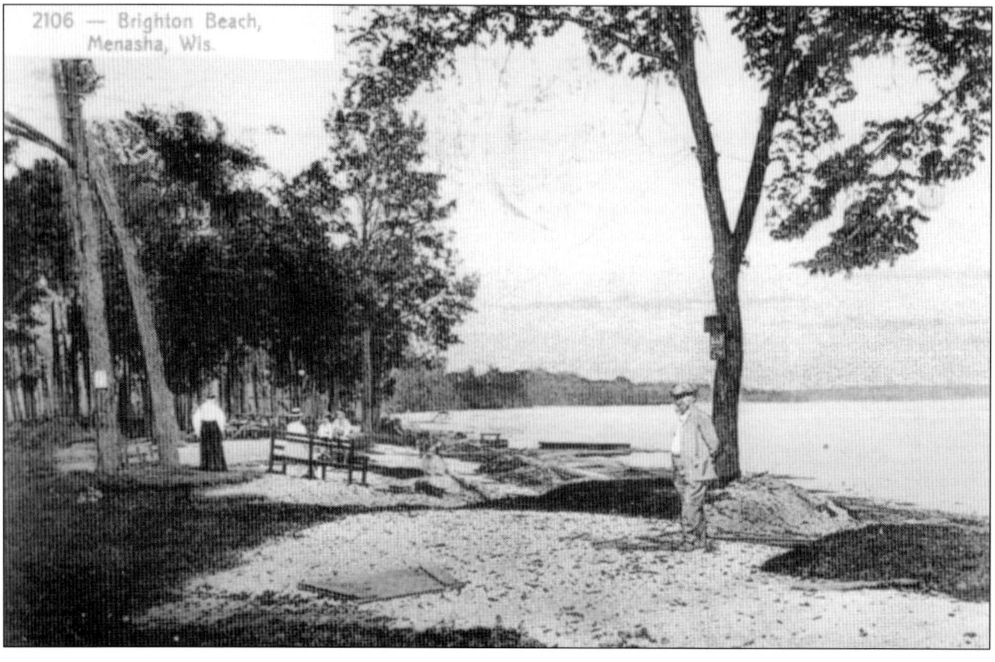

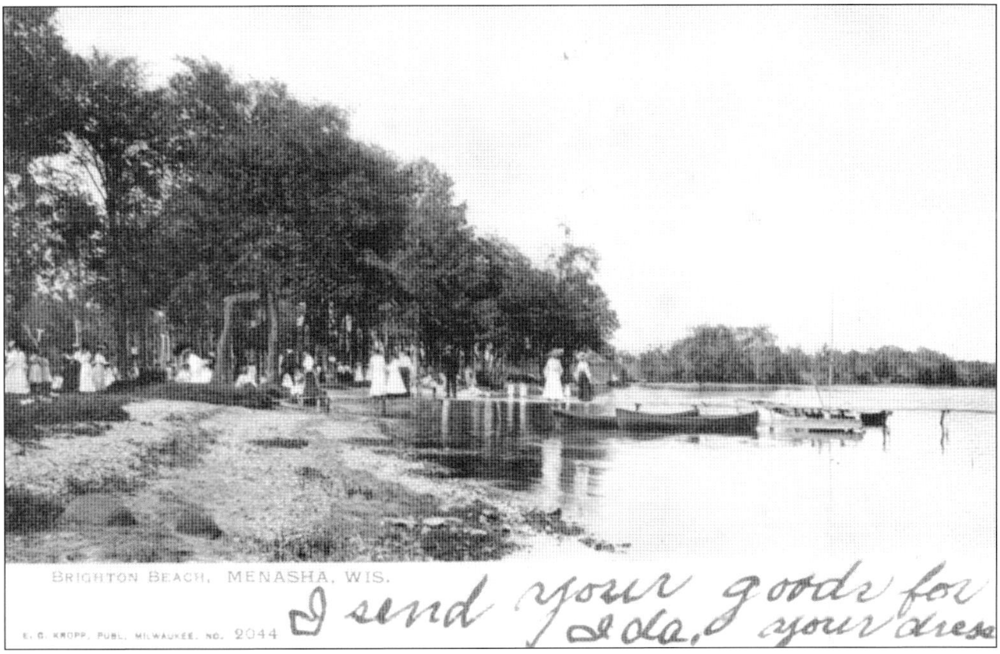

For all their good intentions at providing a safe and enjoyable atmosphere at Brighton Beach, in hindsight, one wonders why the patrons had to endure what looked to be such a rickety and haphazard dock to get to a boat. The whole setup looks to be a disaster in the making! A railing surely would have helped, with the ladies in their long skirts and dresses. But despite this perceived danger, this form of amusement was surprisingly affordable for the time. One could ride the streetcar from downtown Menasha one way for 5¢. The postcard above dates to 1906, and the one below is from 1908.

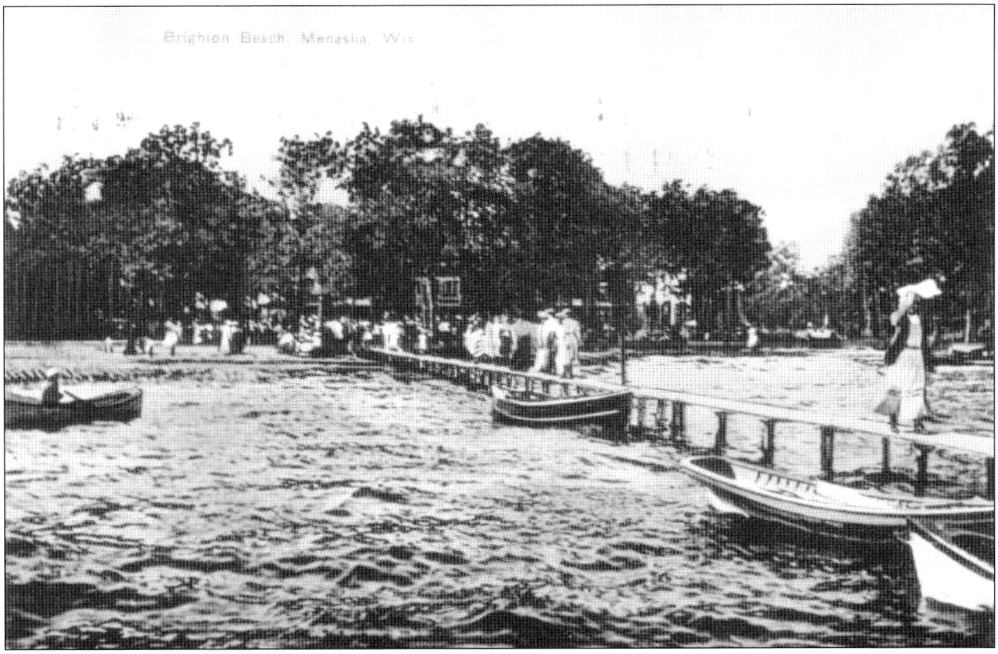

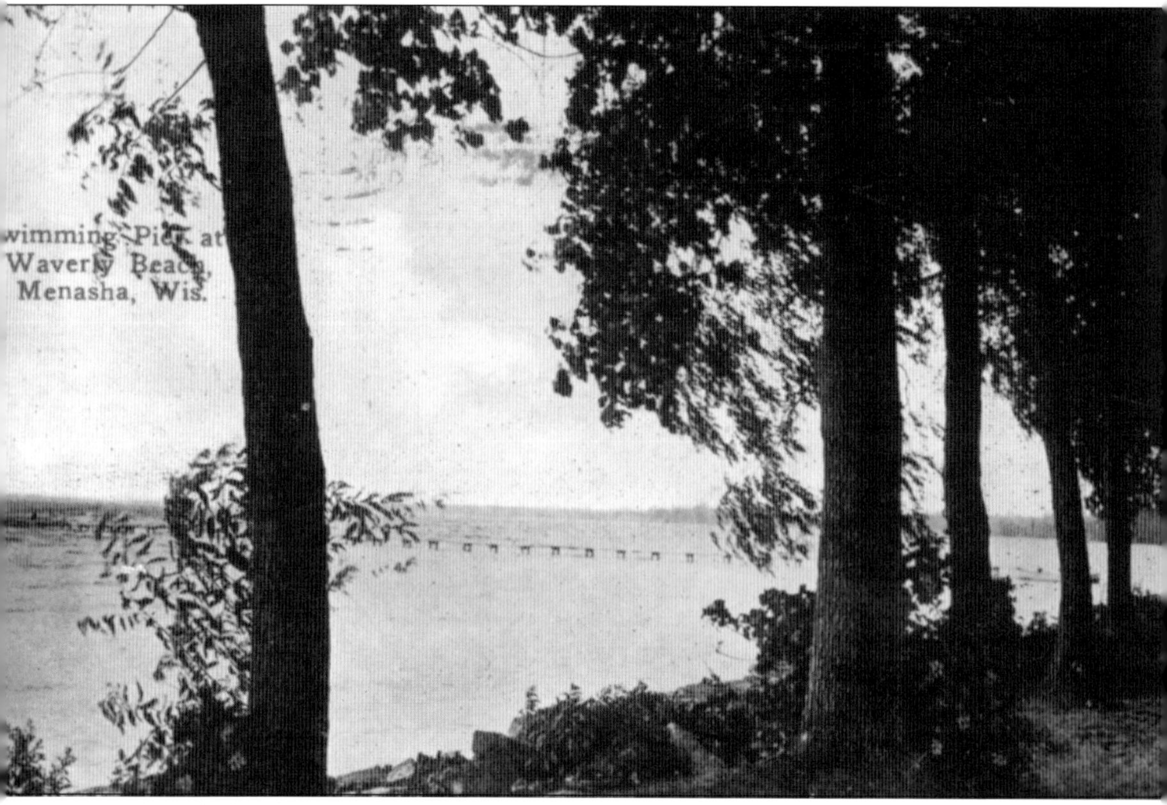

As described earlier, Waverly Beach was another entertainment venue for late 19th and early 20th century Menashans. Sometimes attributed to Appleton but just as often to Menasha, this entertainment outpost on the northern shore of Lake Winnebago, east of Menasha proper, was a go-to destination for many years. Started in 1886, the recreation area went through many phases to satisfy the entertainment-hungry consumer. Originally just a beach and bathing facility, it evolved to include a ballroom, a roller rink, a penny arcade, a shooting gallery, an amusement park featuring a wooden roller coaster known as the Jack Rabbit, and even a zoo over its lifetime. For a time in the 1920s and 1930s, it was a regular stop on the Big Band circuit for such luminaries as Benny Goodman, Harry James, and Tommy Dorsey. And as with Brighton Beach, this was another stop on the electric railway or streetcar, with a low toll of 10¢ for a round trip.

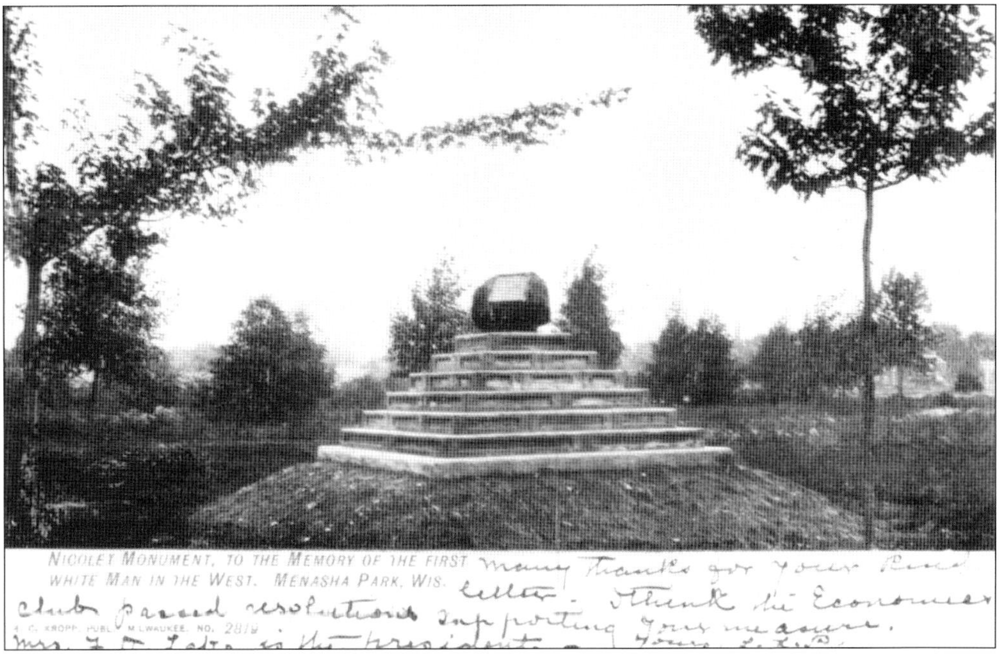

In 1634, Jean Nicolet, an emissary of Gov. Samuel de Champlain of New France (Quebec, Canada), landed at Red Banks on the shore of Green Bay. Nicolet expected to meet Asians on his voyage and donned an elaborate Oriental robe before landing. Brandishing two pistols, he fired into the air to impress upon the Winnebago Indians who met him that he was in authority. Later, after traveling down the Fox River, Nicolet came ashore near what is today's Smith Park. This monument sits in Smith Park and was provided by the Women's Club of Menasha in 1906. It is said to be made of basalt rock and is known as the "Winnebago Manitou Stone" or "Spirit Rock," as described in a 1909 issue of *Popular Mechanics*.

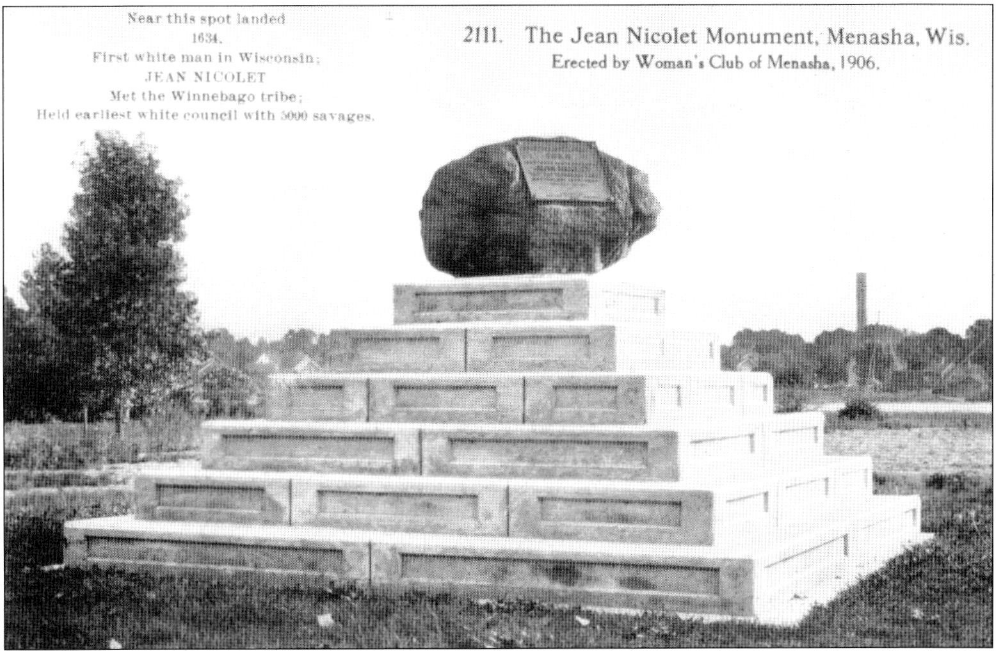

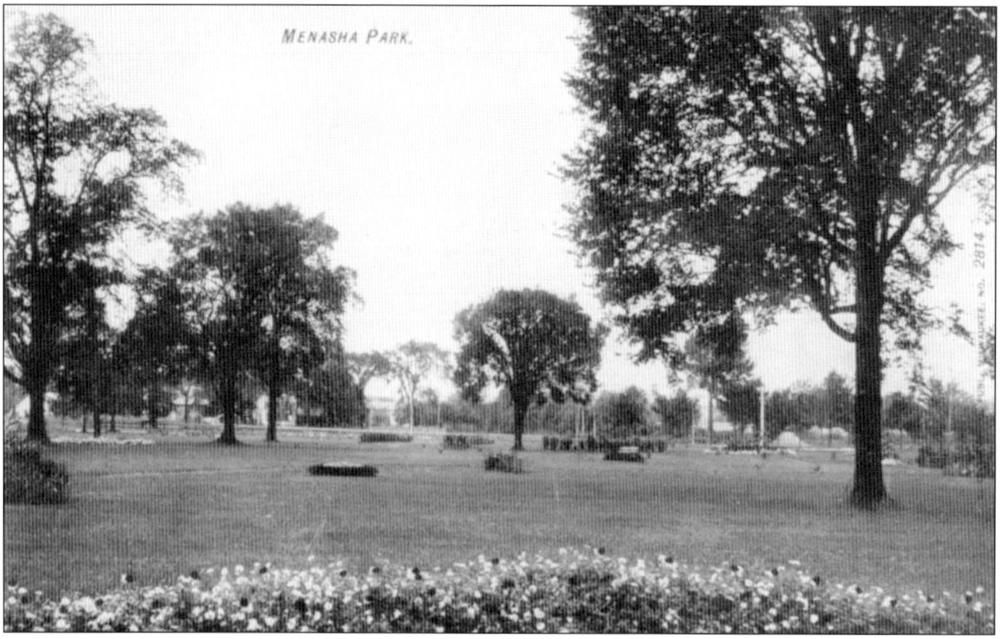

In the 1890s, Menasha Wooden Ware founder and city benefactor Elisha D. Smith attempted to attract Downer College, then located at Fox Lake, to move to Menasha. He was disappointed when the school's leadership decided to merge with Milwaukee Women's College and move to Milwaukee. Smith decided that the rejected 40 acres he had offered Downer should instead be offered to the city of Menasha to become a park. This donation was made in 1896, at about the same time as his offer to build the city a library. Many years later, Downer College merged with Lawrence University in Appleton.

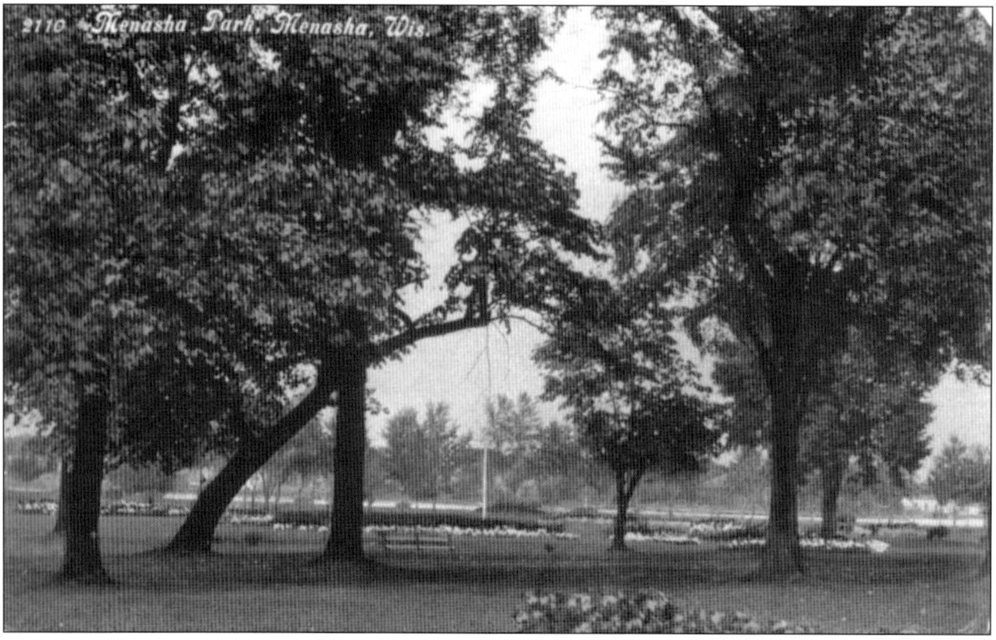

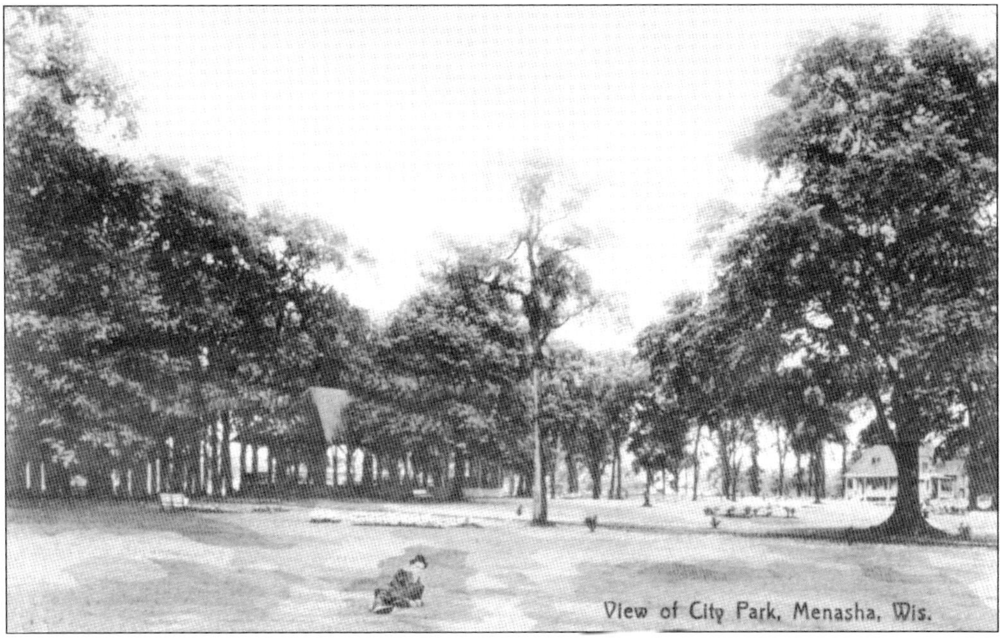

The heavily wooded property Smith had selected was located between "the Avenue" (Nicolet Boulevard) and Cleveland, Keyes, and Park Streets on Doty Island. Before the park development, Doty Island was, in part, quite undeveloped. The brush grew wild in the area, and hayfields even extended from Naymut Street to Cleveland Street. Along with the land, Smith had a pavilion constructed to encourage use of the park. A pious man, he stipulated that there be a strict ban on alcohol, circuses, gambling, sports, and dangerous machinery at the park. Of course, this ban also included Sundays, except for religious activities and temperance meetings. Originally known as "City Park" or "Menasha Park," it became Smith Park after his death.

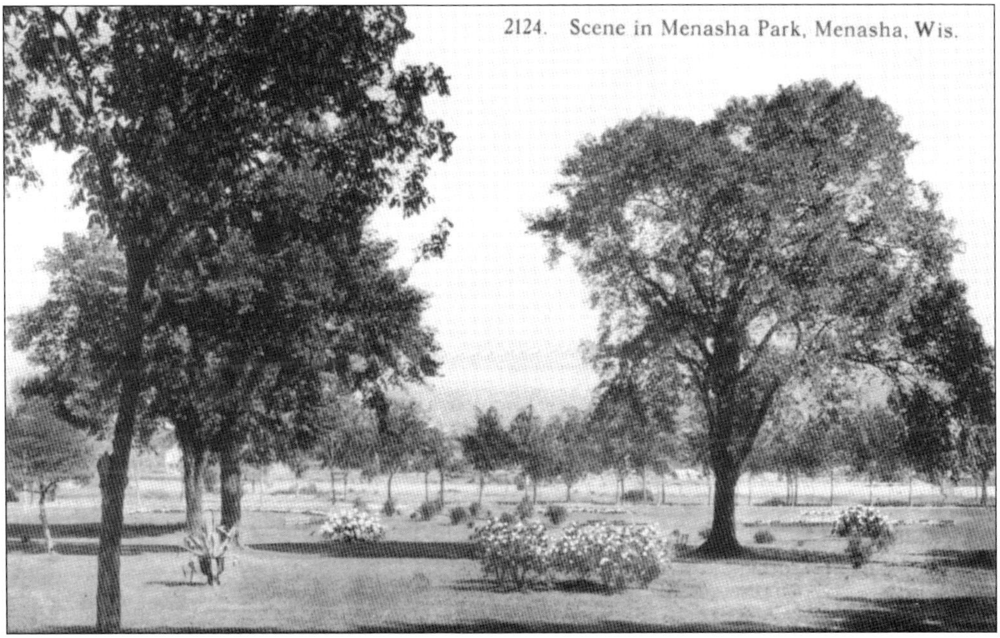

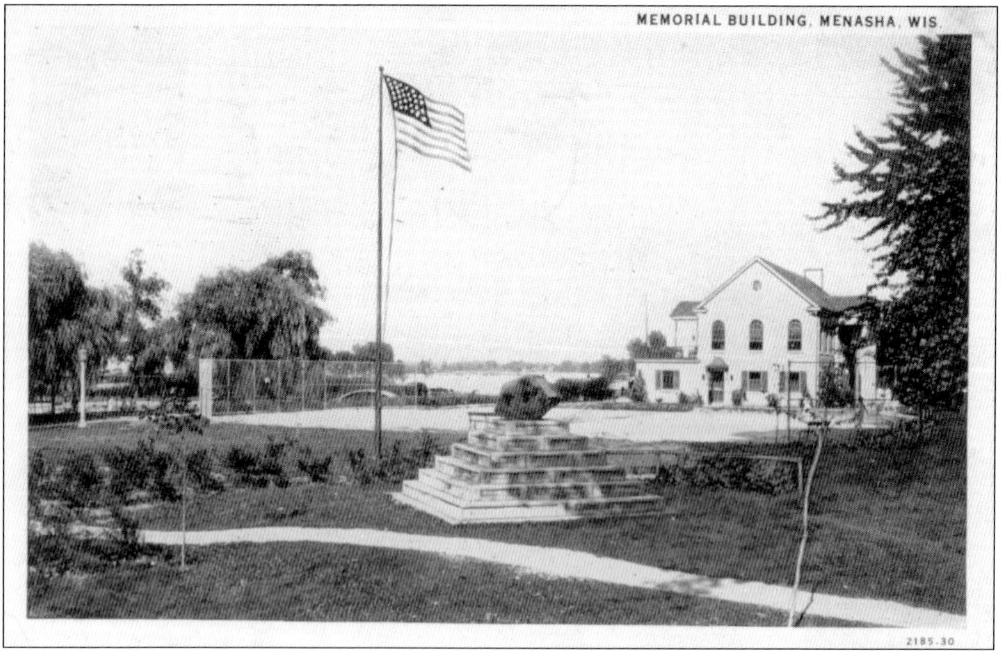

The Memorial Building, or "the Mem" as it was affectionately known to its users, was constructed in Smith Park in 1928 and is officially known as the Soldier and Sailor Memorial Building. It was dedicated on July 4, 1928, as a memorial to those who gave their lives in World War I, or as it was known then, the Great War. Local newspapers reported that over 20,000 visitors came through its doors to see it in person. The Colonial-style edifice, with four handsome columns flanking its entrance, has been many things over the years: a community centerpiece for park dances, changing rooms for swimmers, and classrooms for arts and crafts; in its current incarnation, it houses the city's historical society.

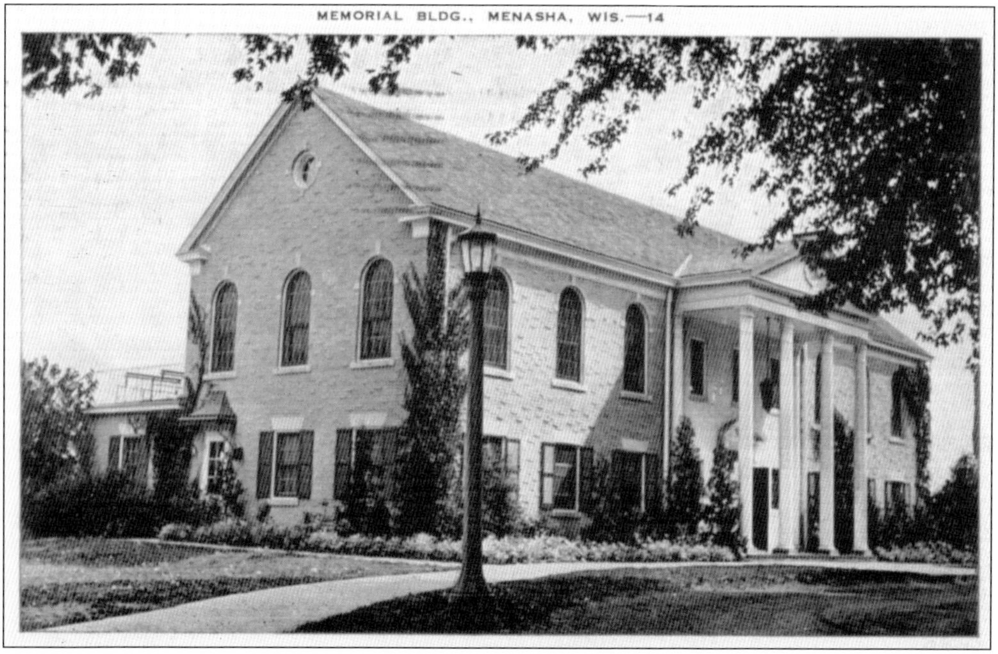

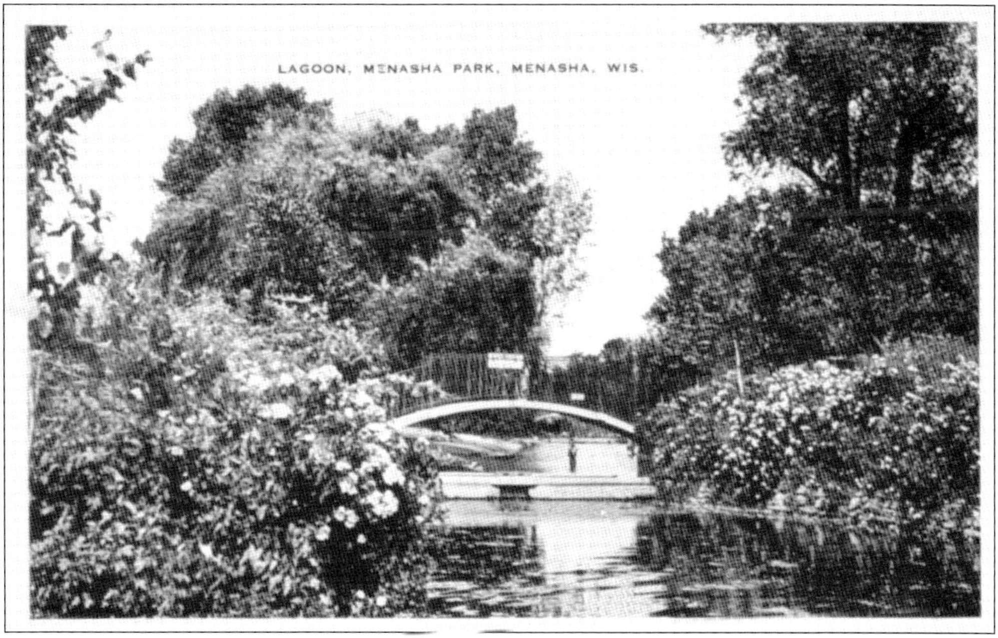

These two views provide a distinct contrast in postcard styles. The above image of what was known as "Picnic Island" is a 1930s–1940s linen postcard, whereas below is a 1958 chrome postcard. Until 2007, when the Isle of Valor was constructed, this was mostly a picturesque site for wedding photographers and a quiet place for contemplation. The Isle of Valor was constructed to honor Menasha's two Medal of Honor recipients, Kenneth Stumpf and the late Elmer J. Burr, and the other Menasha residents who exhibited bravery or valor in military or civilian circumstances. The centerpiece of the isle is a 10-foot monument flanked by plaques detailing the brave deeds of Stumpf and Burr.

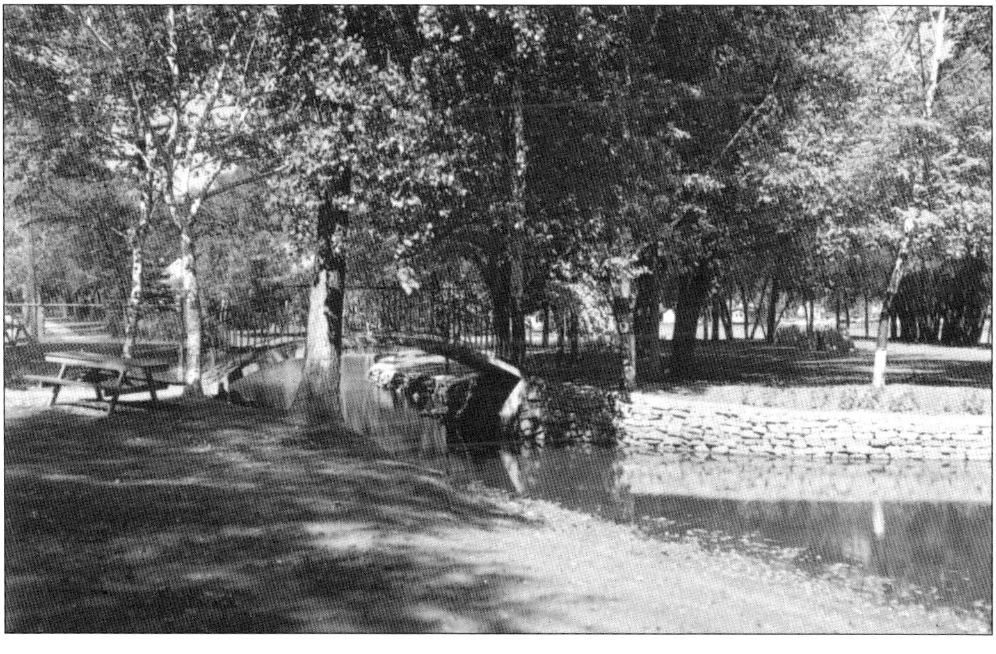

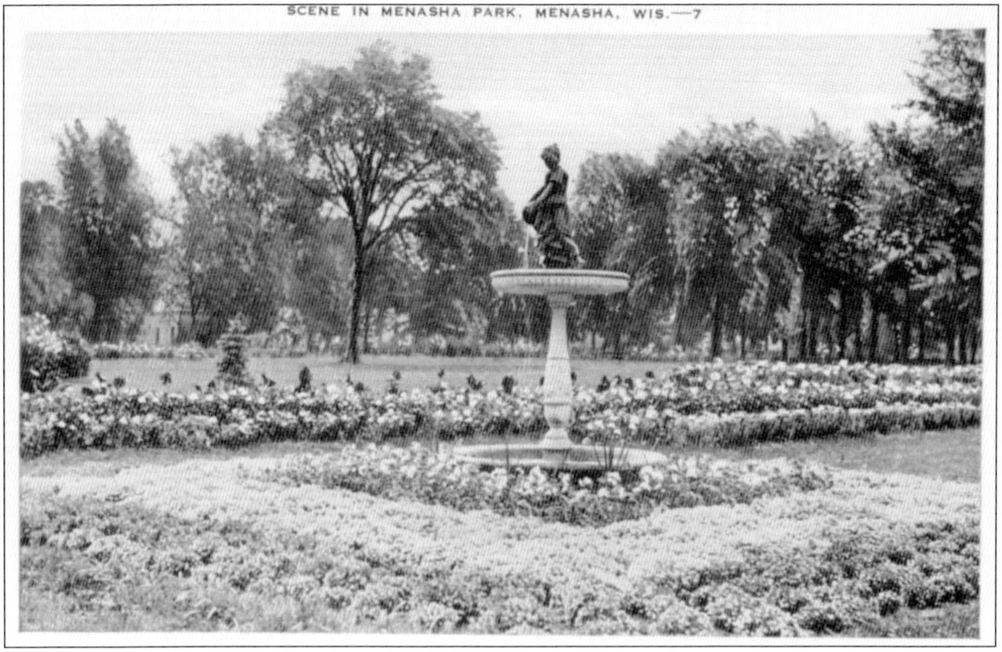

Pretty flower beds are the hallmark of what makes Smith Park a standout in the Fox Valley. Nearly 10,000 annuals bloom from early spring to late autumn each year. Elisha Smith personally selected the designer of Chicago's Lincoln Park, Olaf Benson, to design the gardens and walks within the new park, and when completed, it was the pride of Menasha. These two images represent two distinct eras in postcard collecting. The above image is indicative of the "white border" era of postcards, from approximately 1915 to 1930, whereas the image below represents the photochrome era, most likely the 1950s or later.

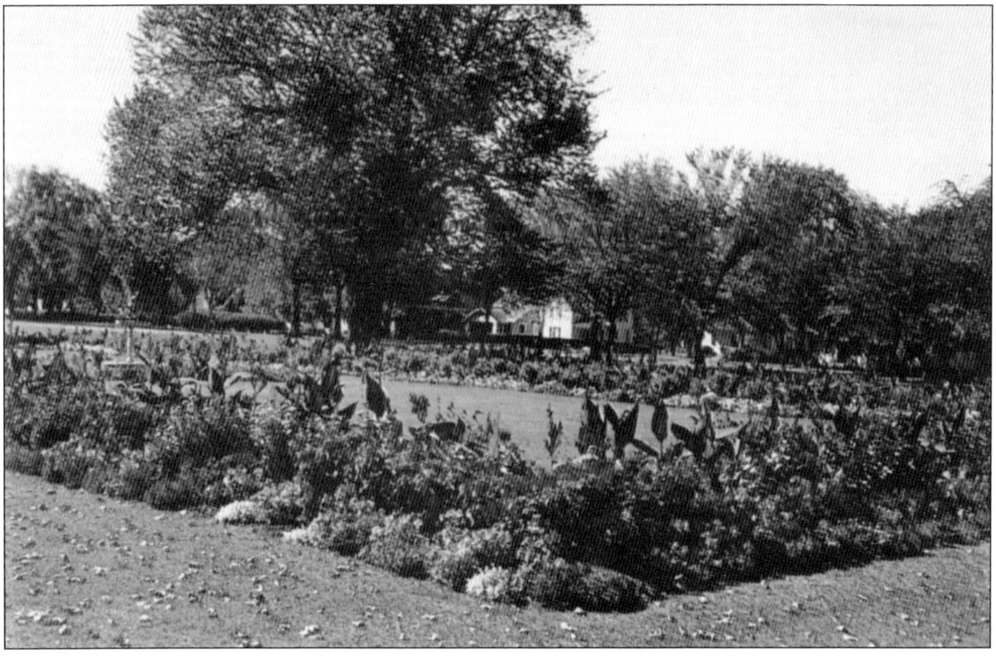

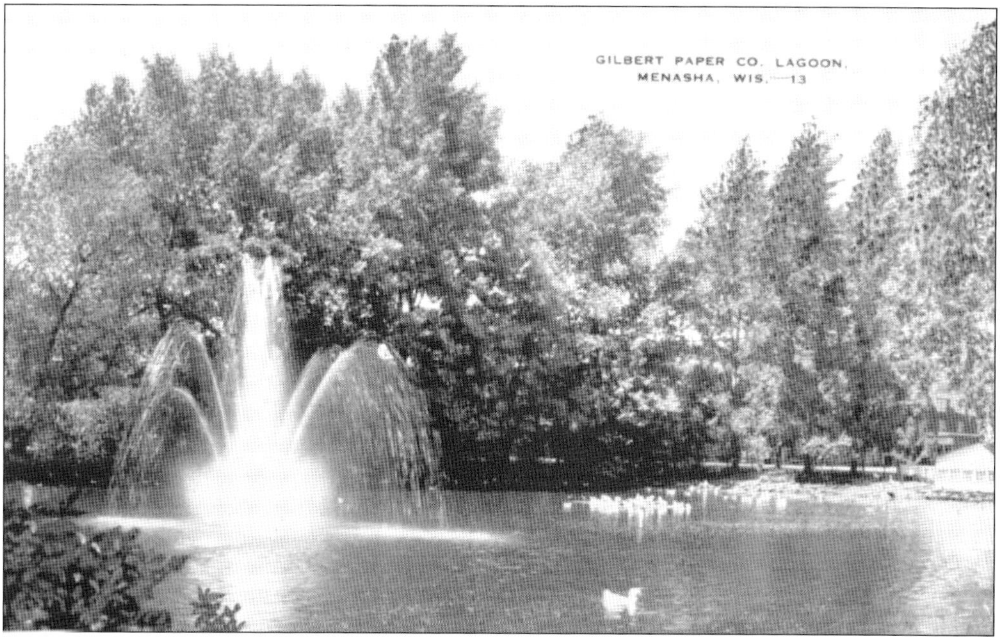

When completed in 1886, the Lawson Canal stretched nearly all the way from the end of River Way to the intersection of Ahnaip and Walnut Streets. Over the years, the length of the canal was reduced due to the construction of the Gilbert Paper Company. The canal ran parallel to Ahnaip Street, with only enough space for an occasional frame boathouse at its western extremity. Clipped by a Chicago & North Western Railway spur line after the turn of the 20th century, the canal was further reduced by the construction of the Gilbert Paper Company offices and machine shop in 1919. What remained became known as the Gilbert Pond. In 1920, the Gilbert Pond was landscaped and surrounded by various conifers and deciduous trees. At some time, a fountain was added. The pond became a year-round home for wild and domestic ducks and geese, numbering up to 500 at one point.

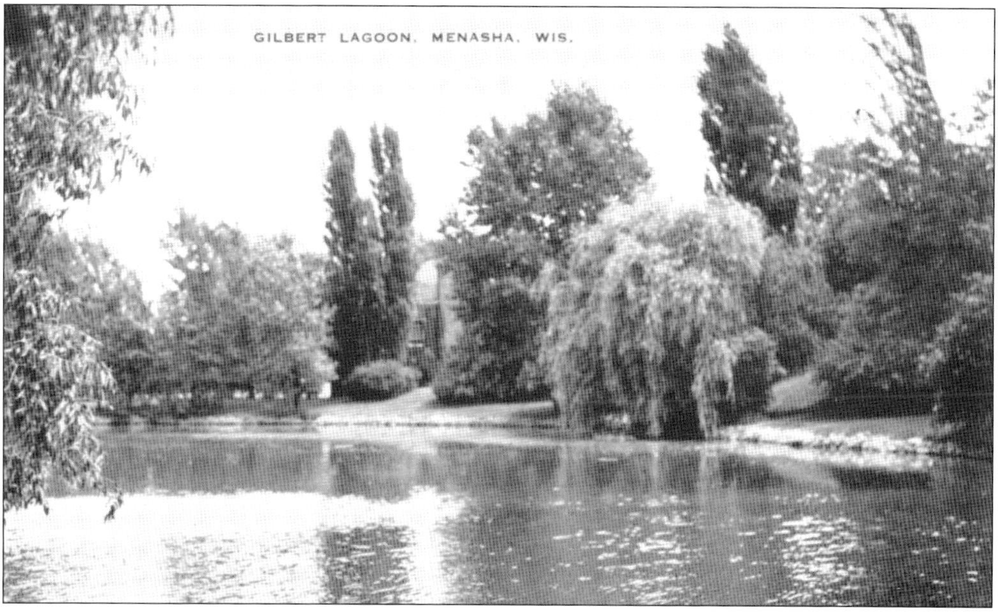

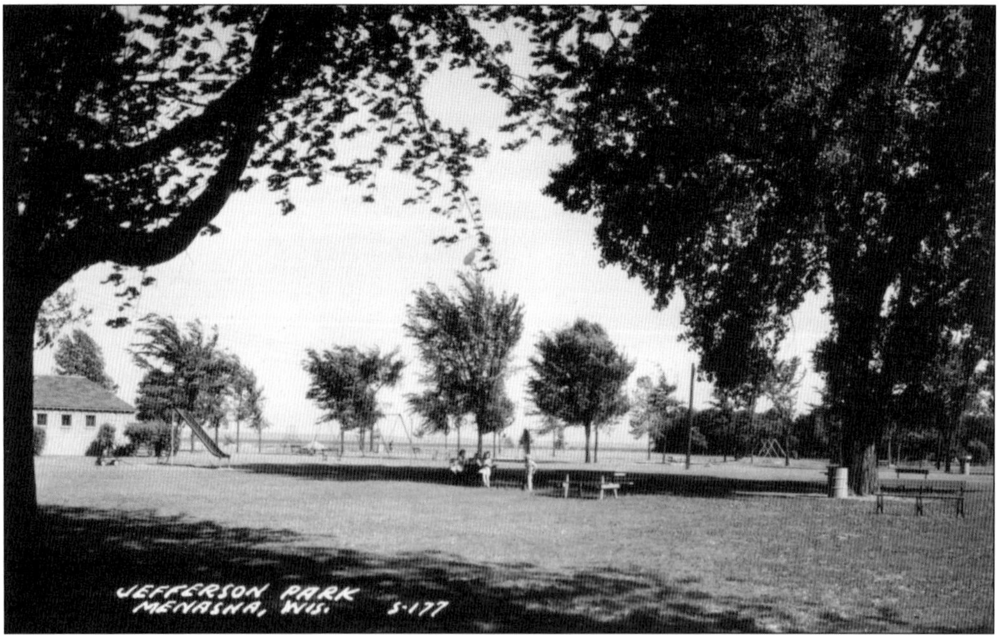

Jefferson Park was built in 1932 and 1933 as a Works Progress Administration project, Pres. Franklin Roosevelt's innovation to provide public works for the country as well as jobs during the Great Depression. Jefferson Park had the advantage of its proximity to Lake Winnebago and the Fox River to provide a striking park facility that is still envied to this day. Jefferson Elementary School, at the intersection of Second and Ice Streets, is adjacent to Jefferson Park. Completed in 1931 at a cost of $125,000, the school had been built at the urging of the city council to provide local employment during the Great Depression. Its unusual styling is categorized as Tudor Elizabethan Revival, and it would look as much at home in medieval England as it does in Menasha.

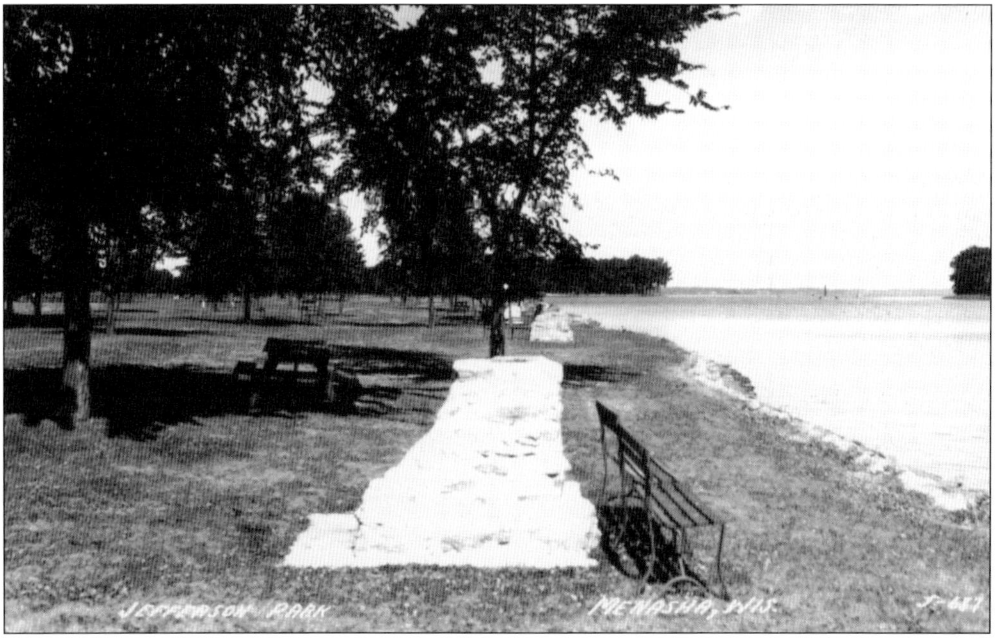

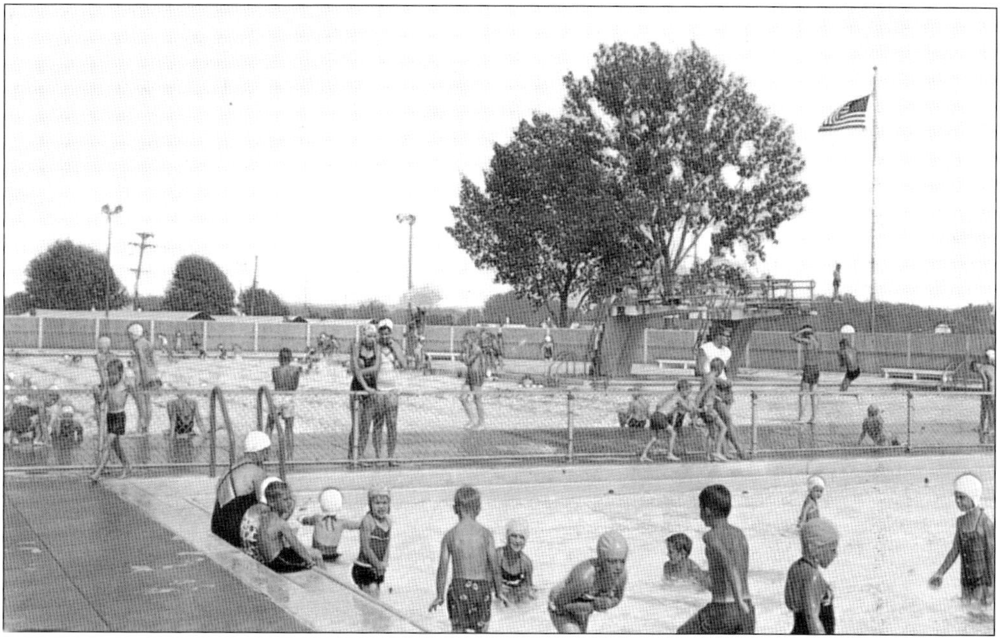

Located in Jefferson Park, the city swimming pool was dedicated on Memorial Day 1957. The *Oshkosh Daily Northwestern* of July 26, 1957, stated that "Capacity of the Menasha pool, when the two smaller pools are put into use, will be 1,300." Before completion of the pool, organized swimming was offered at Smith Park adjacent to the Memorial Building.

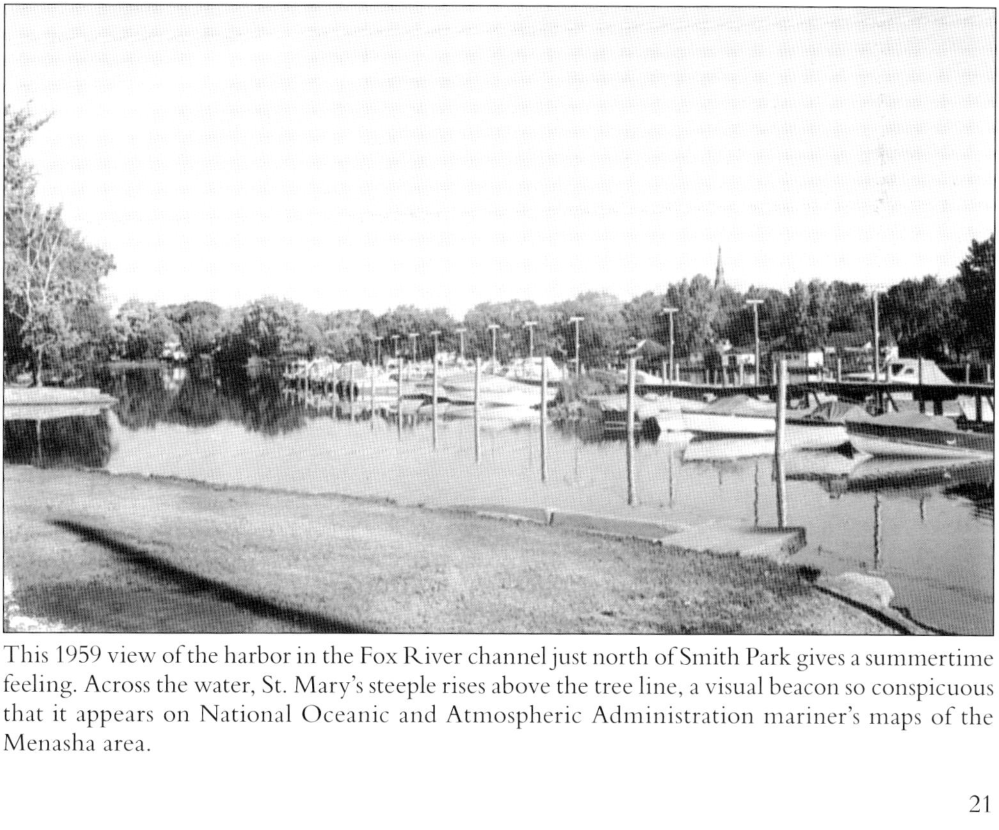

This 1959 view of the harbor in the Fox River channel just north of Smith Park gives a summertime feeling. Across the water, St. Mary's steeple rises above the tree line, a visual beacon so conspicuous that it appears on National Oceanic and Atmospheric Administration mariner's maps of the Menasha area.

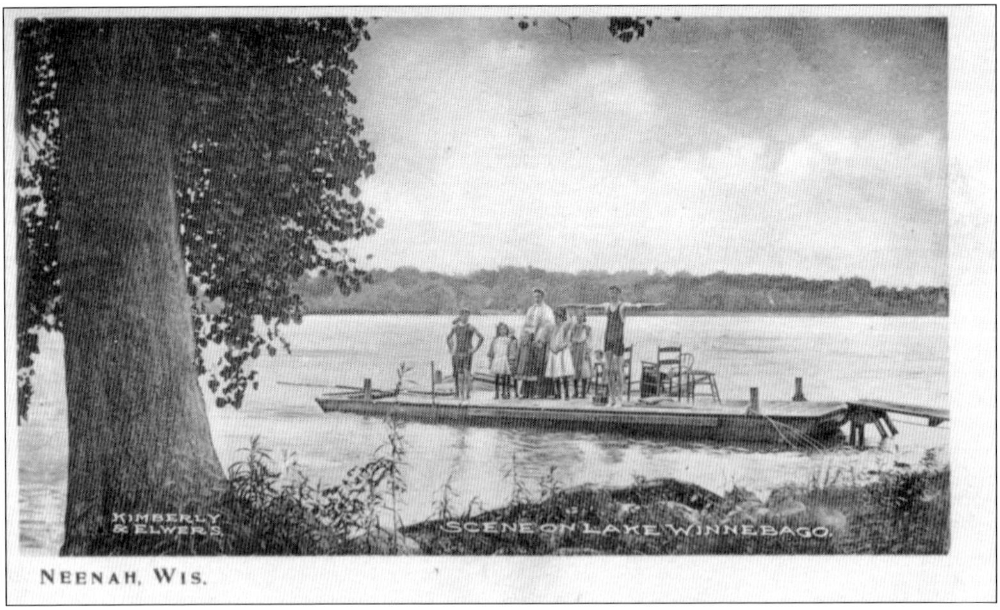

The name Kimberly & Elwers appears on these two postcards featuring scenic views of Neenah—a view of Lake Winnebago and an illustration of Riverside Park. Kimberly & Elwers was a pharmacy on Wisconsin Avenue, one partner of which belonged to the famous Kimberly family. The new popularity of postcards in the early 20th century brought a flurry of activity and new distribution systems for postcards to an eager populace. Soon enough, photographers cashed in on this newfound fad by representing printers who obtained deals with general stores, variety stores, five-and-dimes, pharmacies, and the like to put local attractions in postcard form.

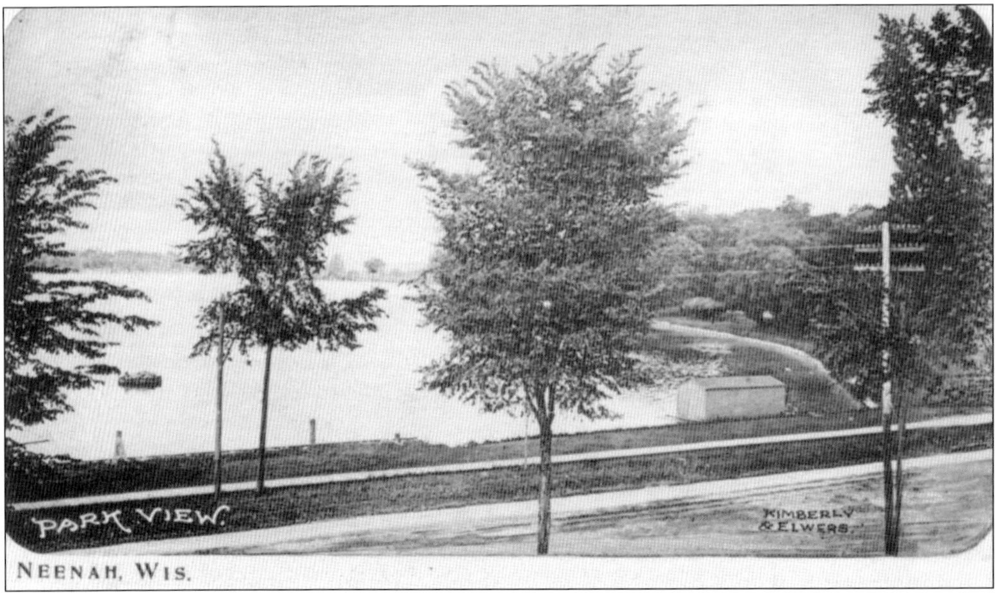

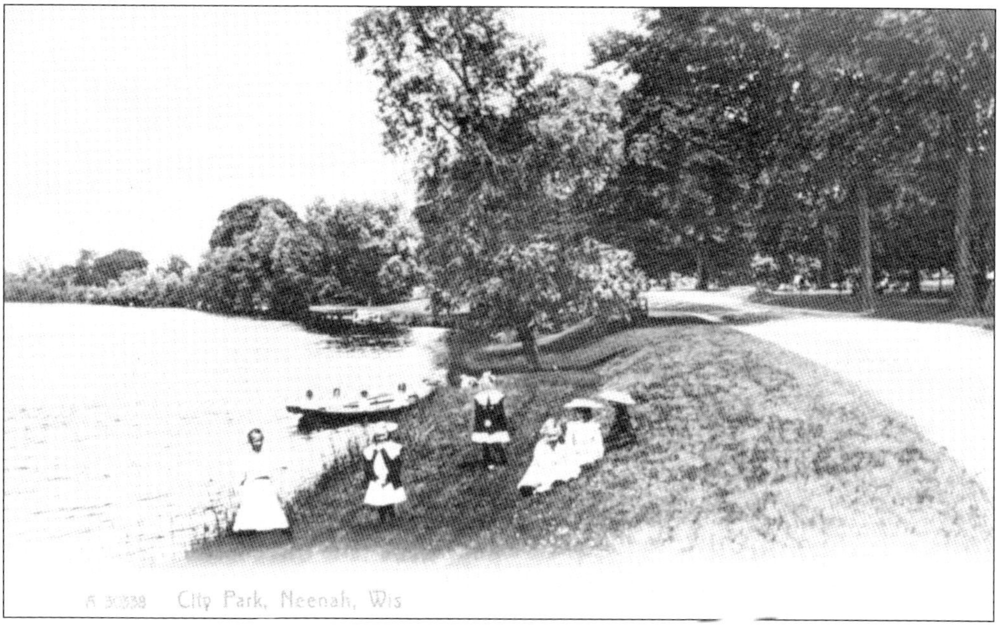

As will be seen throughout this postcard history of the Twin Cities—and especially in Neenah's case—boating, or more specifically yachting, has been a watchword in the community since the late 1850s—so much so that even the well-regarded history of Winnebago County by P.V. Lawson Jr. is chock-full of year-by-year yachting statistics of races won, prizes, and boat names attributed to the Neenah Yacht Club. But that does not even approach the subject of simple "rent a boat for the afternoon" recreational boating on a lazy Sunday at the park, some evidence of which is seen in the two views on this page.

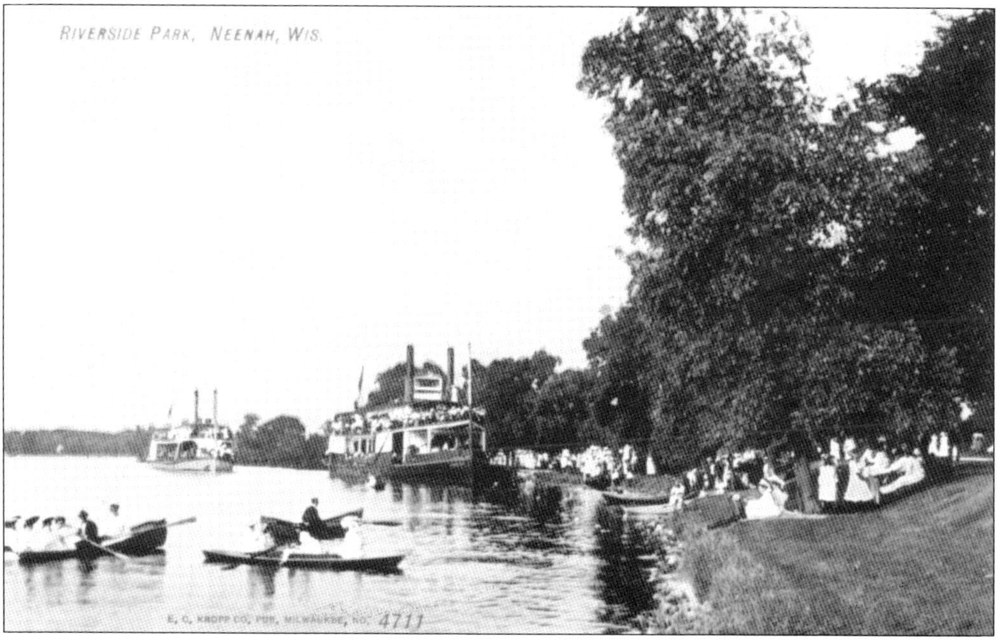

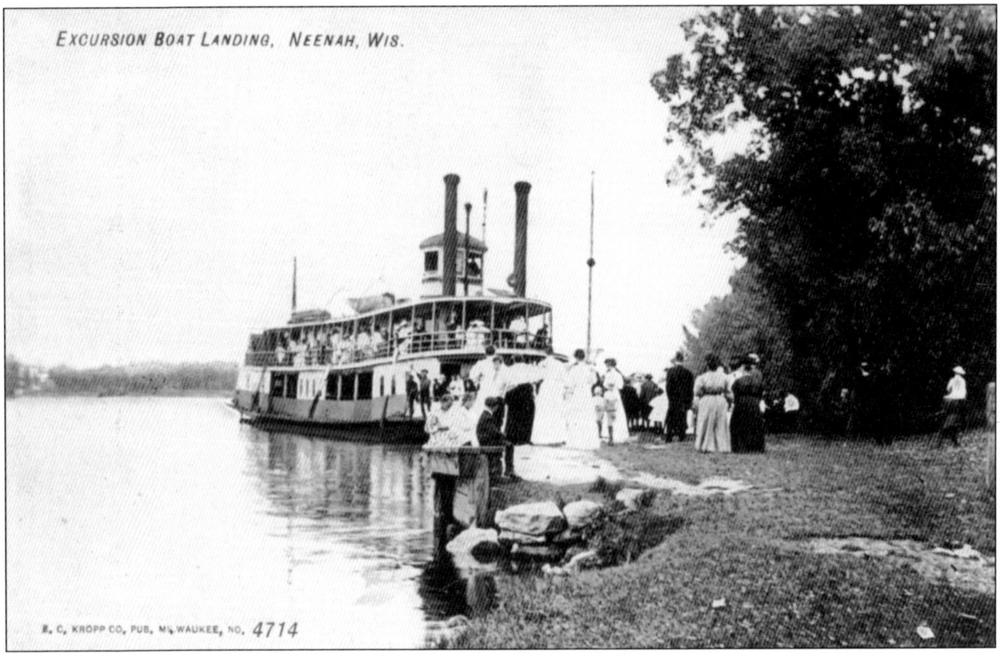

These two postcard views show the excursion boat landing at Riverside Park. From about 1856 until 1927, steamboats regularly plied their trade, traversing up and down Lake Winnebago and the Fox and Wolf Rivers. Until railroads became a reliable means of transport, the Fox River system was the major route from the Great Lakes to the Mississippi River, and steamboats were the vehicles of commerce. Excursion boats offered day trips to High Cliff, Stockbridge, and other destinations on the other side of the 10-mile width of Lake Winnebago, often for fares as low as 10¢. With a road system of muddy ruts and uneven surfaces, water travel was much more reliable.

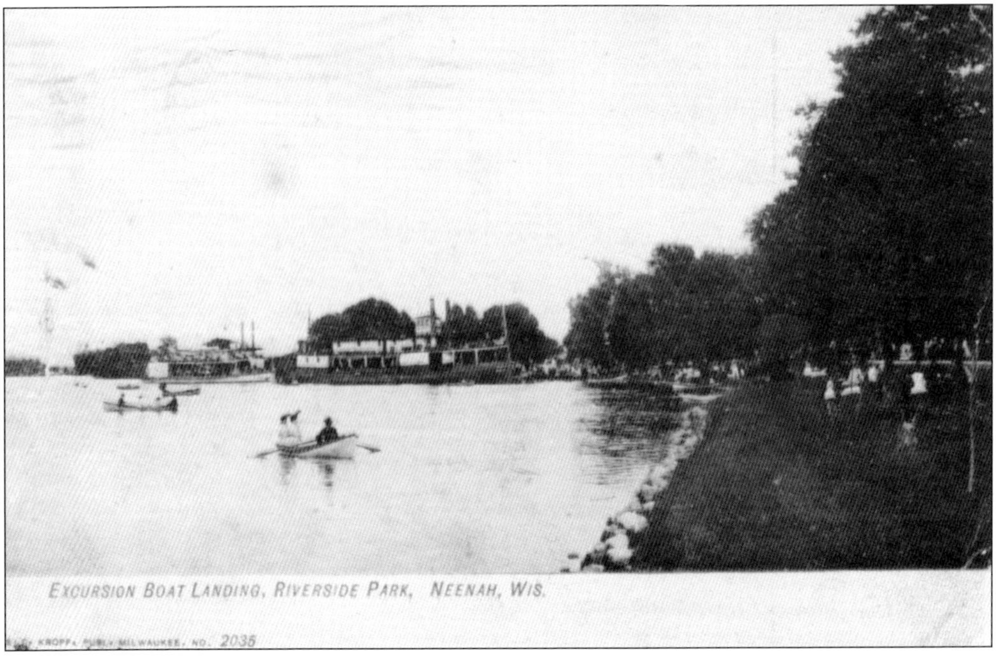

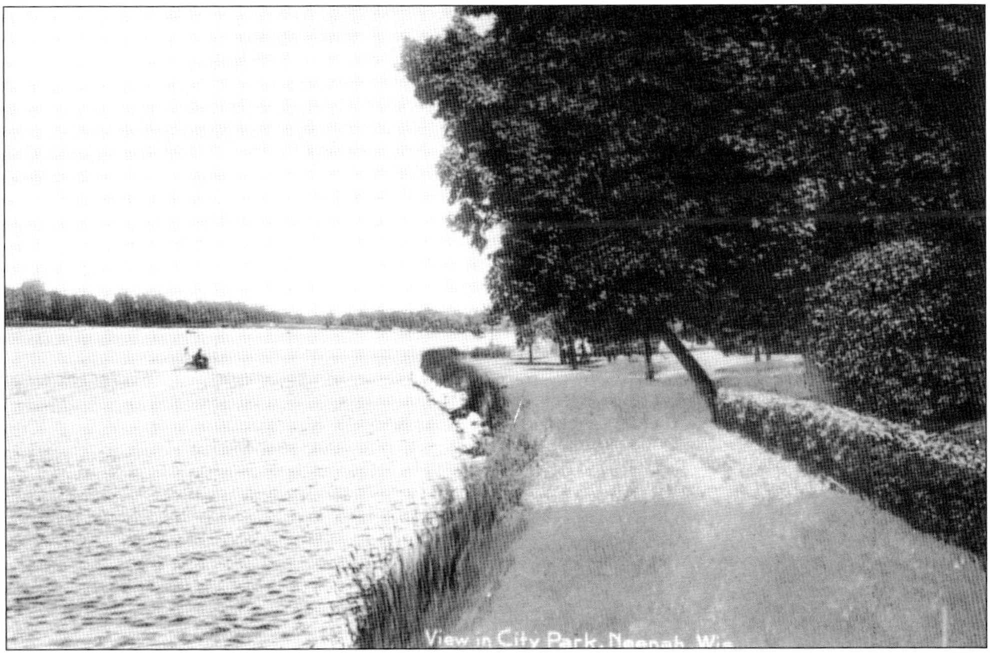

Riverside Park is featured in these two real-photo postcards. The land for the park was purchased by the then village of Neenah in 1872 and has a true history behind it. Though many records of the original Winnebago Rapids mission to the Indians have been lost over time, several of the original mission buildings as mapped in 1839 were on land now known as Riverside Park, beginning from the location of the Old Council Tree and running across the present-day East Wisconsin Avenue up to Doty Avenue. The intense beauty of the park, coupled with its picturesque location on the Fox, has made it a favorite of photographers for many years.

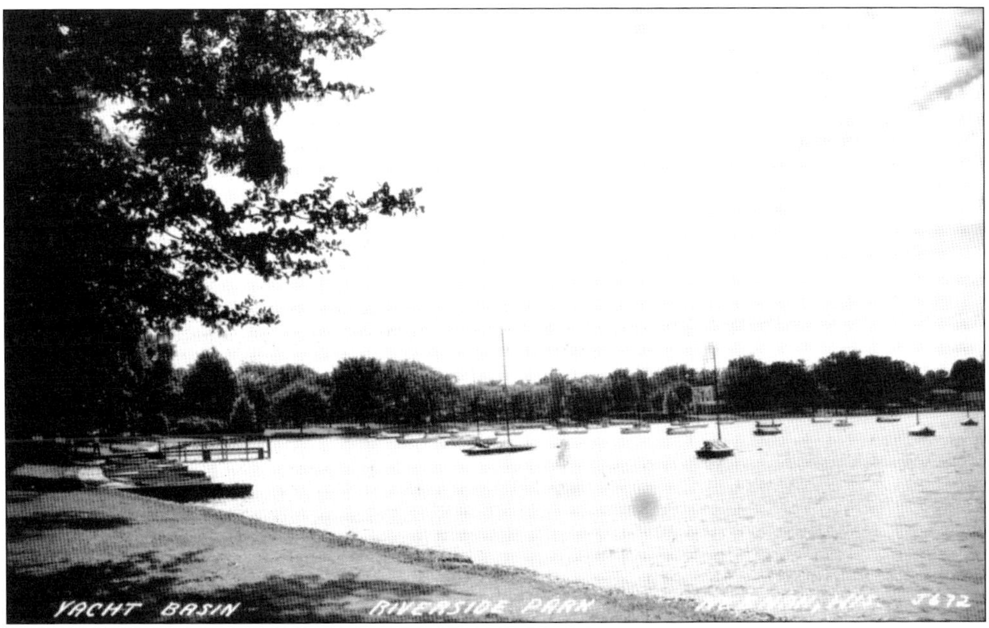

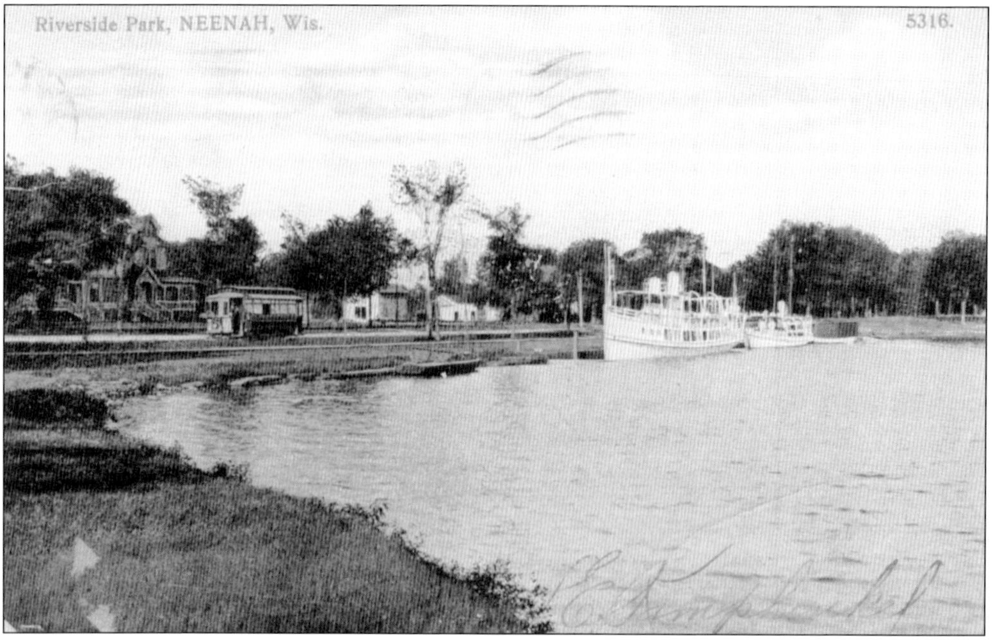

These two postcards show the same area of Riverside Park, though about 30 years apart. One can gauge the improvements to the park and the passage of time with the growth of trees lining Wisconsin Avenue. Most obvious in the view above is the streetcar traveling east on the avenue. From about 1898 to 1927, when the electric trolleys were abandoned in favor of buses, one could travel around the Fox Valley for pocket change. The Wisconsin Traction Light Heat & Power Company was the local trolley line. When the cost of mailing a letter was 3¢, a 5¢ trolley ride in 1918 was affordable. There was even an extended interurban railway that traveled between Neenah and Oshkosh, though one would expect higher rates, of course.

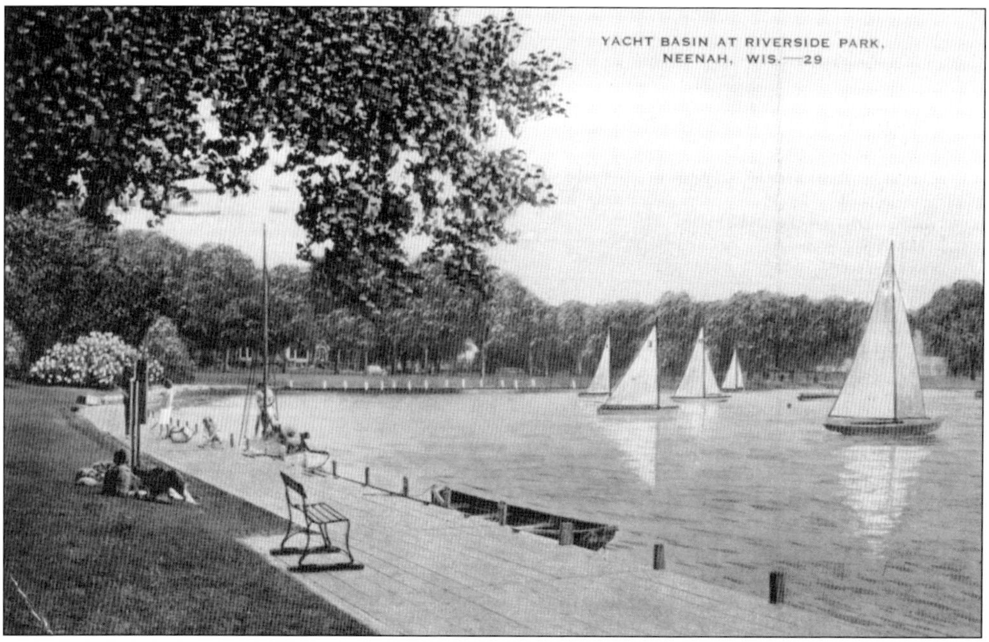

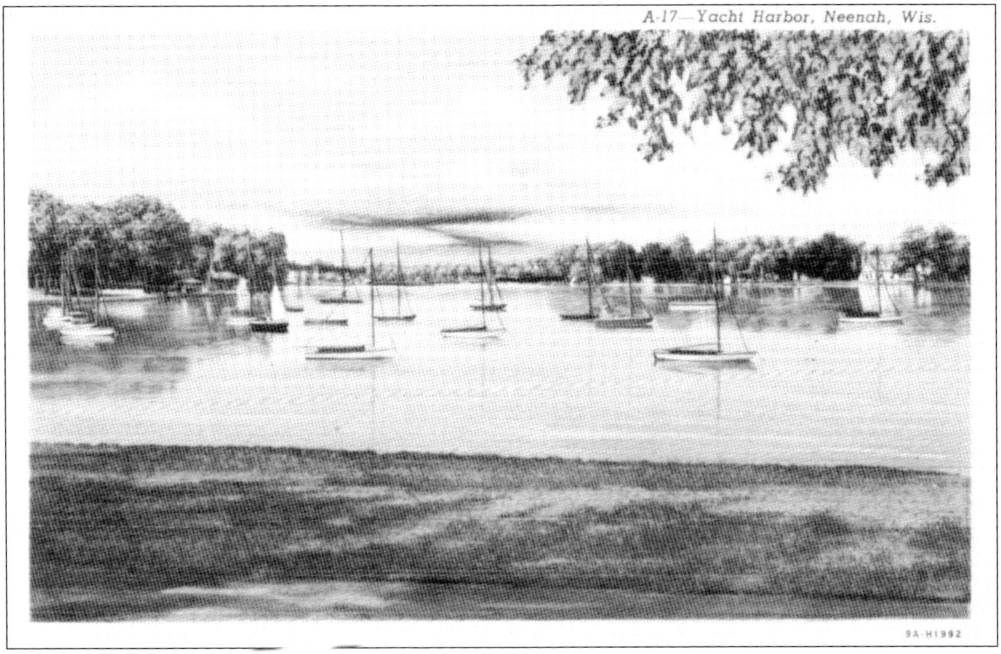

These two cards generally provide the same view, though as on the previous page, they are many years apart. Above is a linen postcard perhaps from the 1930s. Notice the absence of the Oak Street Bridge in the distance. The bridge was not built until 1949, in response to the horrendous traffic tie-ups on the Commercial Street–Washington Street corridor between the Twin Cities. With as many as nine railroad crossings along that route, lengthy delays were frequent and quite frustrating for the burgeoning auto usage after World War II. Below is an early 1960s photochrome card.

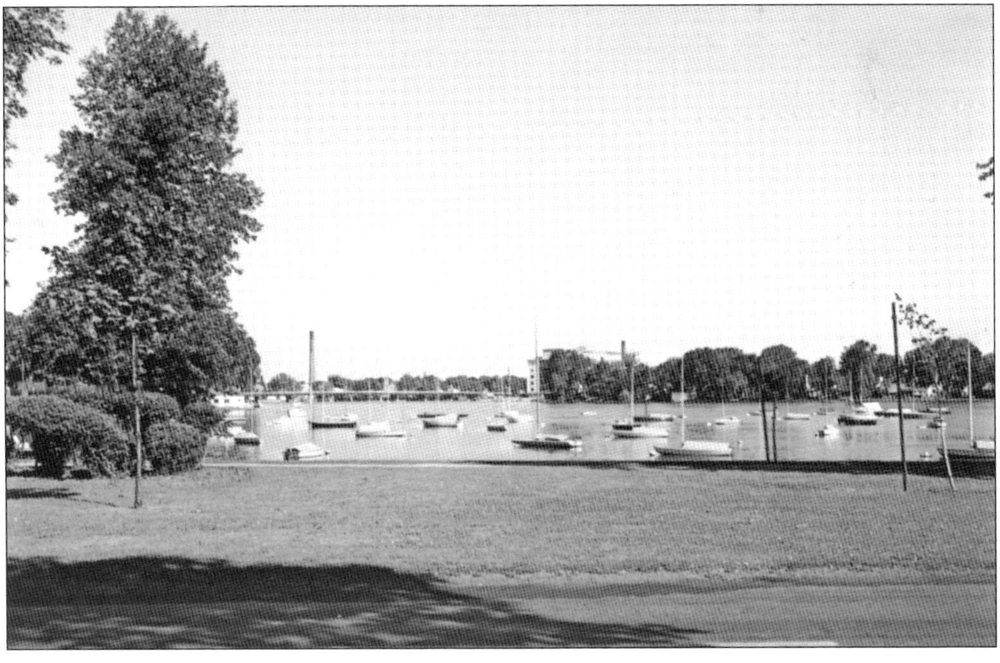

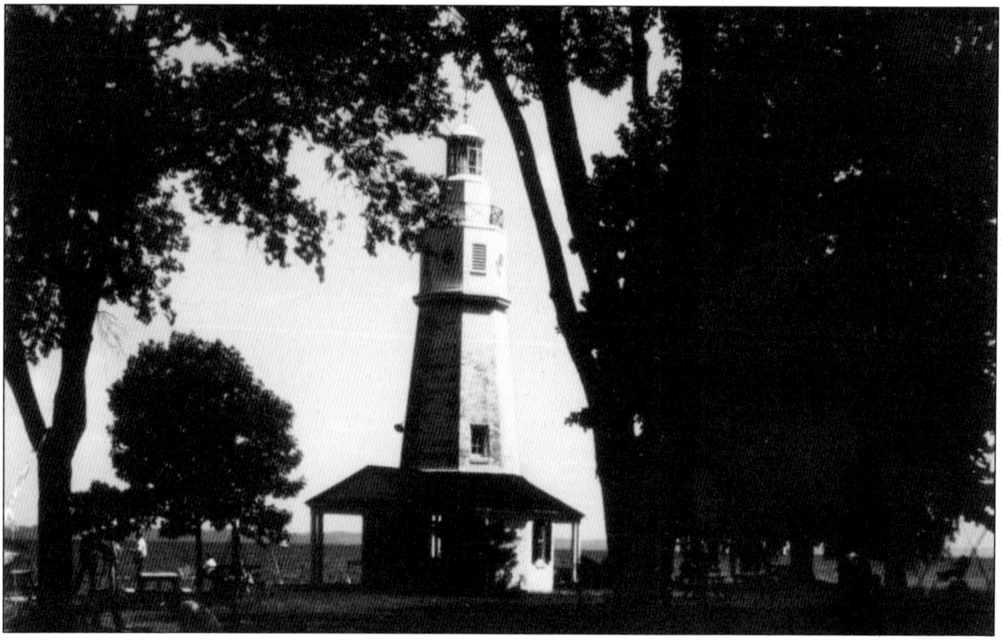

The Kimberly Point Lighthouse was built in 1944 from funds donated by J.C. Kimberly, who recognized a need for a light to mark the entrance to the river. The lighthouse cost $7,500 to build and first saw service in 1945. It was built on land that had been donated by Helen Kimberly Stuart in 1929 as a park that bears the Kimberly name and which was the site of the famed Old Council Tree from Neenah history. It was cut down in 1885 by the US Army Corps of Engineers when the river channel was dredged and widened, but a historical plaque marks the site.

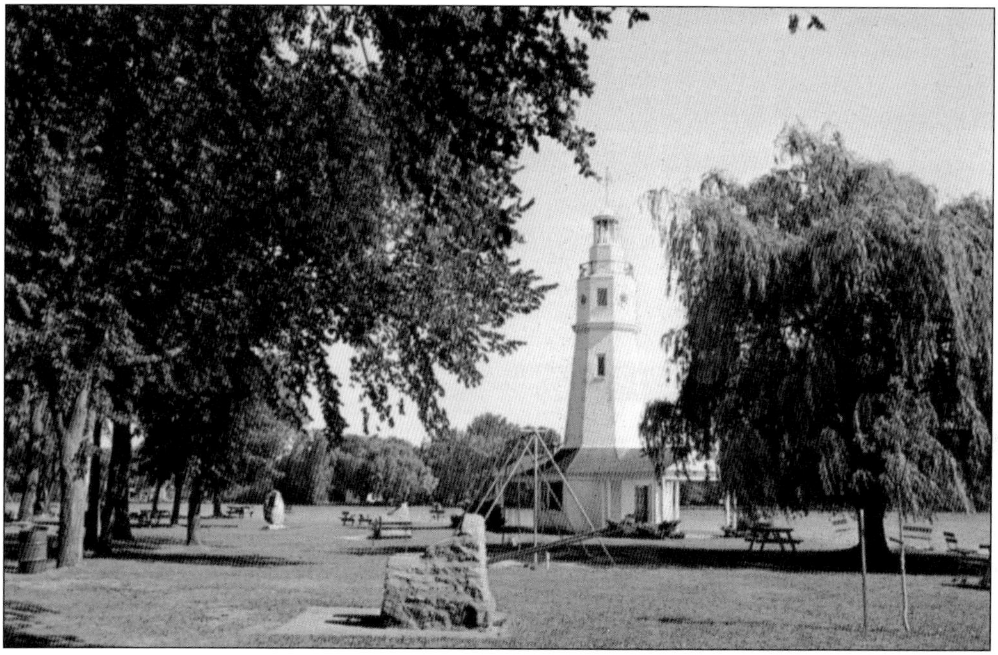

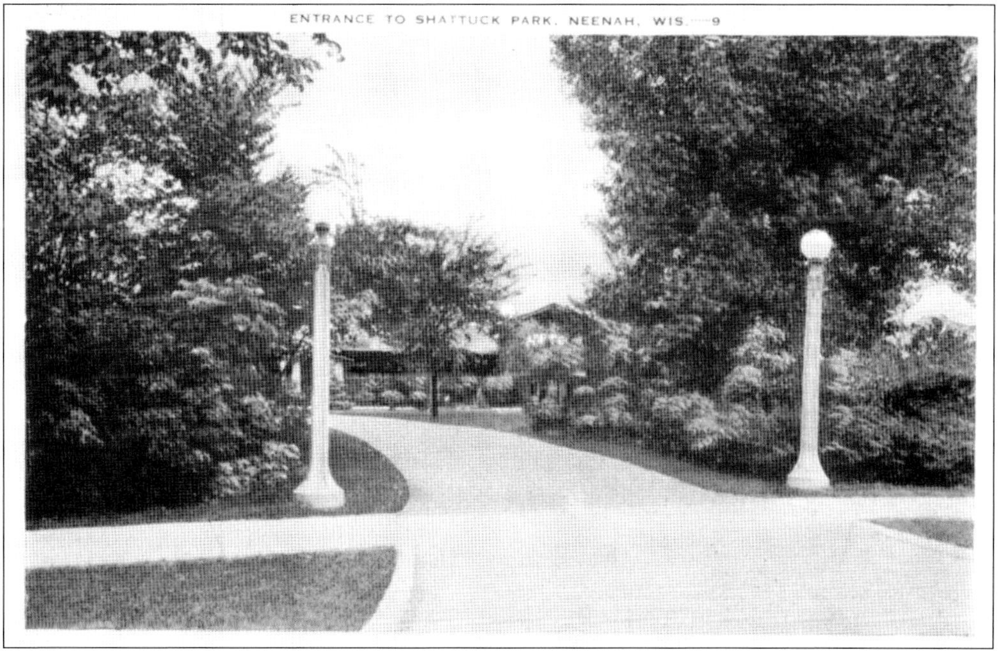

The land that later became Shattuck Park had an ignoble history. It had been used by a sewer pipe company, a marble works, a coal yard, a boat works, and a steam laundry. Part of it was a swamp, and by 1910, it had become a dump. Clara Shattuck, wife of a Kimberly-Clark founder, F.C. Shattuck, purchased the land in 1912 and developed it into a showplace that was deeded to the city in 1915. The landscaping of the park is believed to be the work of Eunice Fenlon, a landscape architect for Weyauwega who also designed the landscaping for the Havilah Babcock home on East Wisconsin Avenue. Babcock was one of the original four partners of Kimberly-Clark.

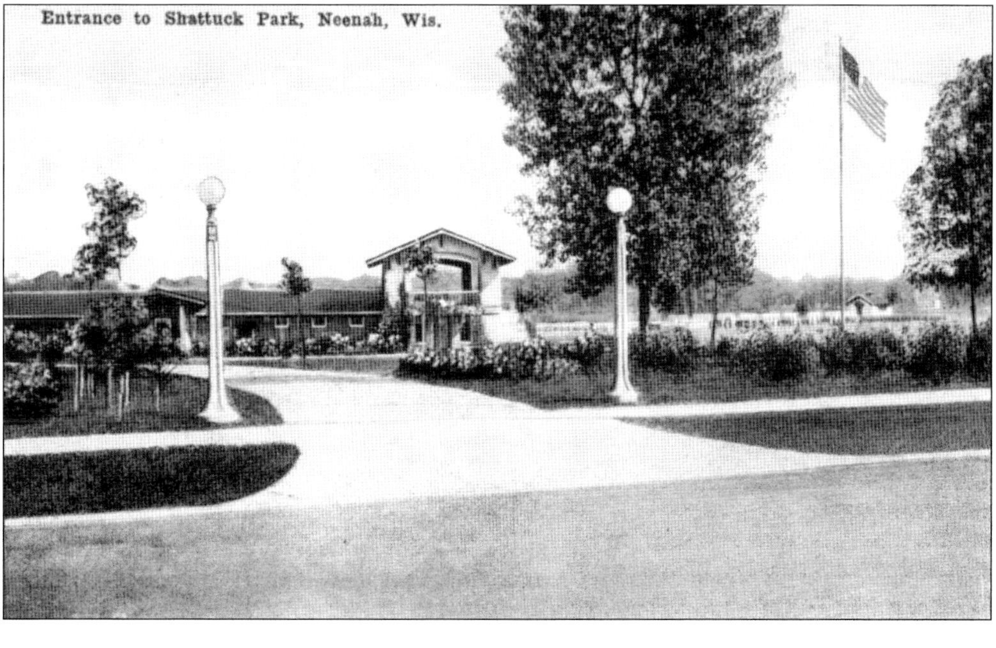

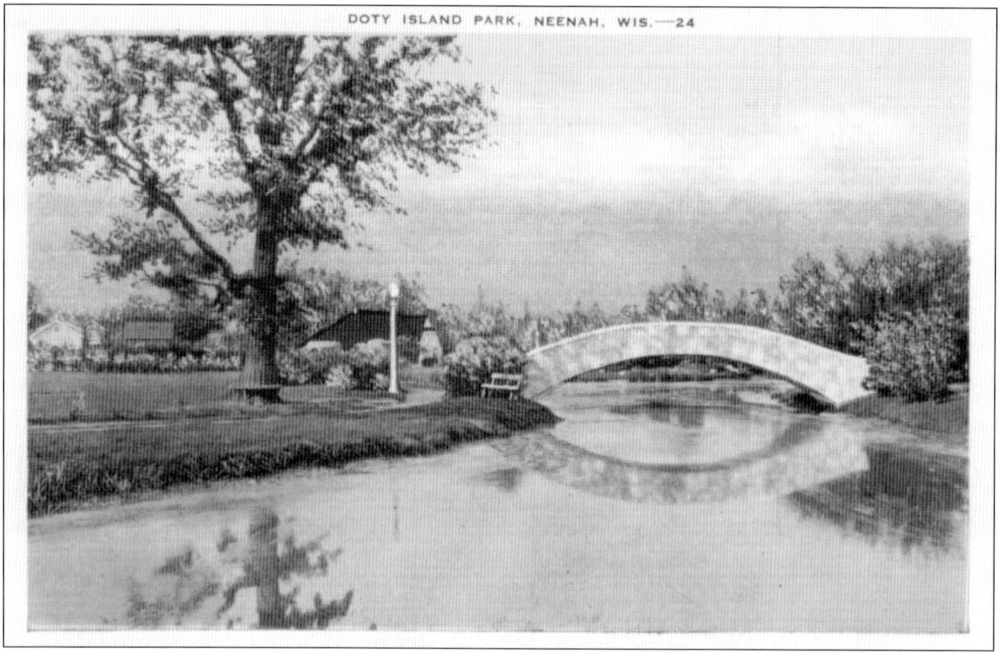

C.B. Clark Jr. was considered one of Neenah's "first citizens." Among his accomplishments were the presidency of Riverside Paper Company, developer of Theda Clark Hospital, alderman, mayor, school board president, director of Kimberly-Clark, and donor of the Park & Recreation Building. Clark donated much of the property for Doty Park in 1922 and improved this once-marshy wetland into a playground for the city to cherish. It was originally known as Island Park, but when Gov. James Duane Doty's cabin was moved here in 1925, the park was renamed in his honor. Doty was Wisconsin's second territorial governor and the namesake for the island on which the Twin Cities' history began. To this day, the site is maintained as a historical museum.

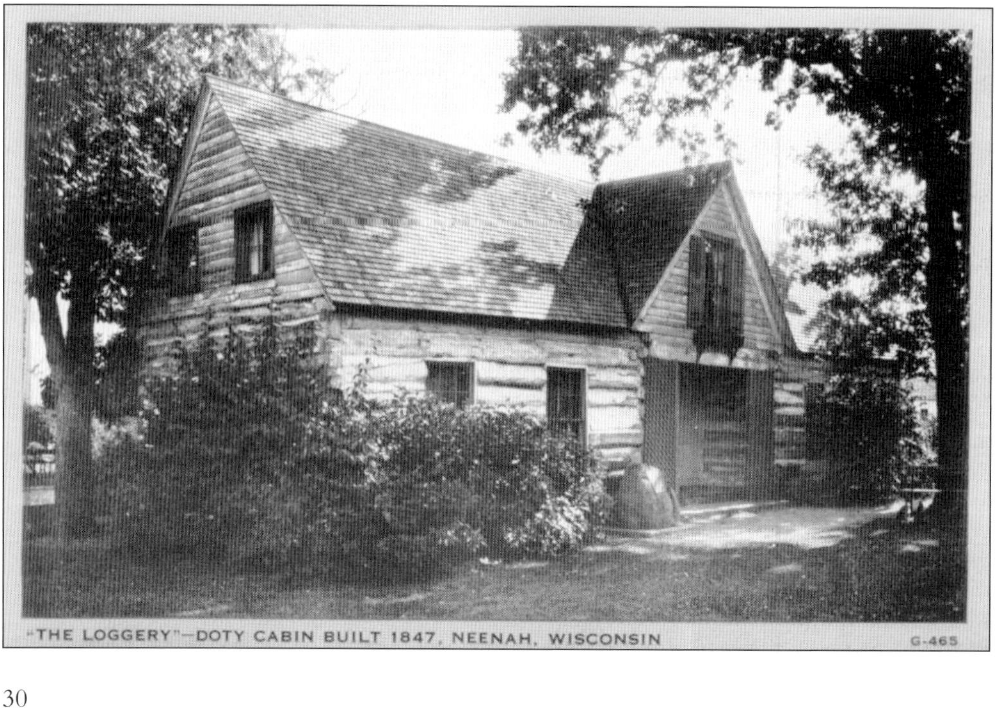

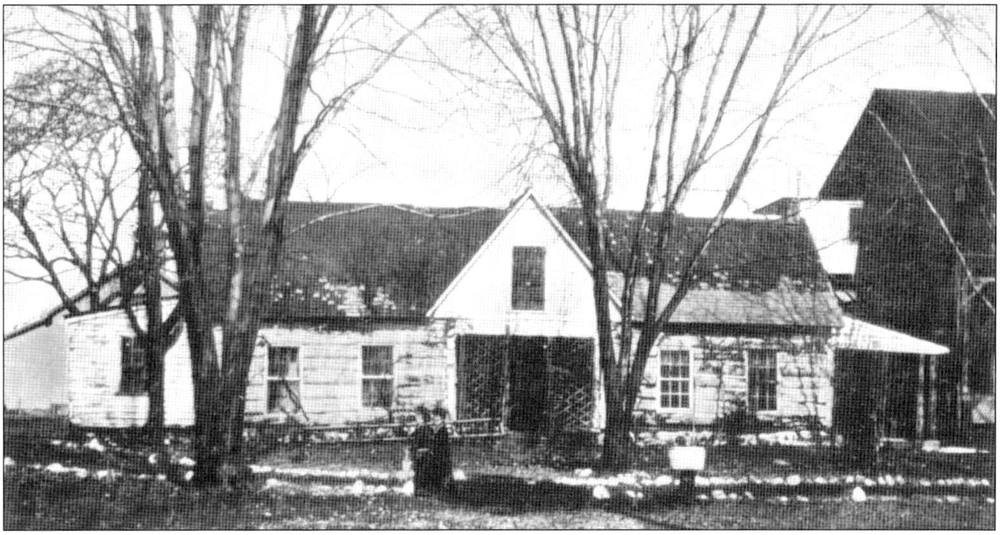

John Roberts was an innkeeper who, in the 1870s, was proprietor of the National Hotel in Menasha. Later, he gained much notoriety and fortune as the owner and keeper of Roberts Resort in Neenah, built on the grounds of Governor Doty's former farm in 1877. The Roberts Resort property (below) was sold in 1905 to John Strange, who remodeled the hotel as his home. He donated Doty Cabin to Neenah in 1923 and had it moved to the park just west of his property. The property remained within the Strange family until 1965, when it was sold and subdivided and the old resort was razed.

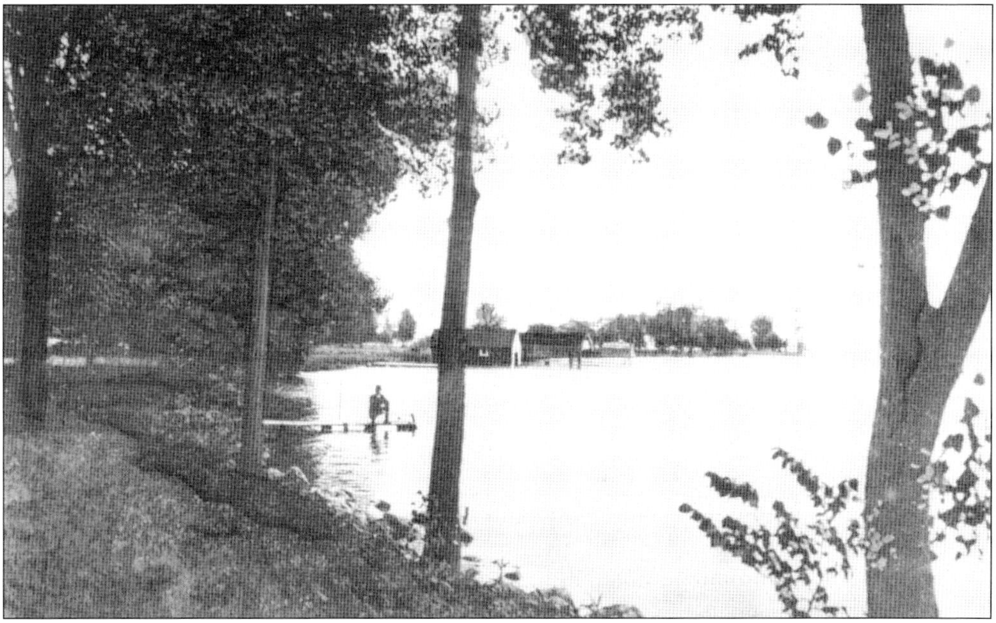

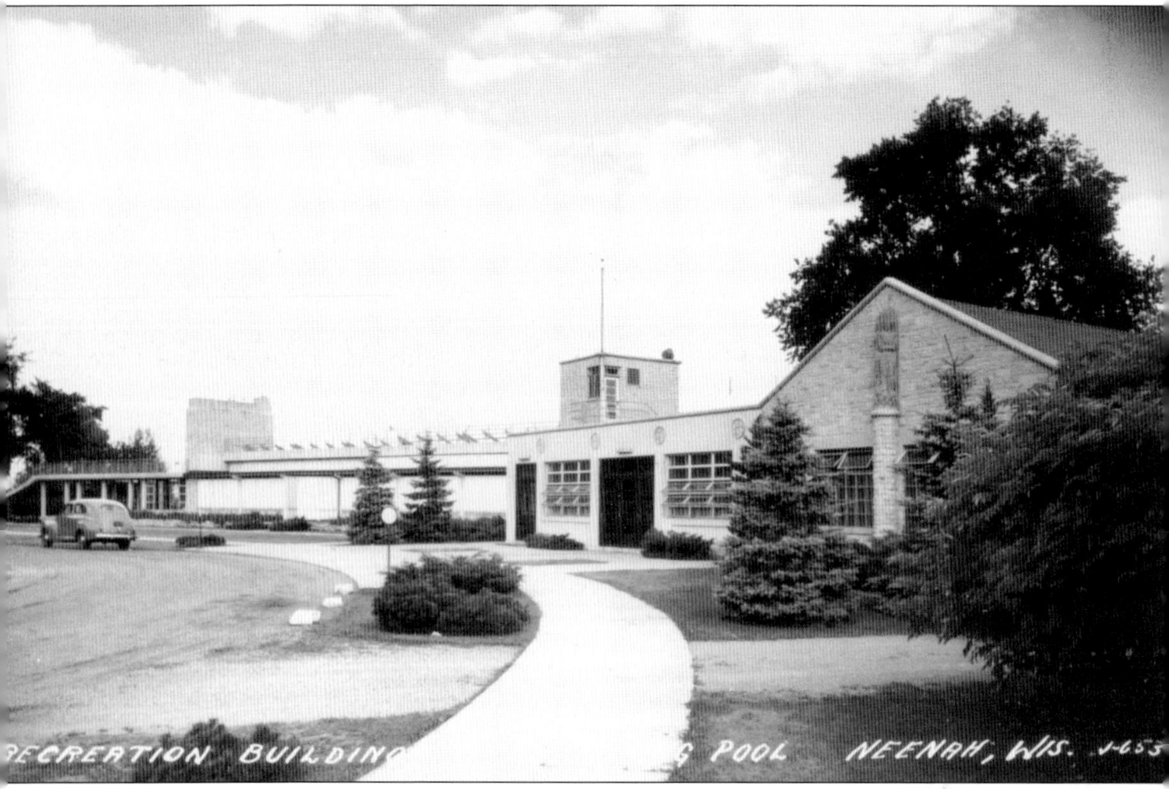

During the planning stages for the Neenah swimming pool, Ole Jorgensen conducted extensive research on swimming pools, and he later became the facility's supervisor. The pool and recreation building was completed in 1940 on land donated by C.B. Clark and S.F. Shattuck. Pool attendance was 70,831 for that year, including 22,142 for the year-round indoor program, proving that a solid recreational program could enhance the quality of life for its citizens while providing healthful and affordable benefits to its patrons. The Amateur Athletic Union Women's Swimming and Diving Championships were staged at the Neenah pool during August 1942. This brought national recognition to the Twin Cities, even more than usual due to Word War II's preempting of the 1940 and 1944 Olympics. Many world-class female swimmers and divers who normally would have placed at the Olympics competed in Neenah.

Two

Bridges, Dams, and Transportation

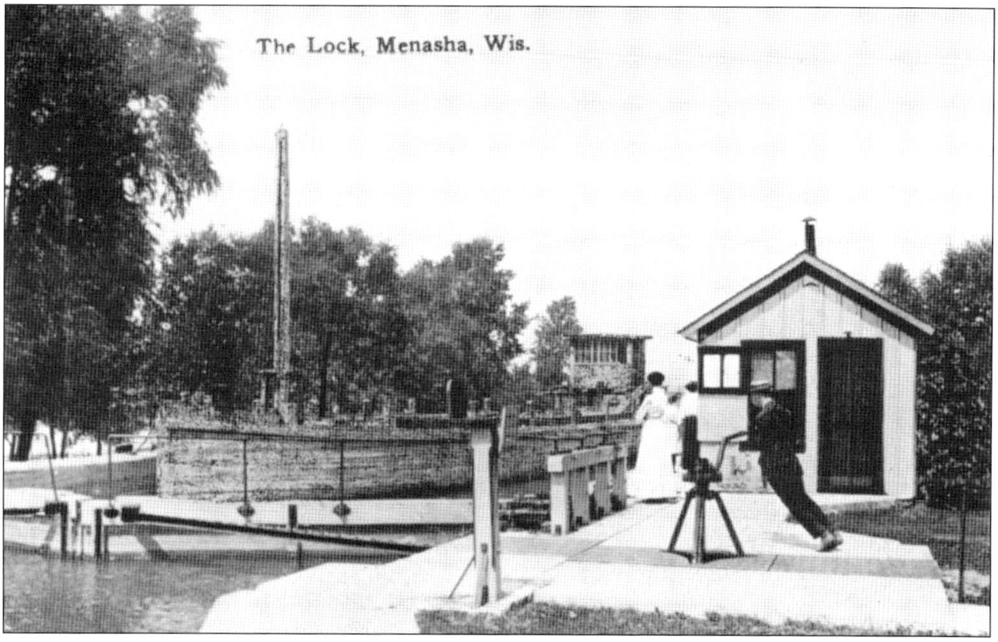

Operating continually from the 1850s, the Menasha Lock is a part of the historic Fox River lock system. Constructed between 1848 and the late 1870s, this was once part of a 24-lock system connecting the Great Lakes with the Mississippi River and the Gulf of Mexico. This hand-operated lock permits passage of boaters from Little Lake Butte des Morts to Lake Winnebago, though invasive species have recently shut down operations.

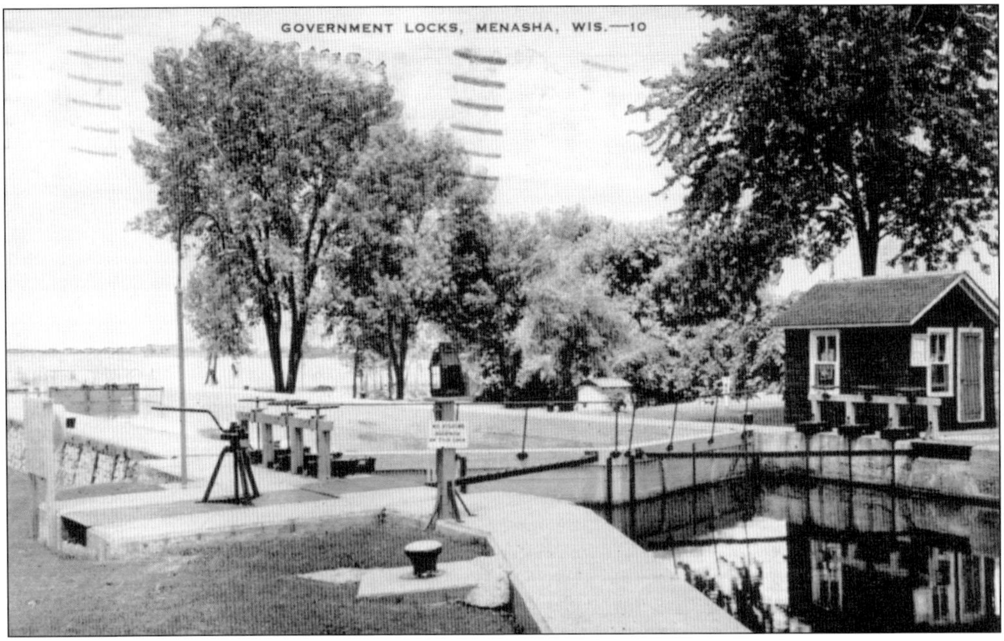

In the early 20th century, Menasha and Neenah were among the world's largest producers of paper. From the 1850s through the early 1900s, the steamboats, tugs, and freighters that passed through the Menasha lock fueled this industry, bringing in timber from the north and carrying paper to ports throughout the world. In the early 1970s, a major reconstruction occurred, and steel gates were added. In 2004, the Fox River Navigational System Authority (FRNSA) was established by the State of Wisconsin to revive the system. The real-photo card above is from the 1940s. The photochrome card below dates to the late 1950s.

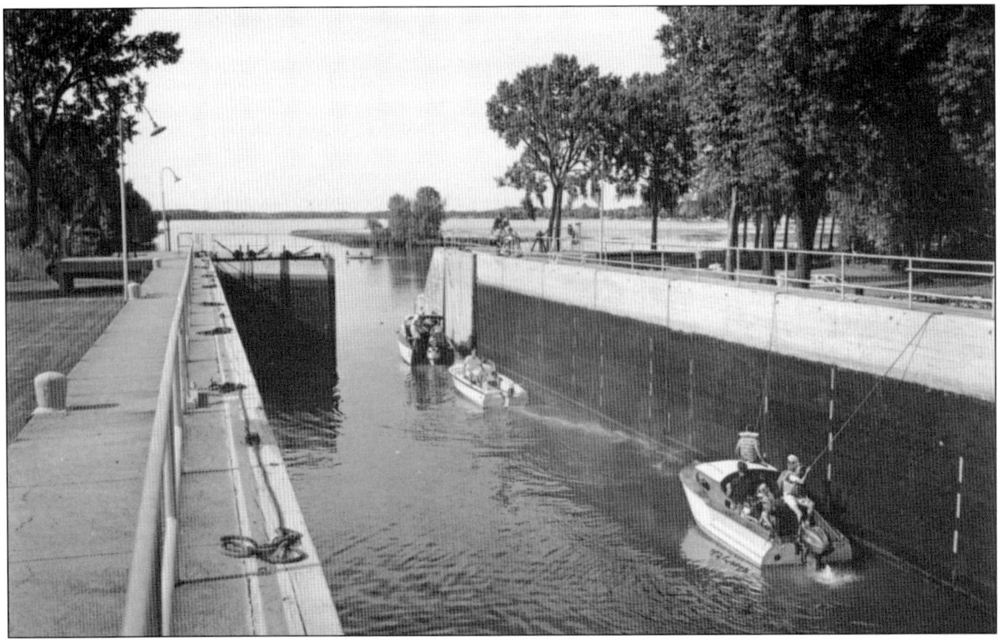

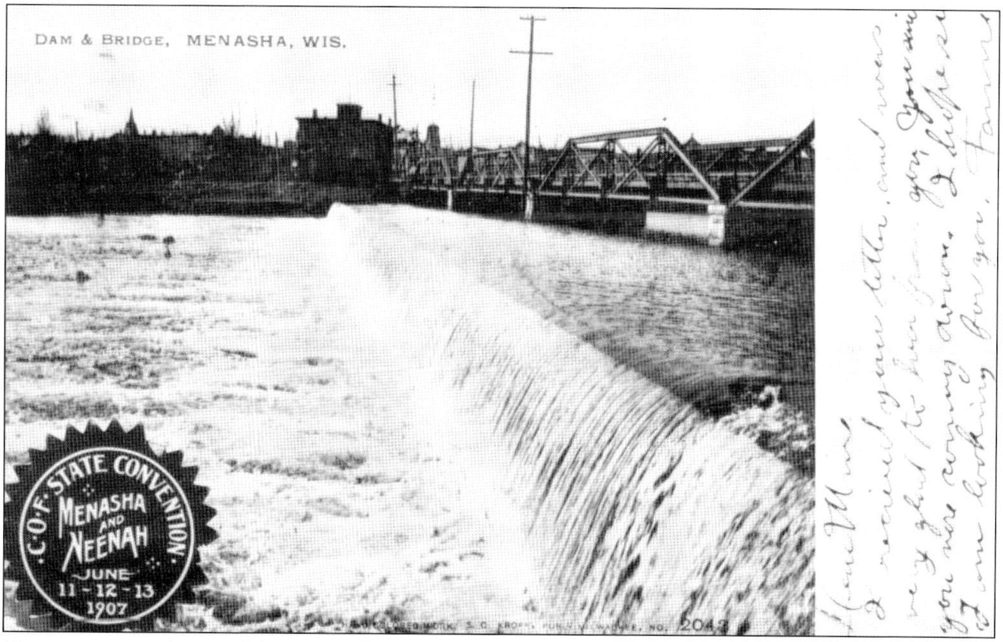

Here are two views of the Menasha Dam and the Mill Street Bridge. The card above shows a view to the north, taken from the vantage point of the Island Paper Company and looking toward downtown. This bridge preceded the current Racine Street Bridge, which was built around 1951. After crossing the bridge, travelers would first encounter the magnificent public library, an imposing sight welcoming them to mainland Menasha. The view below looks to the south toward the Island Paper Company. Though changing hands many times since its inception under different ownership in 1876, this is the oldest paper mill in town. About the time of this postcard, the mill made corrugated paper that aggravated the citizens because of the odor it emitted. They called it "strawboard."

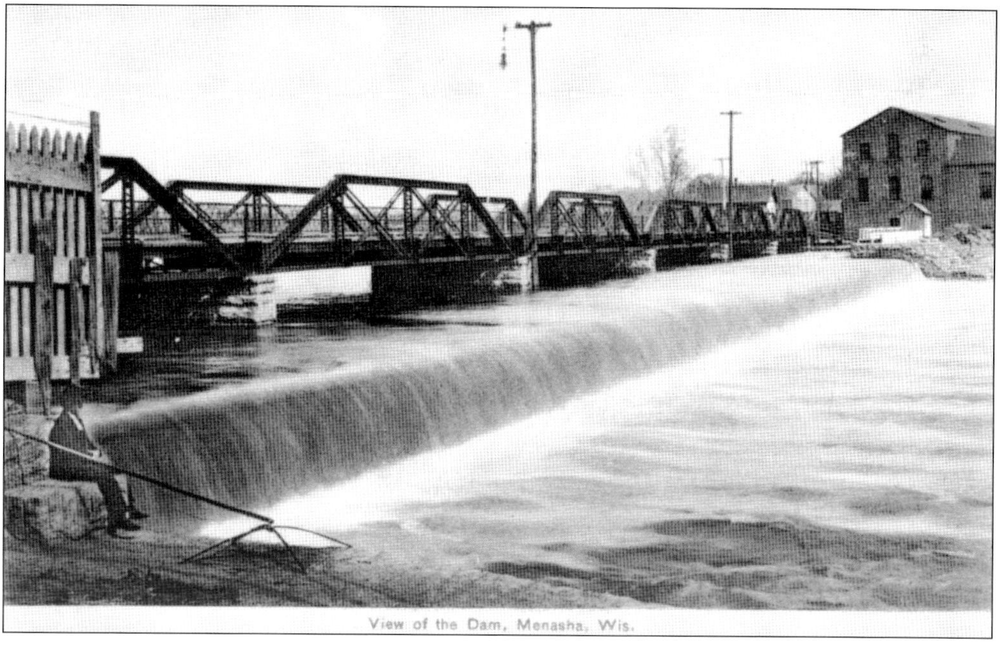

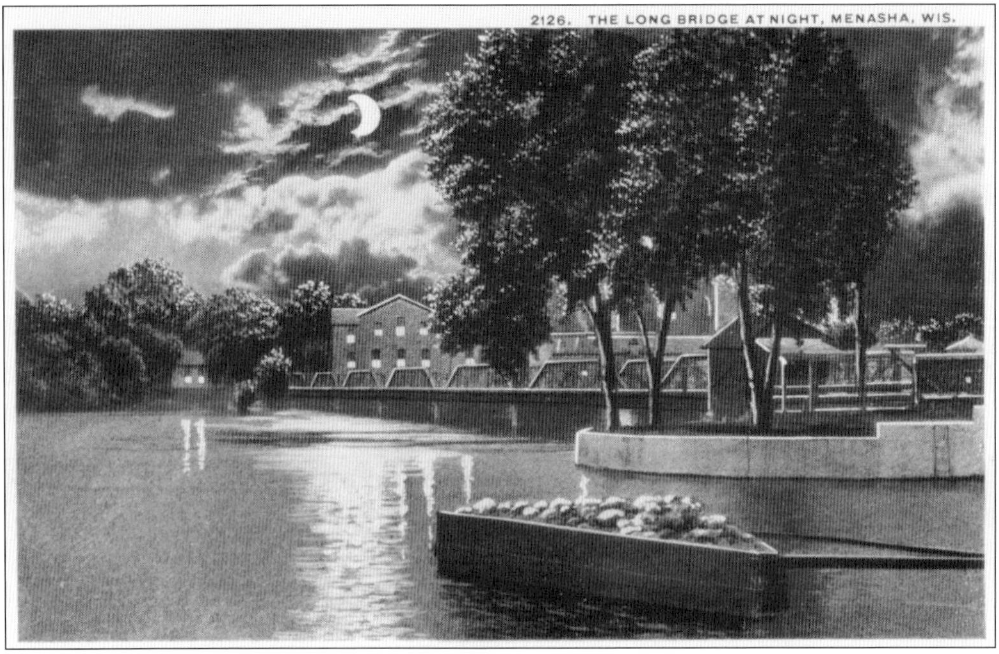

The postcard view above shows the same Mill Street Bridge at night. The view below shows a dreamlike moonlit scene near the present-day intersection of Main and Racine Streets. This type of postcard was very popular in the early to mid-20th century in the pre-photochrome era. What is remarkable about such cards is that they appear to have detail that would not necessarily show up in a true night-time photograph, leading one to conclude that these are composite illustrations with hand-painted highlights to give the illusion of night. Nevertheless, they are a charming addition to most postcard collections.

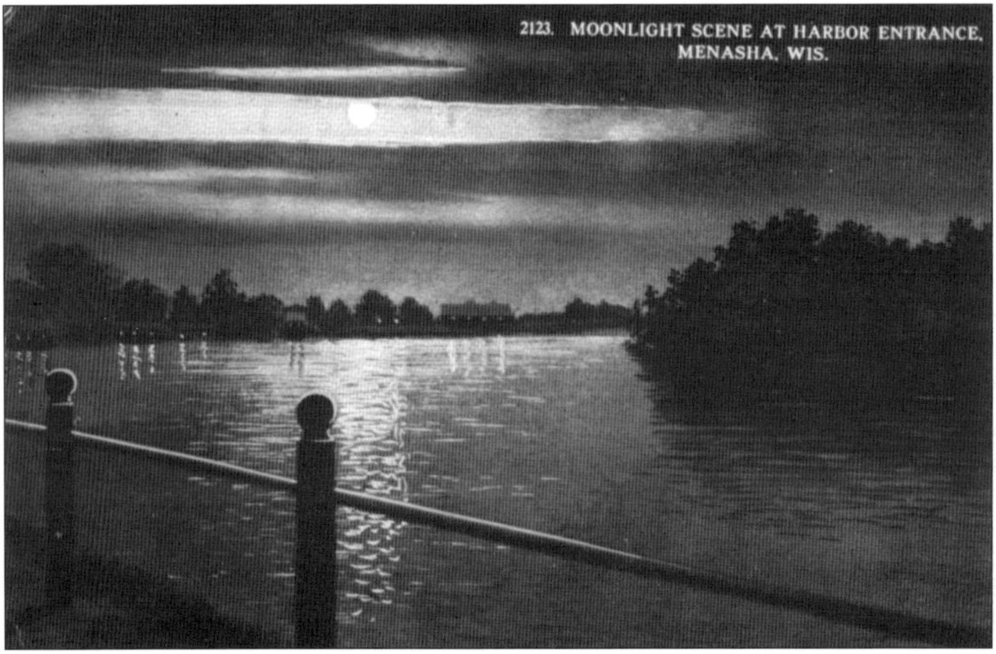

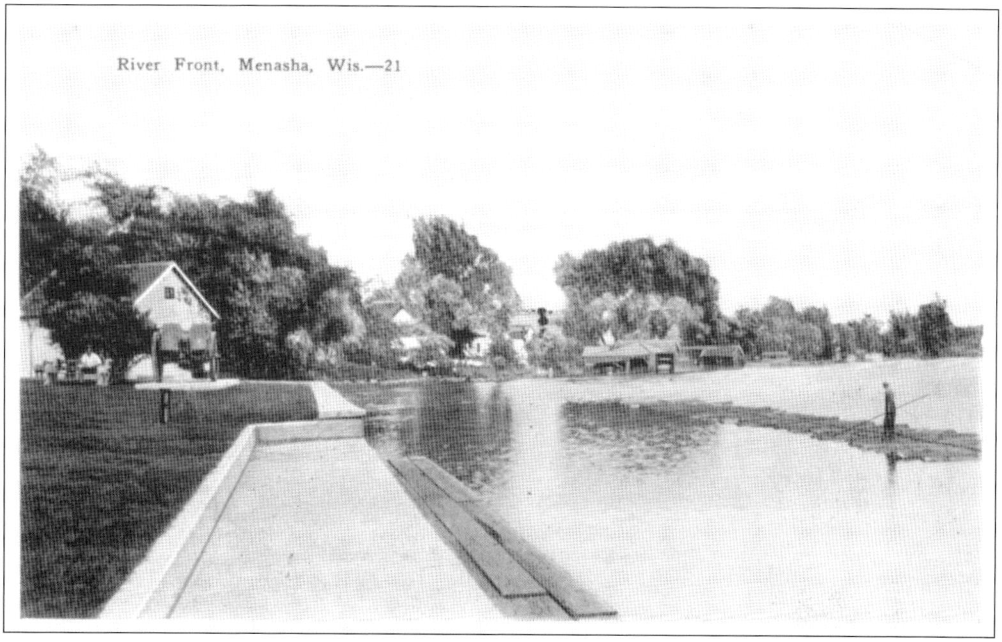

The view above predates the Racine Street Bridge and portrays a bygone era when logs were traditionally floated down the Fox River to the sawmills. This area would be the north terminus of today's bridge. The card below shows the Racine Street Bridge in a photochrome format from the 1950s. One cannot fault the realism inherent in such a highly detailed photograph. On Saturday, August 25, 1951, the new Racine Street lift bridge was dedicated in memory of Curtis Reed, and the old Mill Street Bridge was demolished shortly afterward. Built at a cost of $585,000, the modern structure, with automatic warning lights and power-driven lifts, is a far cry from the first crude bridge that the early settlers threw across the treacherous stream.

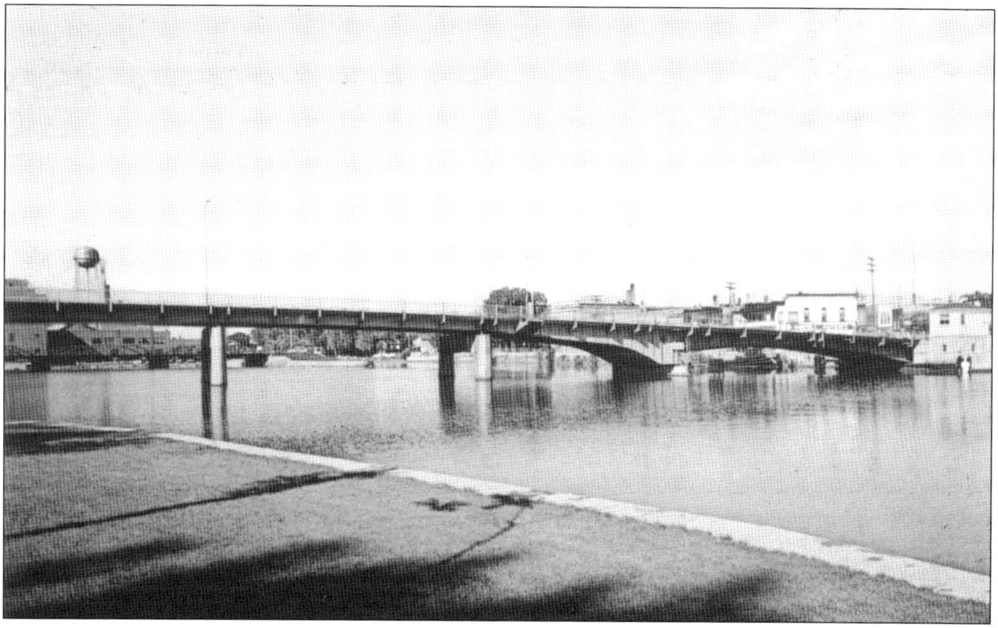

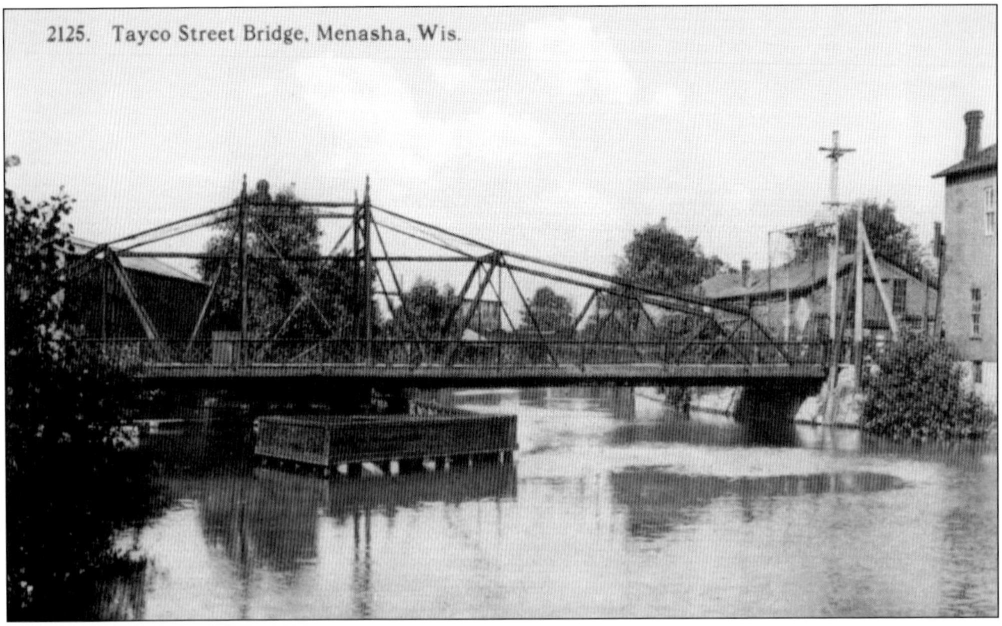

From 1859 until 1886, a wooden swing bridge operated on Tayco Street. In 1886, the structure collapsed as a large herd of cattle was crossing. A new iron swing bridge was then constructed for $7,500. That bridge is portrayed above; it lasted until 1928, when the familiar bridge with a stone tower at each of its four corners was built (below). The postcard printer was partially correct when he labeled this as the Washington Street Bridge. Actually, this is the Tayco Street Bridge, but at this point moving south from the bridge, Tayco Street becomes Washington Street, where it gains its own bridge with that name. One can see where the confusion lies.

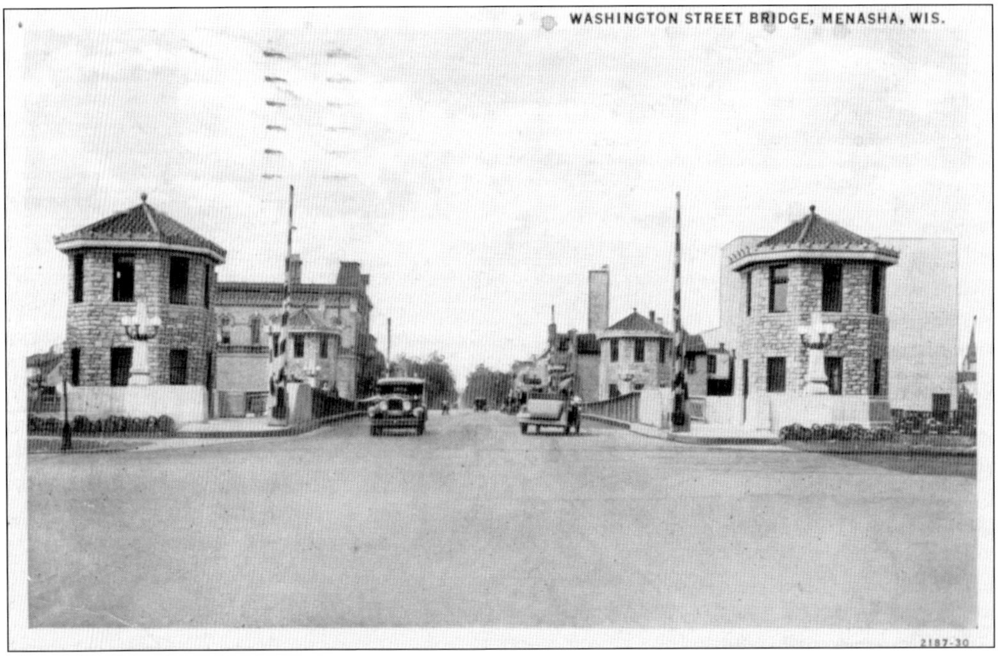

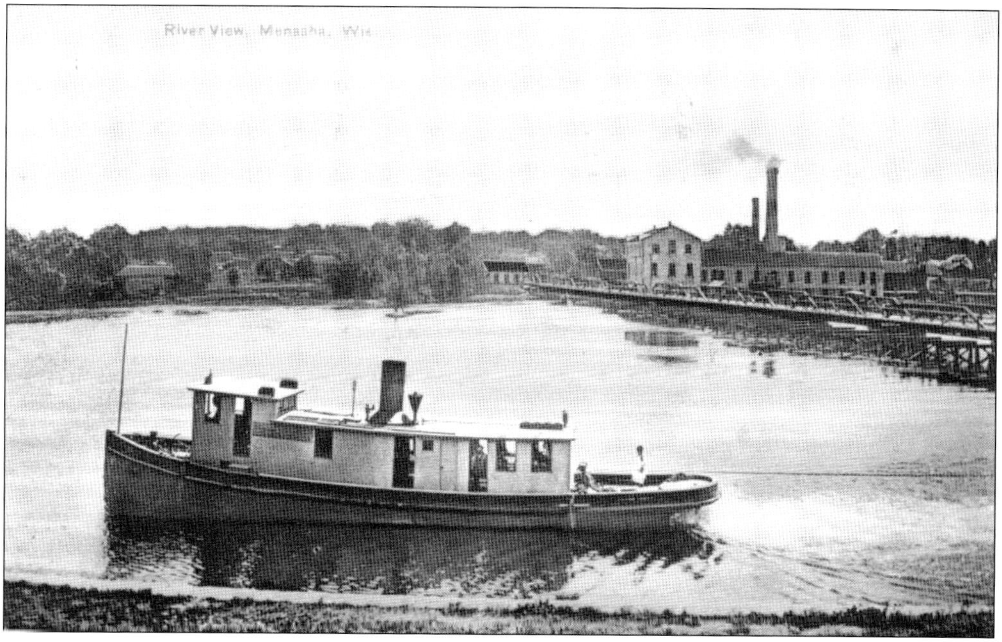

The postcard above from 1908 shows one type of watercraft that trolled up and down the waters of the Fox. This scenic illustration shows the boat heading east toward Lake Winnebago, leaving the manufacturing district of Menasha behind as it looks at the Mill Street Bridge and Island Paper Company in the background. The unique view below is Lawson's Canal, located just west of the street known as Riverway in Menasha. It runs behind the former Banta Company and continues south to the old Gilbert Paper Company. It was constructed in 1882 by P.V. Lawson Jr., mayor, attorney, businessman, and city leader. St. Mary's steeple provides a focal point across the river.

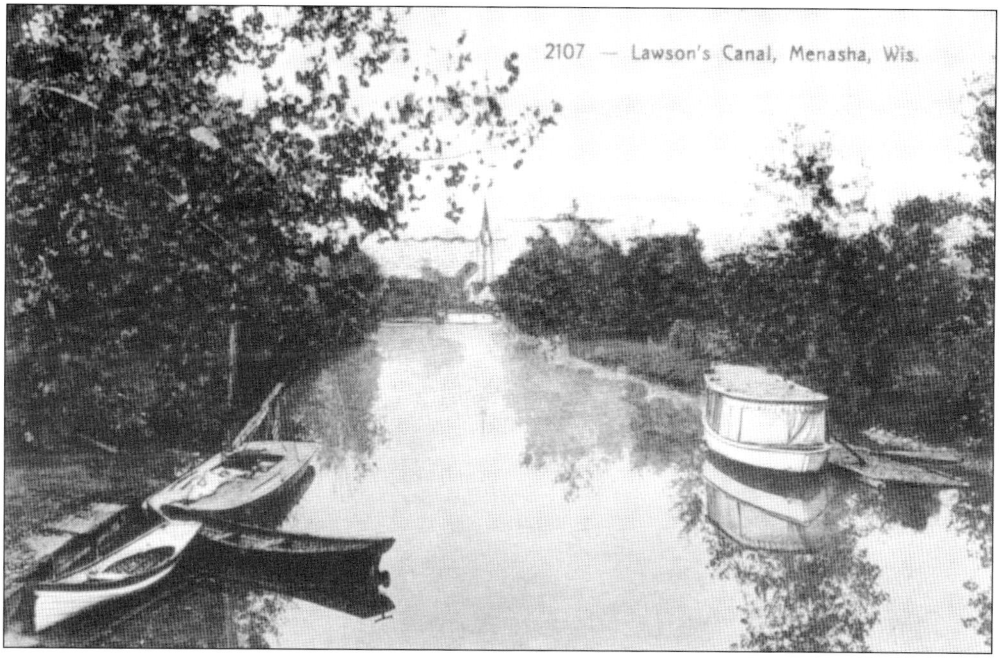

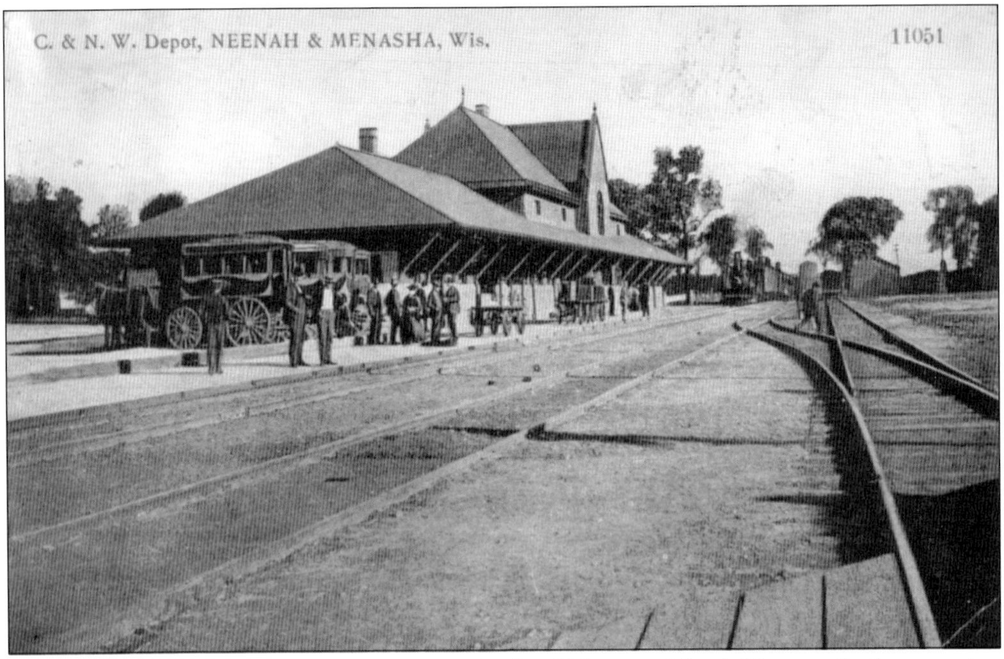

Built in 1892 in a Victorian Romanesque style, the Chicago & North Western Railway station was strategically located on Doty Island, practically straddling the line between Menasha and Neenah. Notice the taxis in the left foreground, ready to take passengers to hotels in Neenah and Menasha or perhaps to Roberts Resort. The citizenry took pride in having a train depot larger than that of nearby Appleton or Oshkosh. Passenger service at this depot lasted until the spring of 1971, when Amtrak took over railroad passenger service and shifted its focus to the northeast corridor of the United States and big cities like Milwaukee and Chicago. As a result, the Twin Cities lost their passenger rail connection to the world.

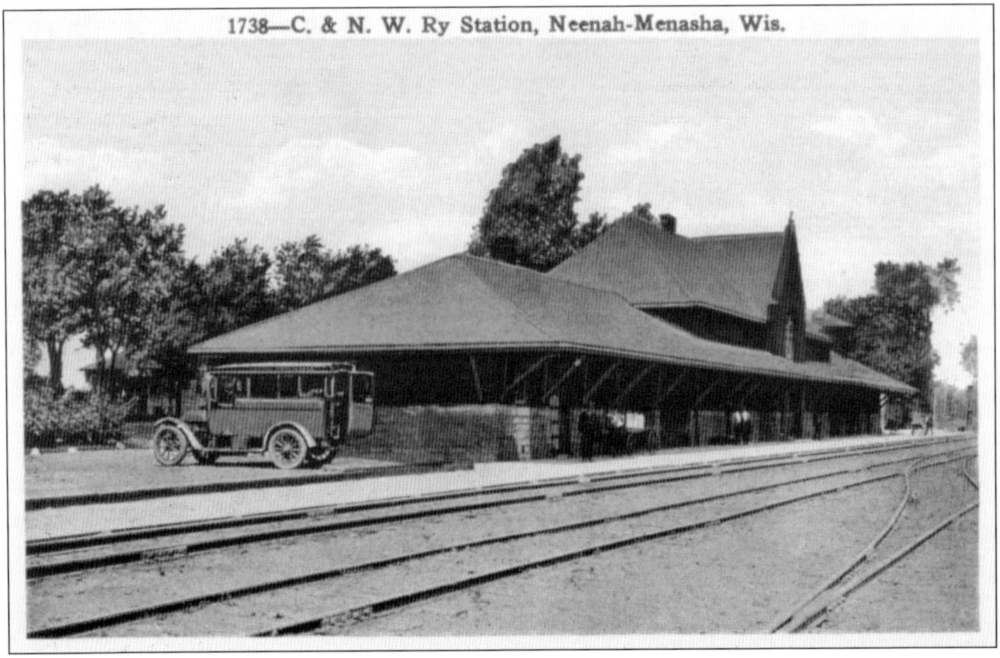

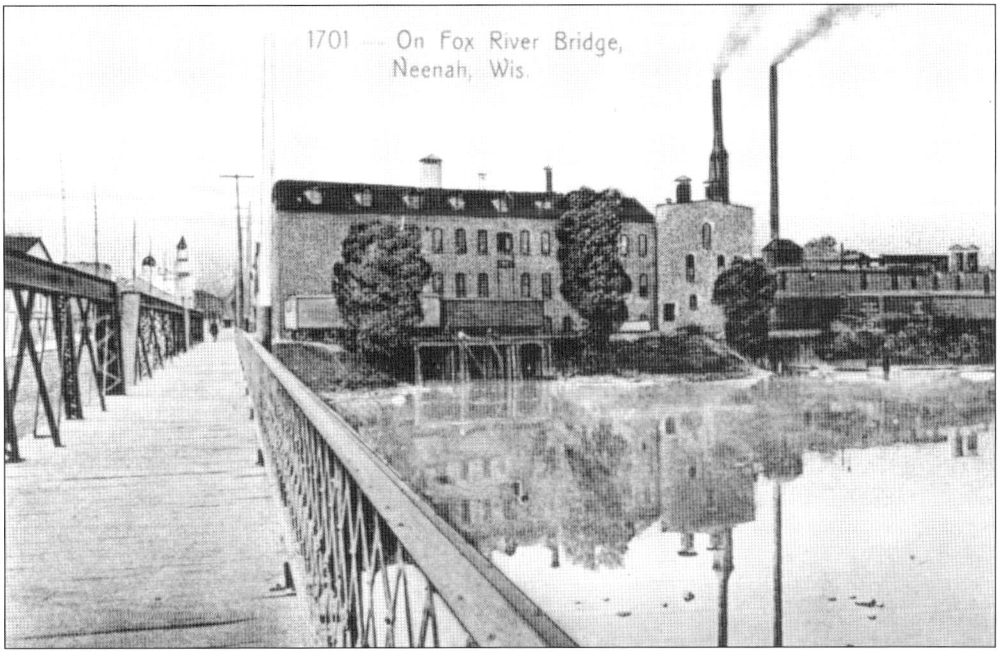

The first bridge to span the river at this point is thought to have been built in 1852. The prominent building here is the Badger Globe Mill, seen from the north and looking toward downtown and Wisconsin Avenue. Notice the overt depiction of industrialization, punctuated by the bulging smokestacks wafting smoke in the air. The same mill makes another appearance below years later in a more modern 1930s view that is more sedate and pedestrian in its orientation. The modern nature of the bridge, coupled with the streetlights, makes for a true "civic pride" illustration portrayed on this linen postcard.

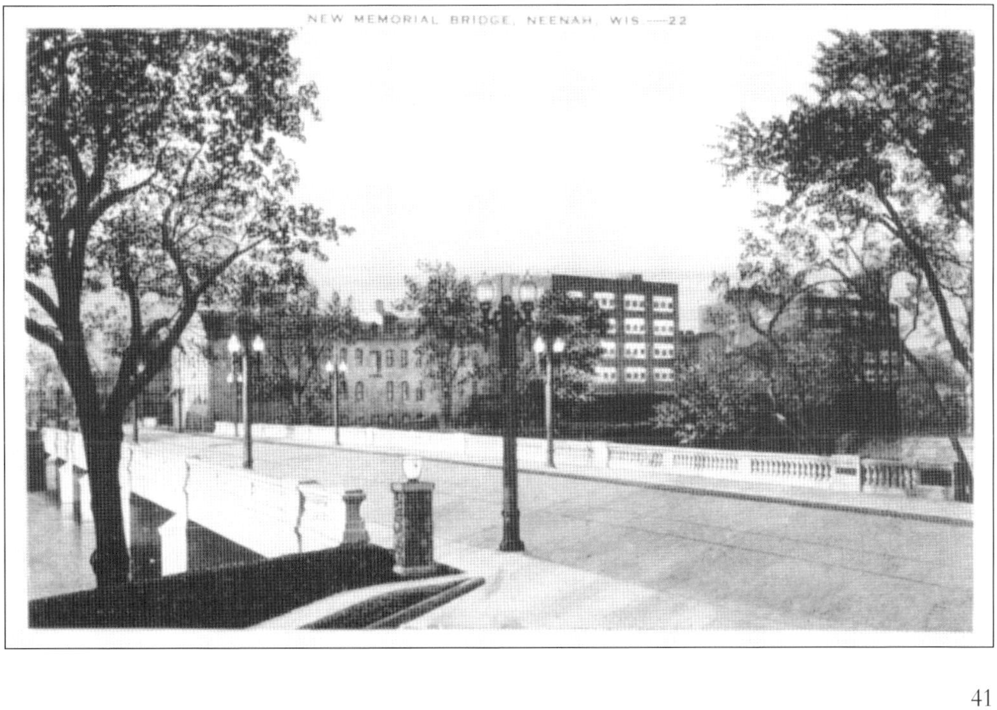

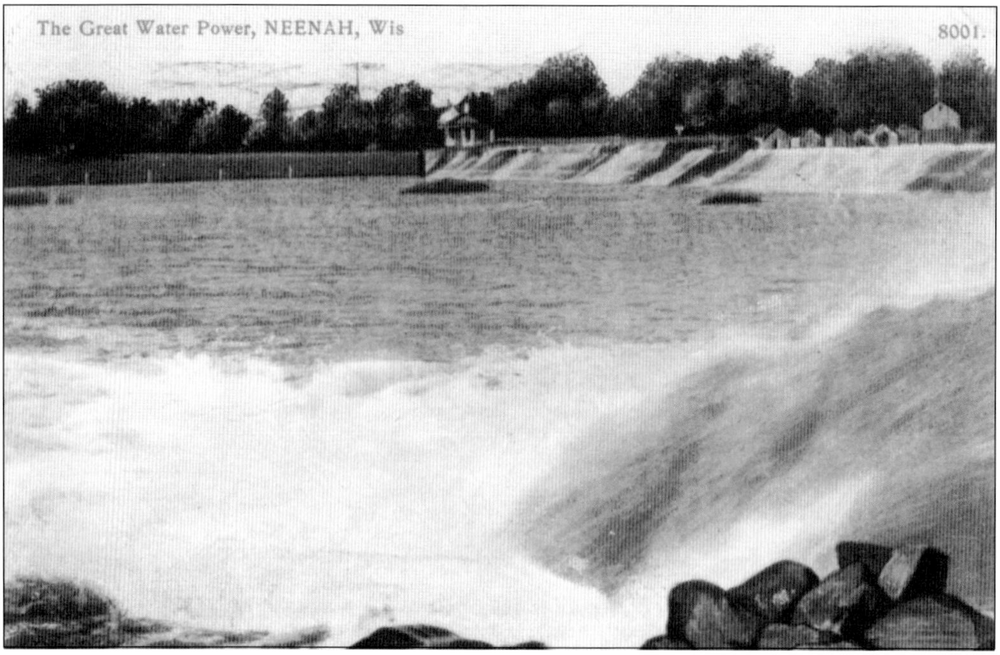

The Neenah Dam was the first to be built on the Fox River, in 1854. The harnessing of waterpower at this location led to a renaissance of building. Numerous sawmills and flour mills utilized the water's power to provide the energy for these concerns. In time, the flour industry died out, but papermaking took over and became the model industry for the town.

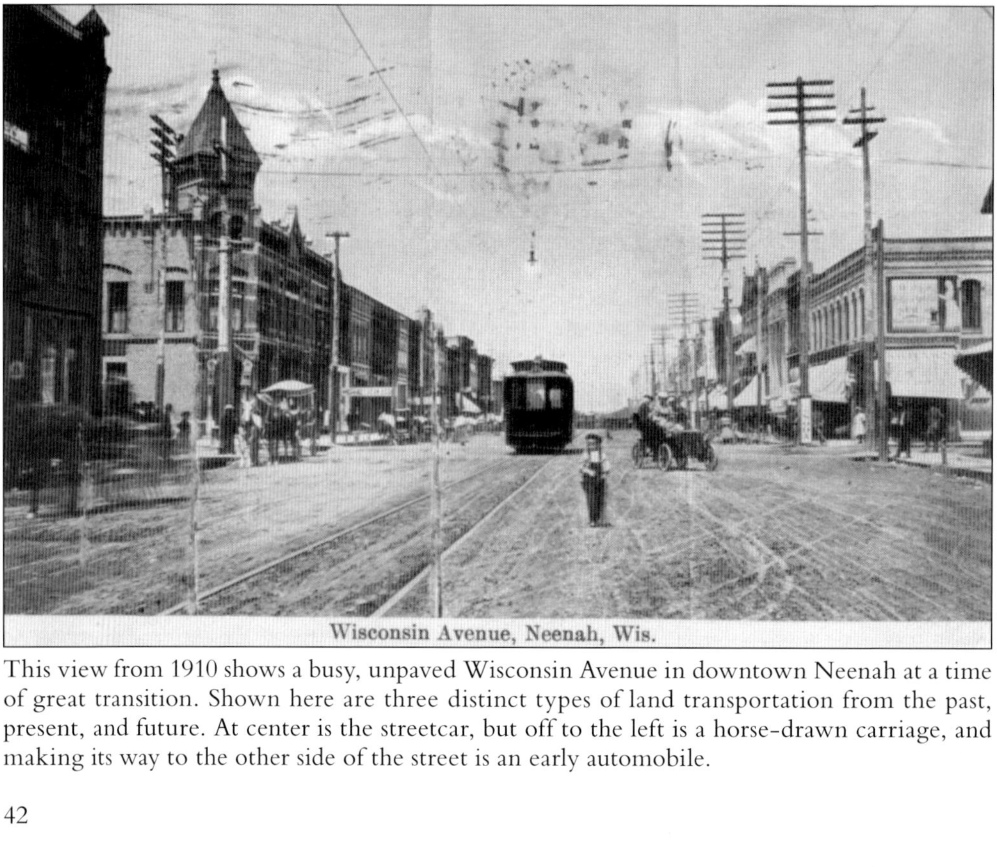

This view from 1910 shows a busy, unpaved Wisconsin Avenue in downtown Neenah at a time of great transition. Shown here are three distinct types of land transportation from the past, present, and future. At center is the streetcar, but off to the left is a horse-drawn carriage, and making its way to the other side of the street is an early automobile.

Three

Industry

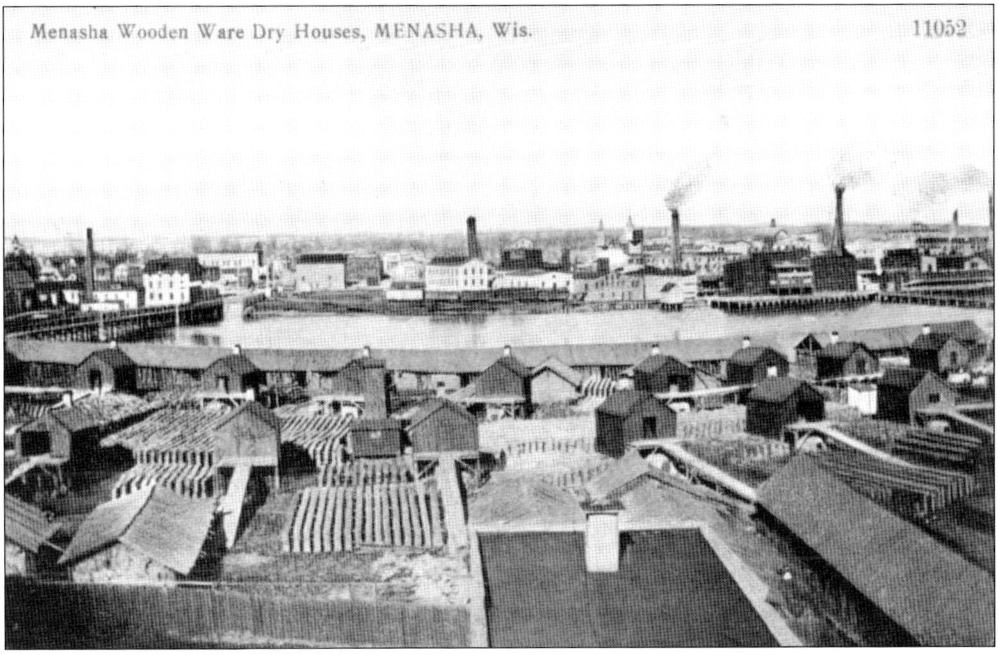

Menasha Wooden Ware was the premier industry in Menasha for many years, and its founder, Elisha D. Smith, ensured that the city of Menasha benefitted from his financial success. Some of the drying yards are pictured in this postcard. The yard in the foreground was used to dry the staves used in making barrels.

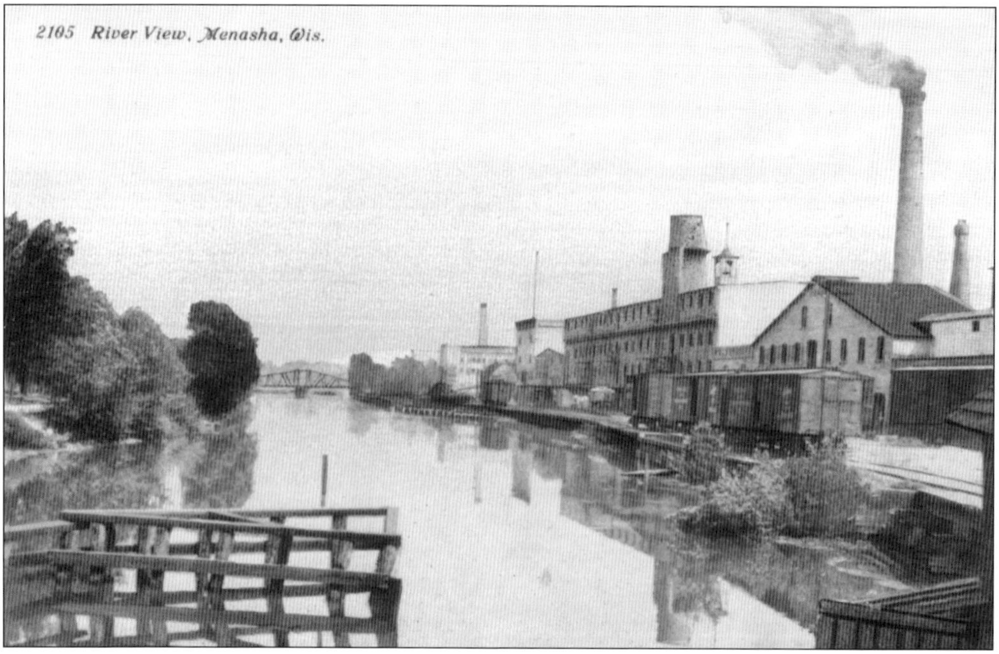

Here are a couple of industrial views of the factories and mills in Menasha. The view above is of the North Channel of the Fox River through Menasha. In the distance, one can see the Tayco Street swing bridge, which was in place until 1928. Mills of all sorts lined the Fox River—sawmills, foundries, papermakers, and even a woolen mill, utilizing the water to power the factories and using the river to float logs downstream to the mills. The image below shows a prominent George Whiting Paper Company plant as the eye moves from Little Lake Butte des Morts into the Fox River channel.

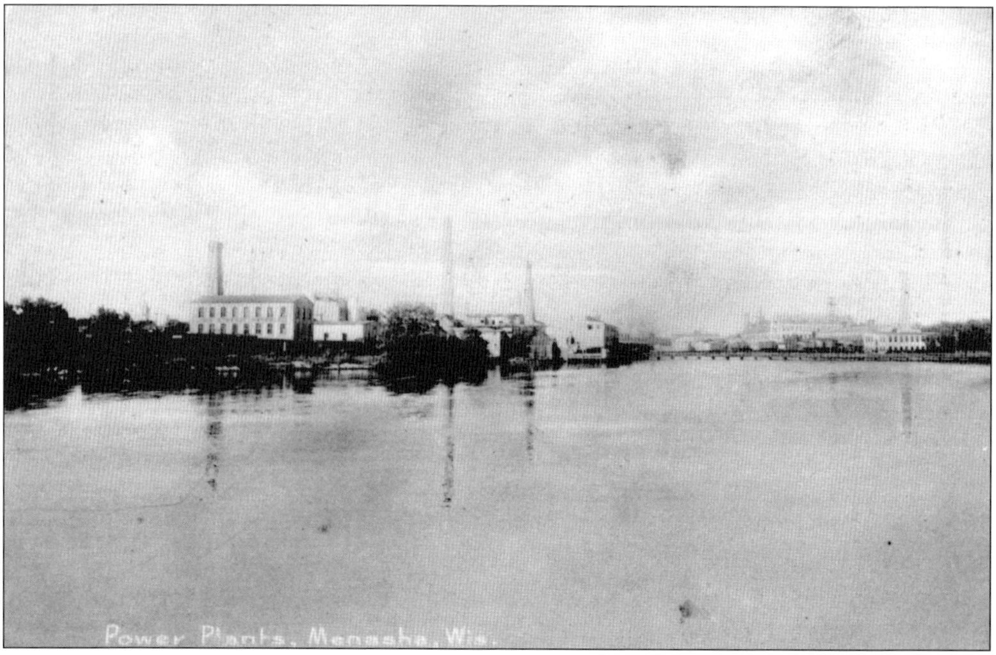

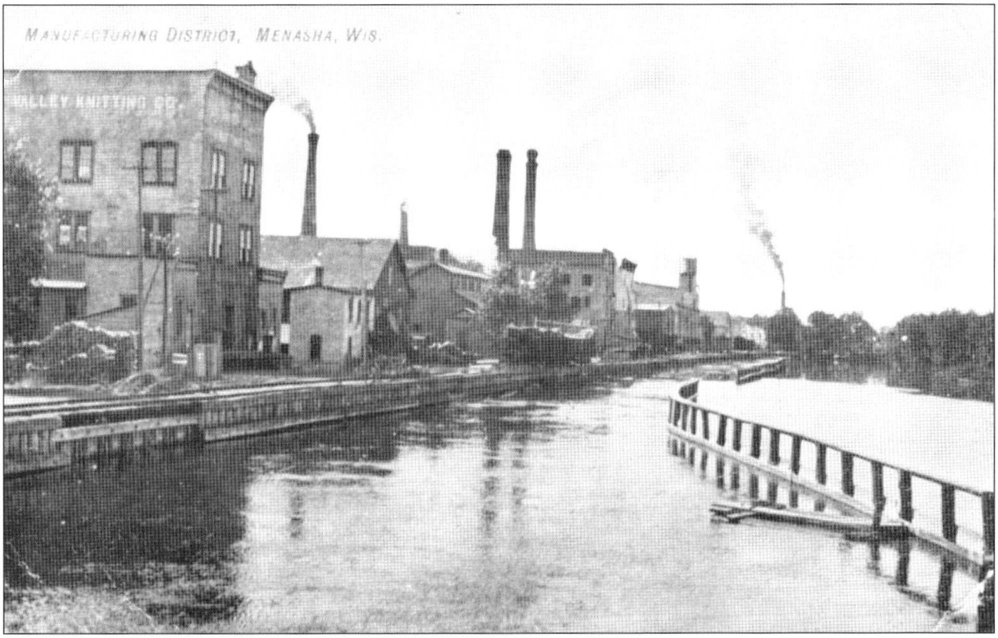

Fox River Valley Knitting Company made what was advertised as "woolen hosiery and mittens, lumbermen's socks and novelties." The plant employed 60 men and women but was destroyed by fire in 1908. The plant was subsequently rebuilt in Appleton. Notice the wooden stanchions in the river channel to keep floating logs away from boat traffic.

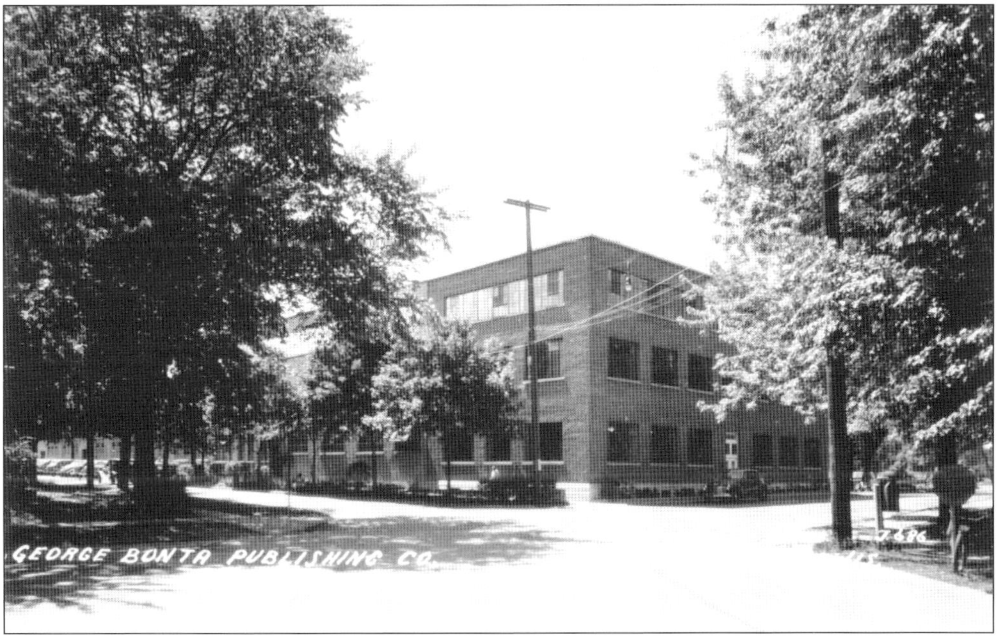

The George Banta Publishing Company became one of the finest book publishing concerns in the state. In addition to book printing, the company specialized in the publications of learned societies and college fraternities, and by 1930, it was printing some 130 periodicals and journals. George Banta originally moved to Menasha in 1885 to sell insurance, but his printing hobby proved to be a more lucrative business.

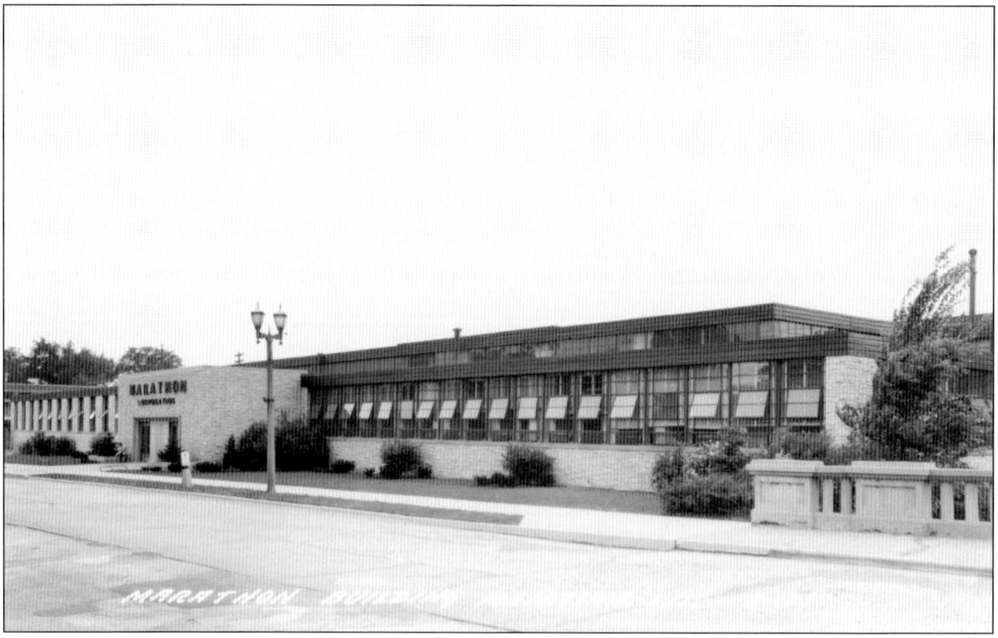

Marathon Corporation was organized in 1909 in Wausau but did not become a presence in Menasha until 1927, when it acquired the Menasha Printing and Carton Company, a manufacturer of bread wrappers, paper food containers, and other materials for food concerns. Later, printing capabilities and its own ink plant were added, making the then Marathon Company the largest printer in the world. In time, and through several mergers, Marathon eventually morphed into American Can in 1957, James River in 1982, and Fort James in 1997 after a merger with the Fort Howard Paper Company. Notice the start of the Washington Street Bridge in front of the Marathon headquarters above.

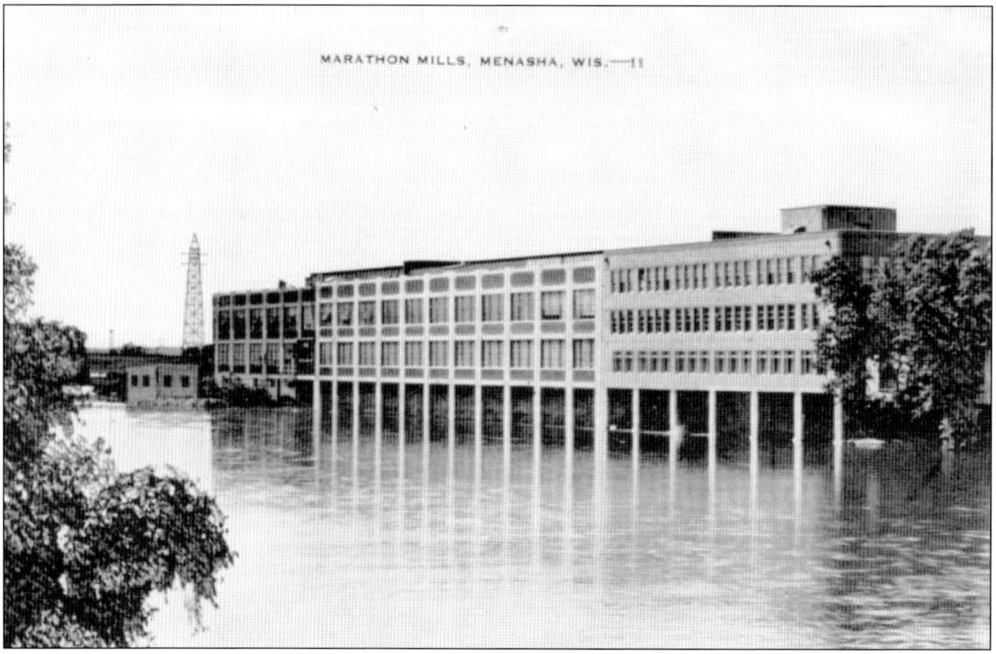

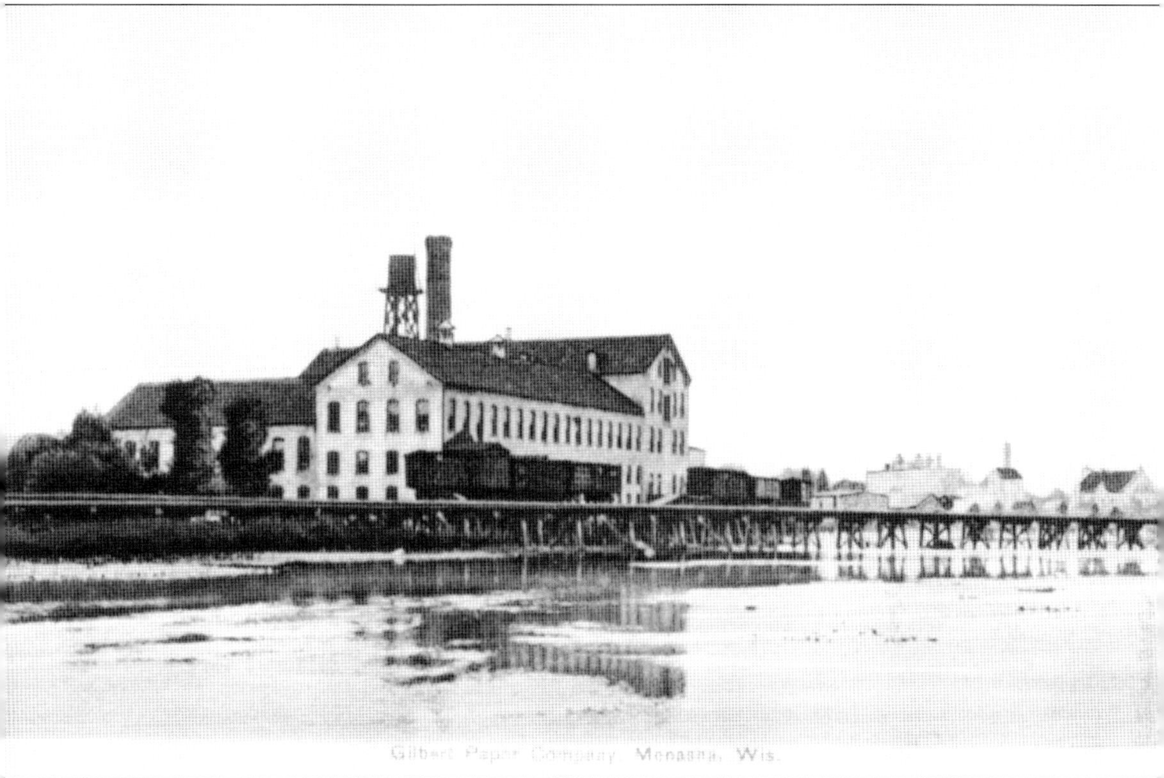

The Gilbert Paper Company was established in 1887 by William Gilbert Sr. and his sons, William Jr., Albert, Theodore, and George. Gilbert Jr. had previously been in business with George A. Whiting, who operated the Whiting paper mill on River Street in Menasha. The Gilbert concern was built on the Lawson Canal the year of the canal's completion and was the third paper manufacturing operation in the city. The firm was purchased by the Mead Corporation in 1960, and in 2001 by the Fox River Paper Company, but ceased production later that year. Throughout its history, the company produced high quality, cotton-fiber paper.

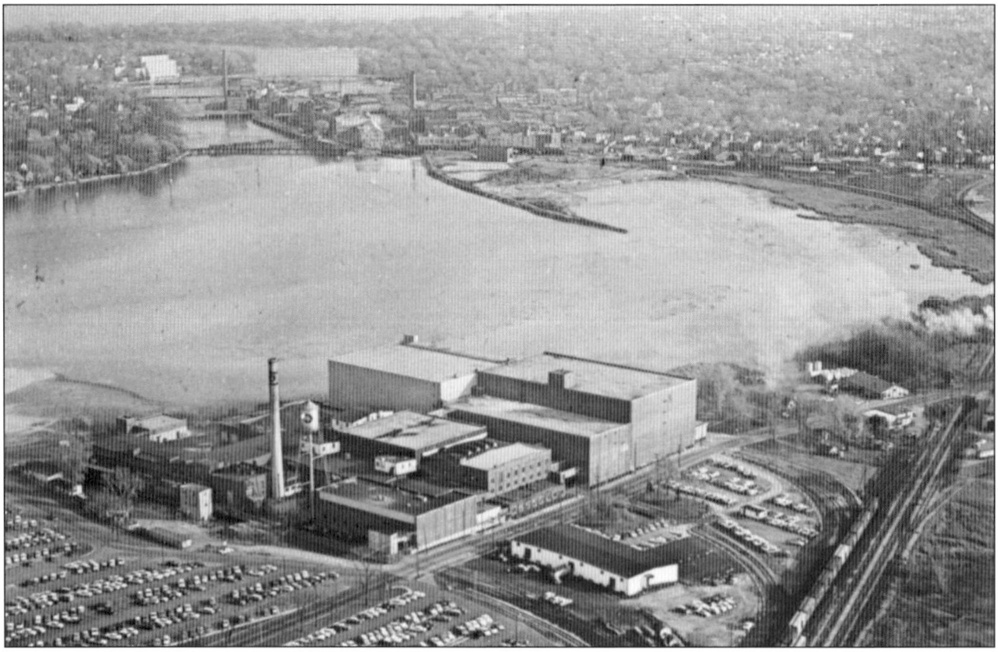

Kimberly, Clark and Co. was founded in 1872 by John A. Kimberly, Havilah Babcock, Charles B. Clark, and Franklyn C. Shattuck. It was said that Clark was an excellent manager, Kimberly a talented buyer and salesman, and Shattuck a skilled accountant. In 1914, the company developed "cellu-cotton," used as a surgical cotton substitute by the US Army during World War I. Army nurses' use of these pads as disposable sanitary napkins led to the introduction six years later of Kotex. Kleenex, marketed as a disposable handkerchief, followed in 1924. Toilet tissue soon followed, as did diapers, training pants, and other consumer paper products.

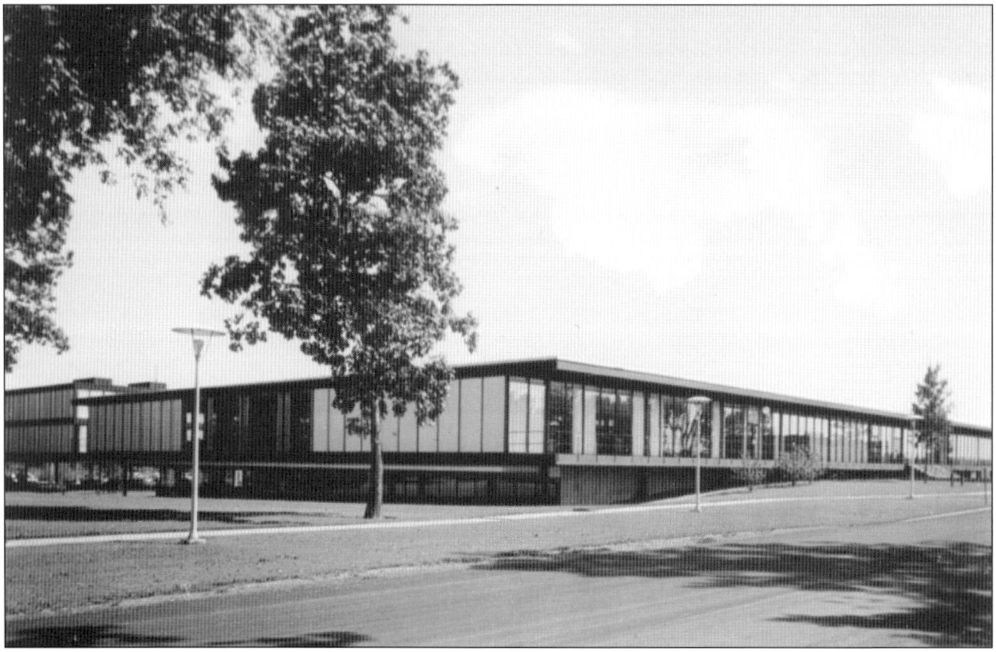

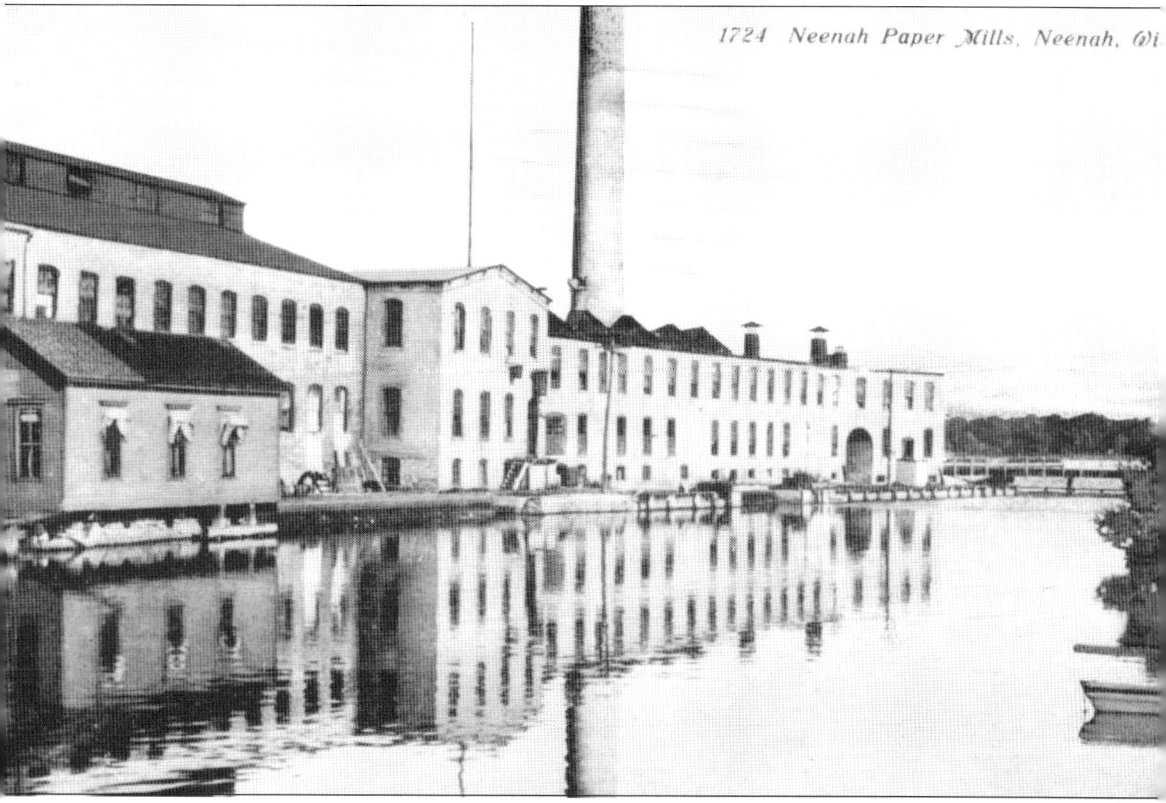

As discussed previously, Neenah Paper Company was first incorporated in 1885 by Samuel A. Cook, Henry Sherry, and Frank T. Russell. Until its sale to Kimberly-Clark in 1892, Cook threw all his efforts into the business. But concurrently and especially after the sale, he branched out into other avenues of commerce, taking an interest in a paper concern in Menasha as well as being elected a one-term mayor of Neenah in 1888. He was so popular as a politician that he was urged to run for Congress and represented Wisconsin in Washington, DC, from 1895 to 1897. The Wisconsin National Guard armory that straddled Neenah and Menasha was named after him.

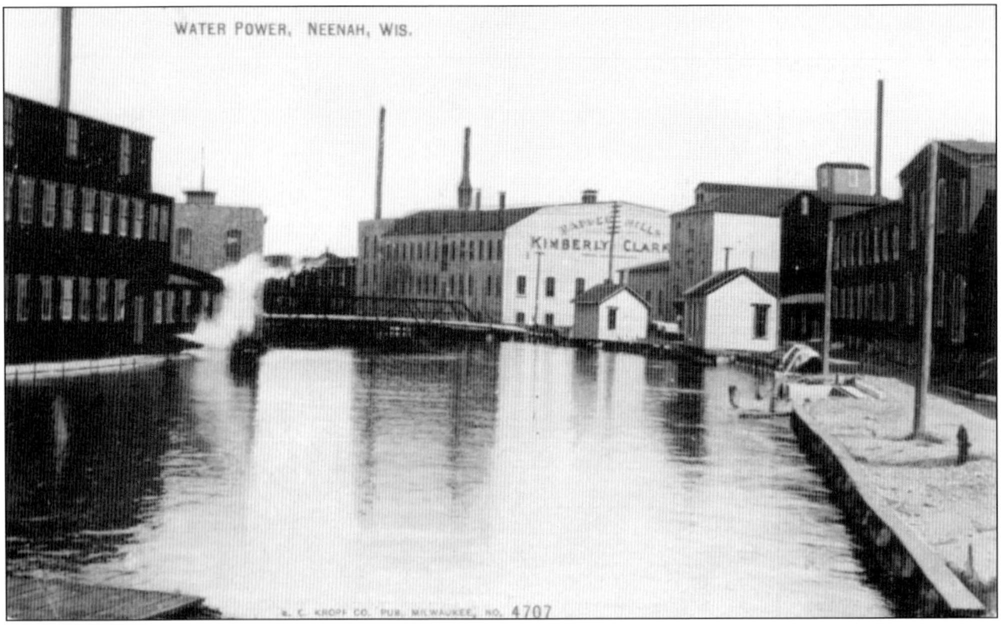

Pictured in this colorized postcard is the Badger Globe Mill. This was the only original Kimberly-Clark mill left in Neenah at the time of its demolition in 1998. It was an incorporation of the Globe Mill and the Reliance Flour Mill, built in 1868 by John R. Kimberly, J.A. Kimberly, and Havilah Babcock, and was the only remnant of the city's once-prominent flour industry.

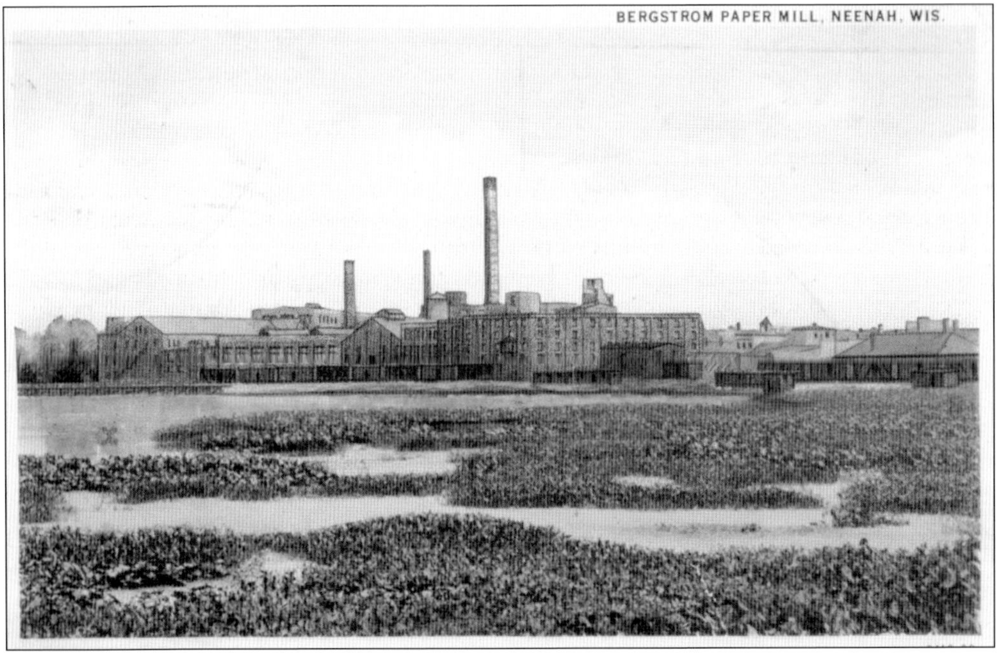

The Bergstrom family originally came to Menasha in 1852 from Norway. John Bergstrom worked on the Menasha lock, later settling in Neenah as a blacksmith. In 1878, his sons Dedrick W. and George O. Bergstrom purchased the Neenah Stove Works from H.P. Leavens, and they operated it jointly until 1904. That year, D.W. Bergstrom purchased the Winnebago Paper Mill from W.L. Davis and formed the Bergstrom Paper Company.

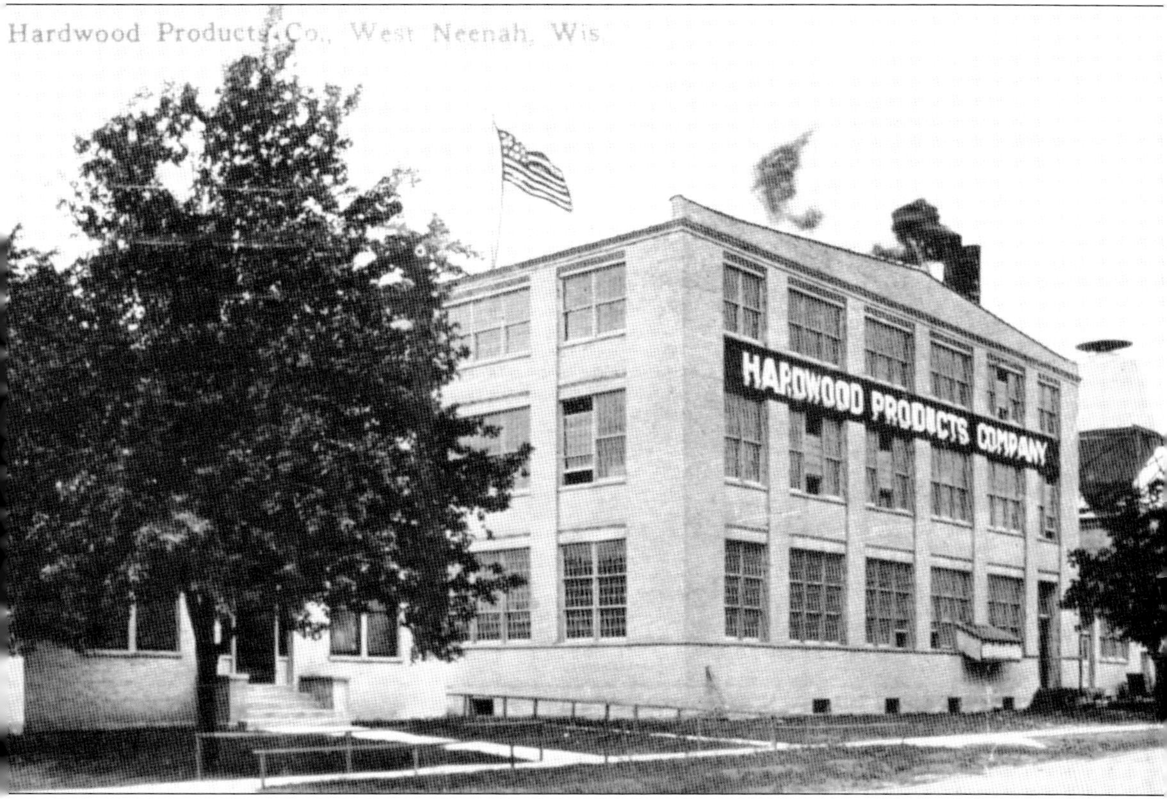

Hardwood Products Company, located on North Lake Street, was a manufacturer of solid-core veneered doors. It was the outgrowth of a small veneer plant near Vicksburg, Mississippi, and was organized by several Neenah men who were still in their 20s. The original incorporators were C.B. Clark, D.L. Kimberly, William C. Wing, and E.D. Beals. The Mississippi plant was known originally as the Kimberly-Wing Company. The name was later changed to the Mississippi Veneer & Lumber Company and finally to Hardwood Products in 1922. Organized in 1908, the plant was completed in the middle of 1911. During World War I, the entire capacity of the plant was devoted to the manufacture of Navy ammunition boxes, and during World War II, the company manufactured numerous items for war use, including its regular chief product, doors, for use on many wartime military installations.

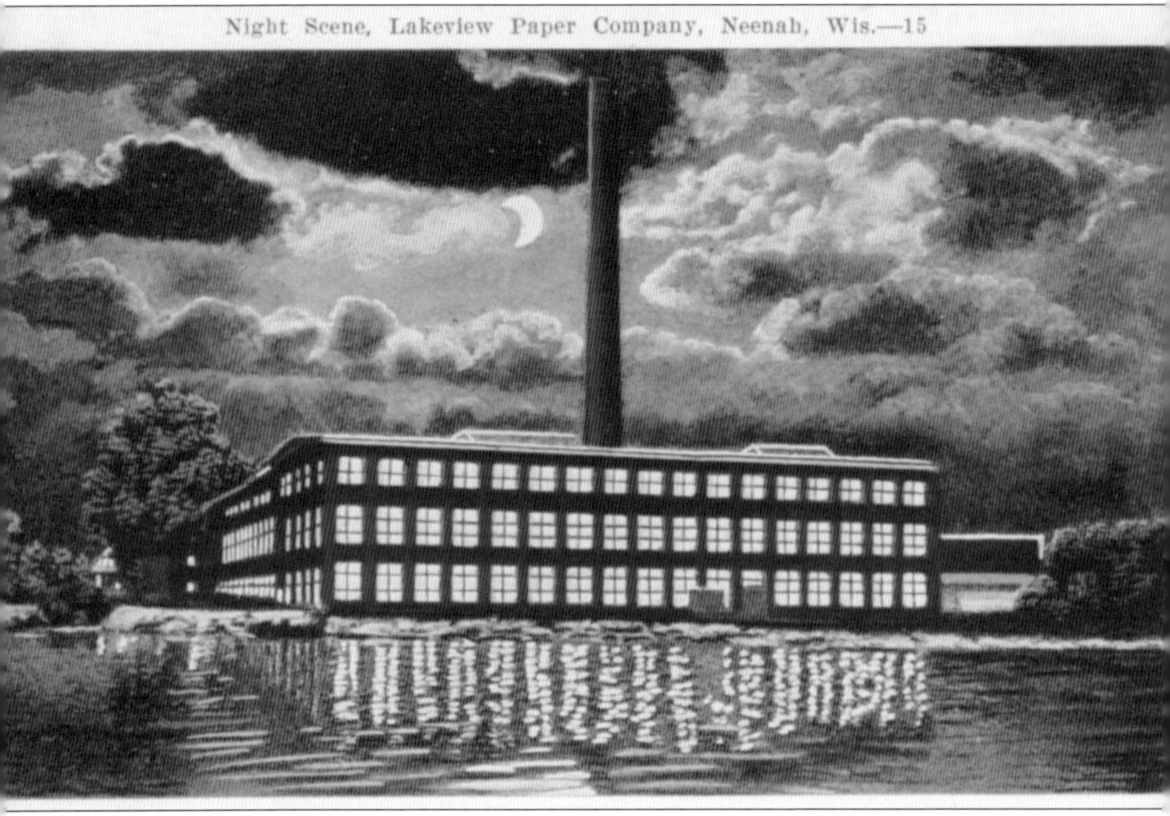

In its prime, this mill was an asset for Kimberly-Clark. But in fact, the Lakeview Mill had a history before Kimberly-Clark purchased it in 1929 from the Fraser Company, which had terminated the facility after taking it over from Sears, Roebuck and Company. Sears had run the mill for nine years, but upon this sale, the Fraser Company shut down the mill and sent the catalogue work to its mill in Maine. This property had been earmarked for millwork for many years before, but technology to convert the meager waterpower available for operations was not sufficient until many years later. Therefore, this mill did not appear until around 1911 as the Lake Side Paper Company. Kimberly-Clark operated the mill until the 1990s, when economics and new mill construction led the company to dispose of it to other concerns.

Four

Businesses and Downtown Views

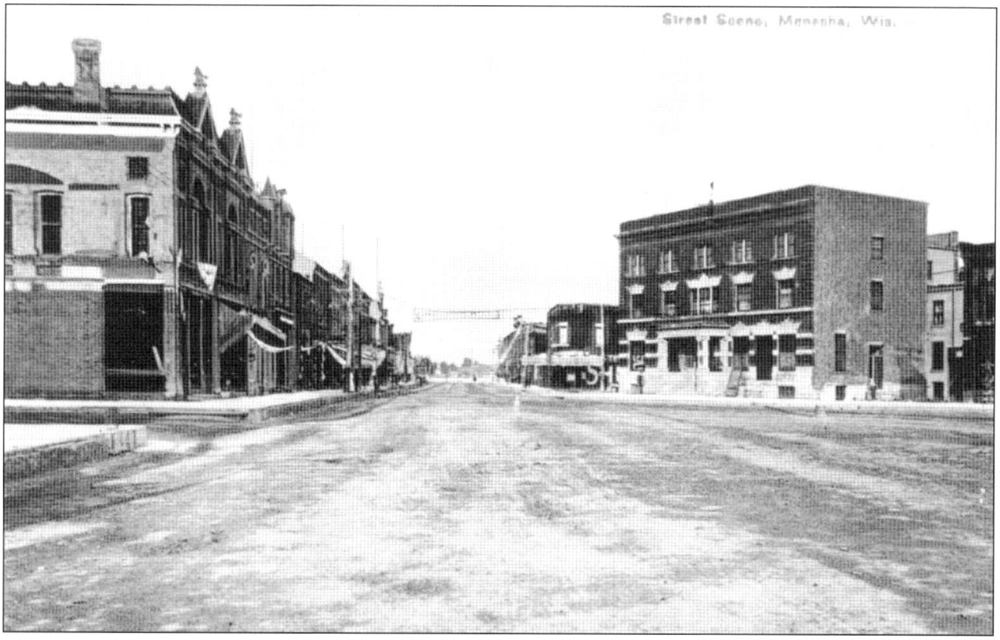

This postcard of Menasha's downtown dates between 1907 and 1910. Notice the dirt streets; Menasha's Main Street was not paved until June 1910 in preparation of the statewide Elks Convention held in the city. In order to keep dust to a minimum, the streets were periodically sprinkled with water by a horse-drawn tanker.

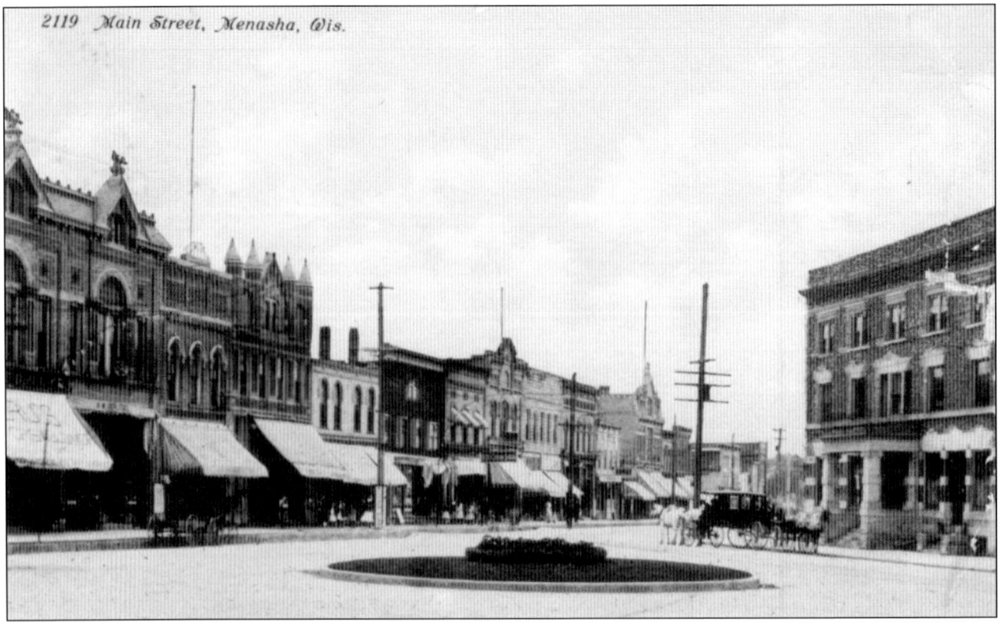

This is another series of Main Street views, taken from the vantage point of the Bank of Menasha. Notice the elaborate awnings to shield the storefronts from the sun. At the center is a prominent sign for ice cream sodas. Menasha mayor and pharmacist John Rosch brought the first soda fountain to Menasha, a very popular amusement for that era. The flowerbed in the center proved to be a point of contention for many years, depending upon who held the mayor's office. With a change in administration, it might appear for that term, only to be torn down to suit the desires of the next office holder, or it might even change shape altogether, becoming triangular, for instance.

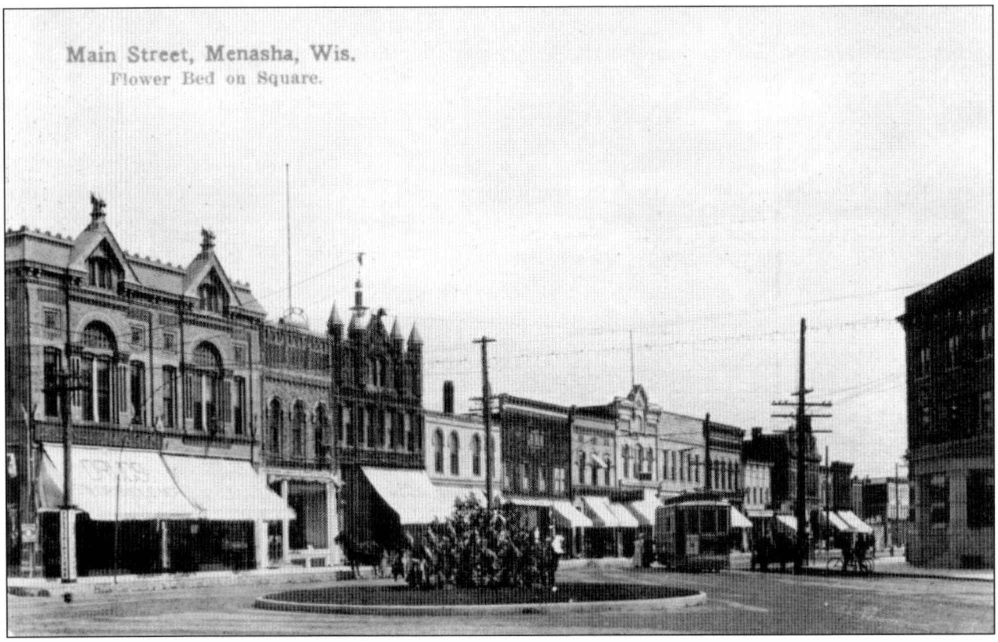

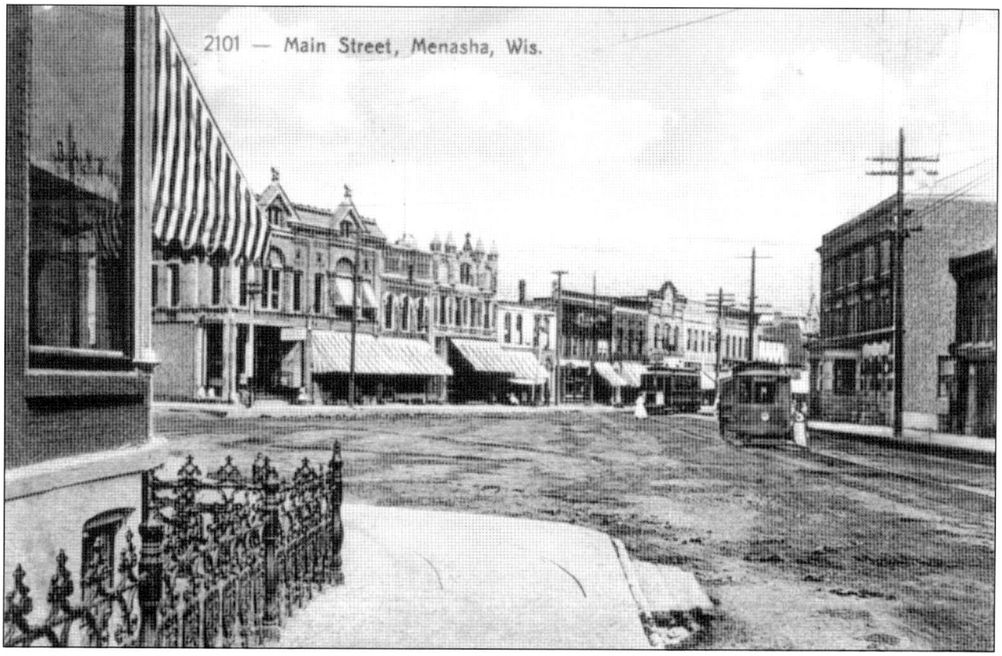

These images predate the previous street views by a few years. The street is still cedar blocks covered with dirt, and the familiar flowerbed circle in the "square" area of Main Street is absent. But notice the streetcar activity in front of the Hotel Menasha. Eager riders could take the trolley to Neenah for a nickel or venture out to Brighton or Waverly Beach for the same one-way fare. The view above gives a better idea of the structure of the Bank of Menasha. As with many cards of the pre–World War I era, these two postcards were printed in Germany.

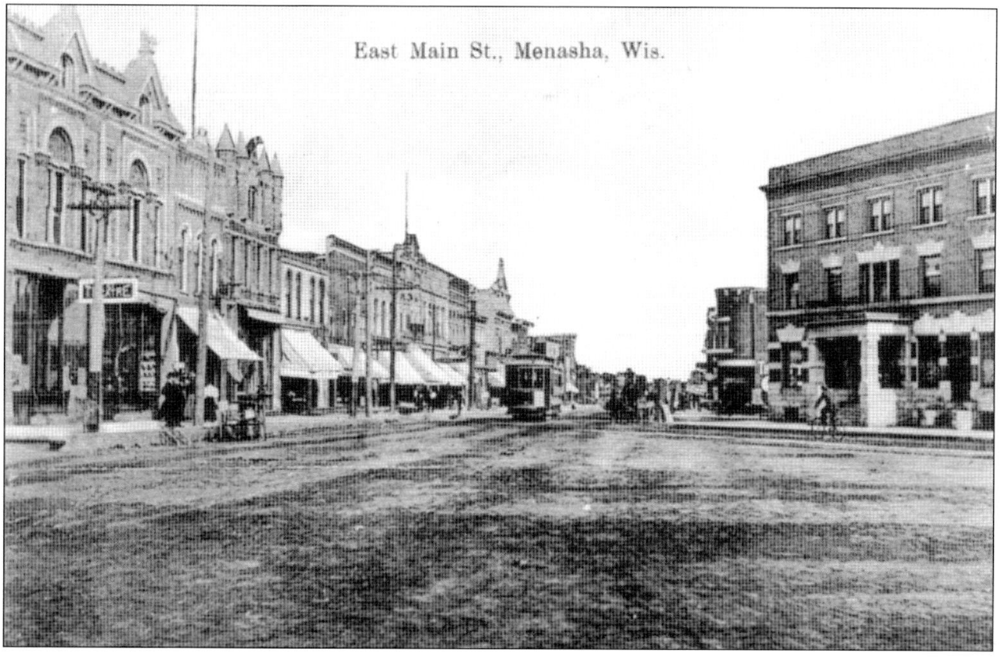

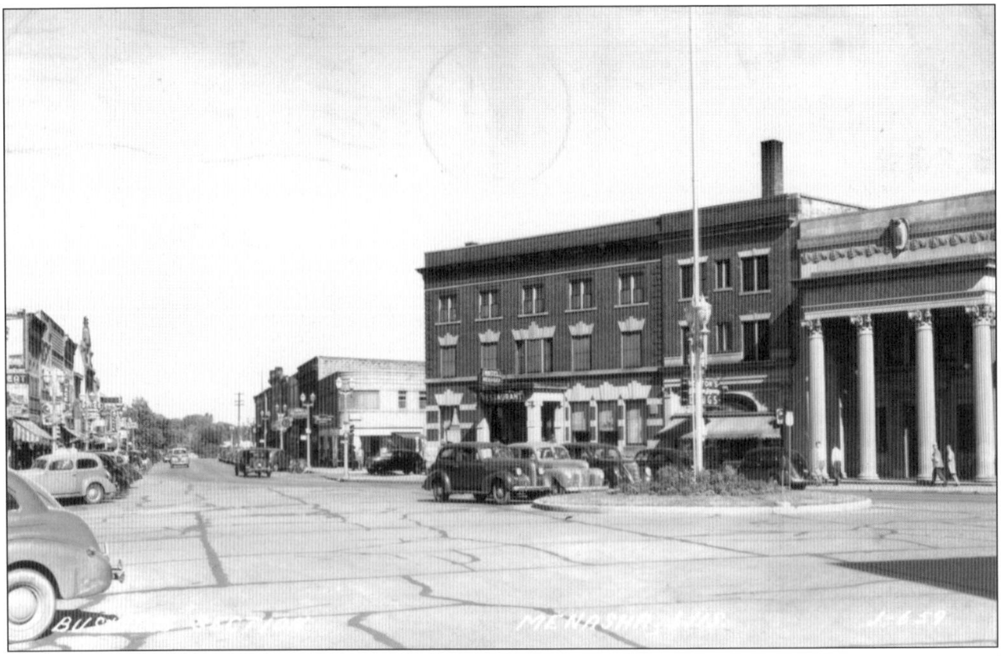

These two real-photo postcards from approximately 1946–1947 showcase the bustling activity of a prosperous Menasha. The stately First National Bank, with its four solid columns marking its entrance, made one feel secure about depositing money there. The unspoken message was one of strength. Across the street, be it the five-and-dime, the grocery, or one of several pharmacies, a thriving downtown business section was sure to deliver what the customer ordered. The corner building on the left was constructed in the 1880s by Reuben Scott, one Menasha's pioneers. In 1869, Scott built the National Hotel, the forerunner to the Hotel Menasha, which was built upon the same site.

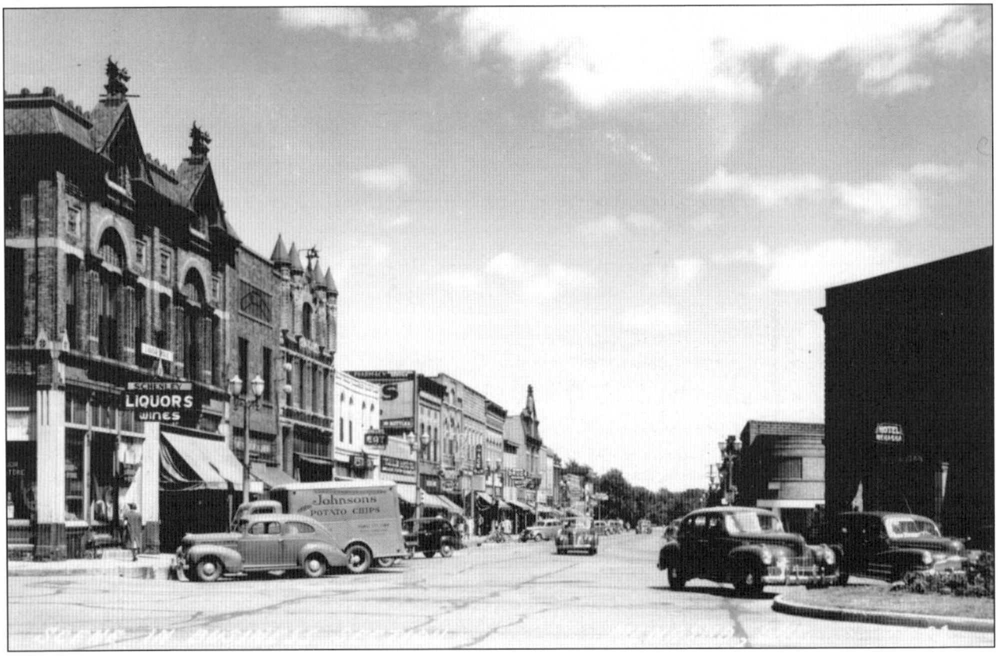

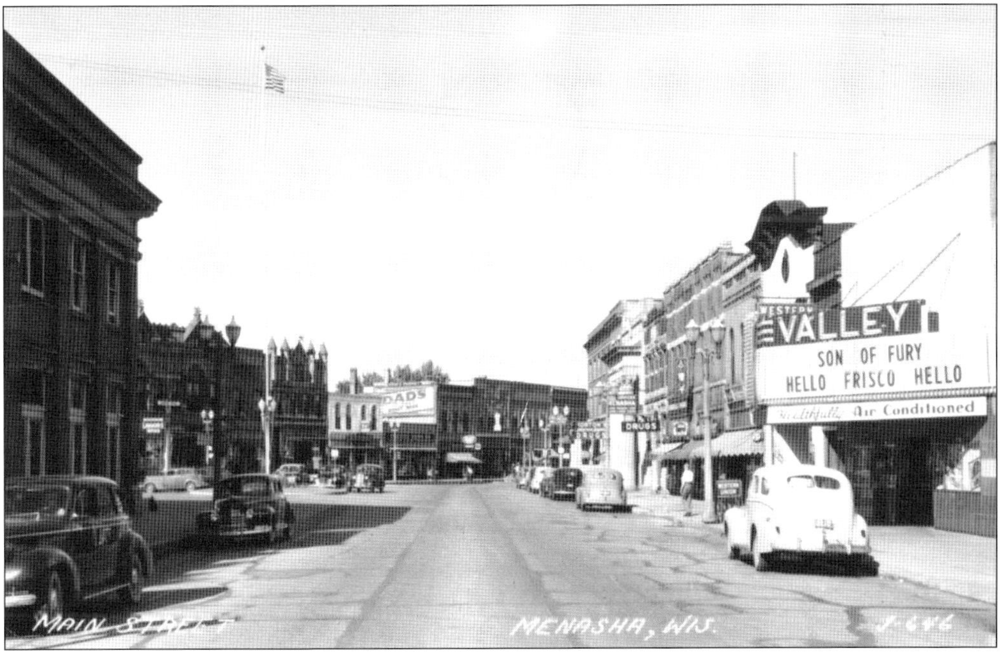

These two cards provide a "now and then" comparison of the same stretch of Main Street looking east toward the heart of downtown. The view above dates to around 1947, similar to the previous views. The view below is from around 1964, as the then-new First National Bank opened that year, taking the place of the movie theater and several other adjacent businesses. The Bank of Menasha is also fairly new, modeling a streamlined appearance. Construction workers in 1962 actually removed the second floor of the bank building and turned it into something deemed more suitable for the ultra-modern 1960s. Another sign of the times, as evidenced in the 1960s card, is the prevalence of TV antennas on the businesses next to the bank.

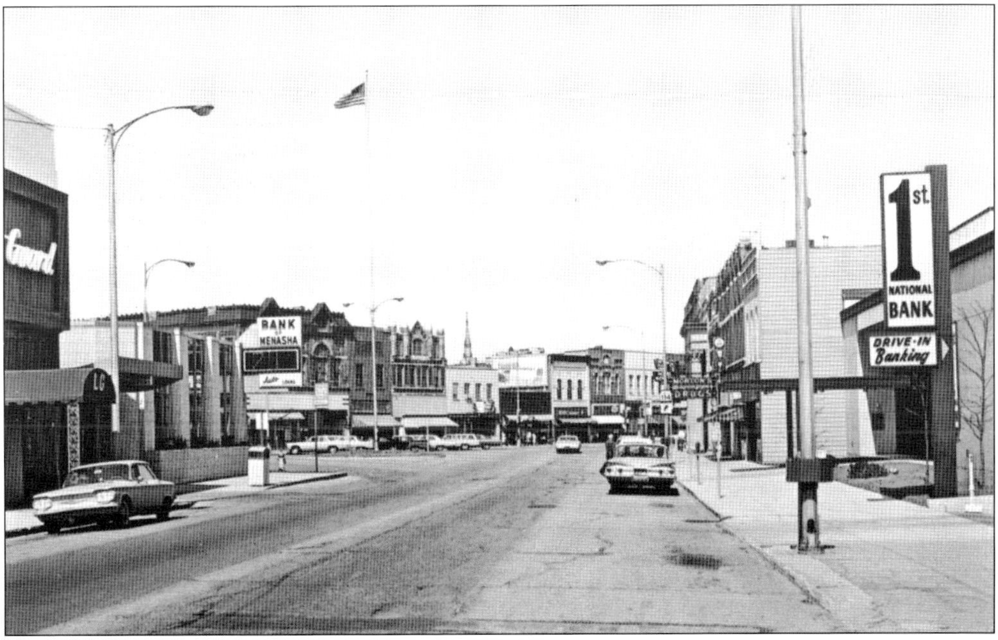

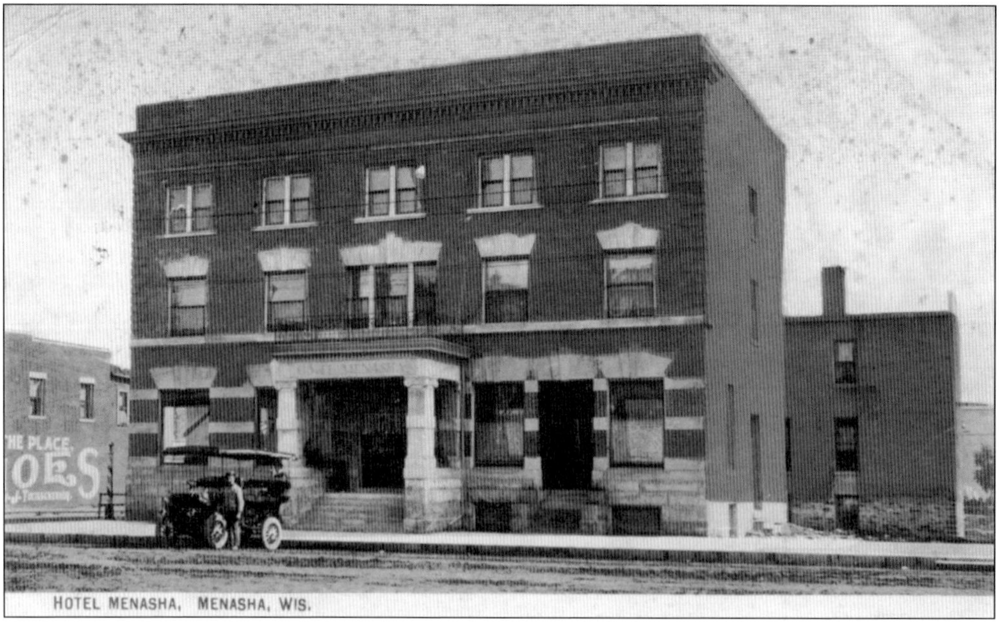

After Menasha's National Hotel burned down in October 1901, Reuben Scott's widow chose to not rebuild on the site, leaving the heart of downtown without a hotel. Plans for a new hotel were developed by city fathers and local manufacturers. Vital to the project were Christ Walter (Walters Brewing), Charles Smith (Menasha Wooden Ware), and Charles Howard (Howard Paper Company), who resourced the project. The town turned out for the laying of the cornerstone in 1905; speeches and a brass band marked the occasion. The new hotel cost $35,000 and became such a hit that it required additions in 1911 and 1916. Notice the prominent signage on the side of Tuchscherer's shoe store across the street, which for years announced, "This is the Place for Shoes."

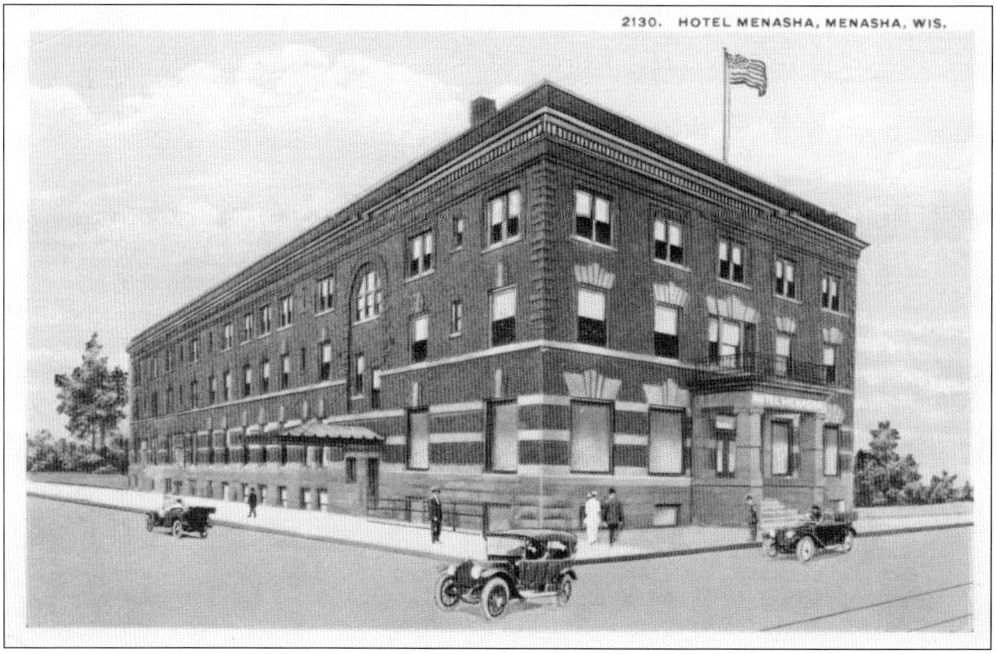

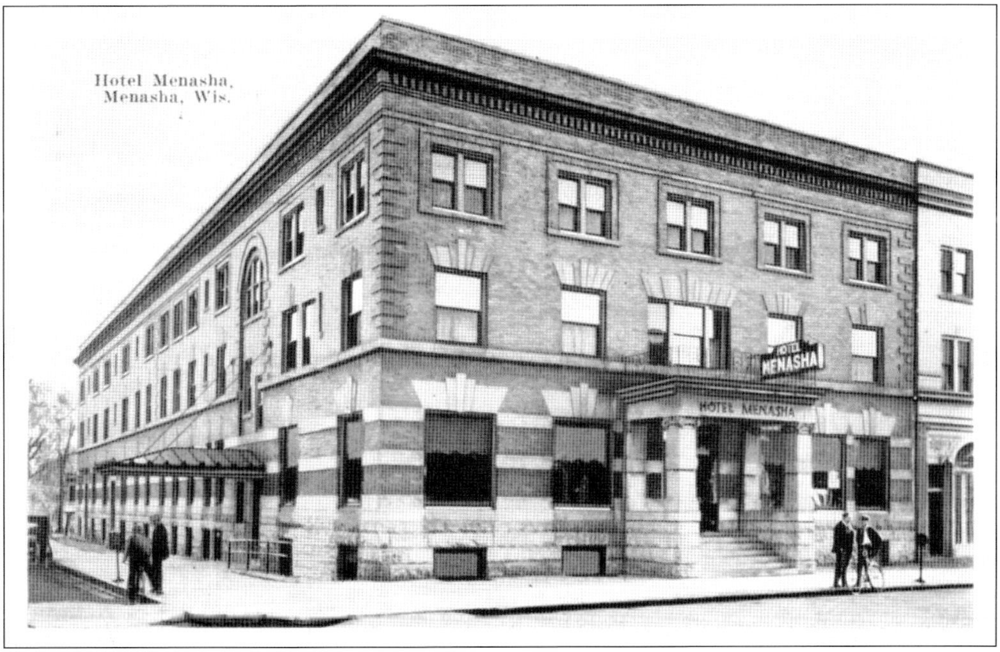

These postcards show the addition to the hotel between the hotel proper and the First National Bank. The main entrance on Main Street would eventually be bricked up in favor of the Mill Street entrance, marked by a dark awning. As with other views of the hotel, automobiles were a significant prop to any photographs of the establishment. The original Wisconsin Central Railroad Company was organized in Menasha on this site at the National Hotel in 1871 and was established by an act of the Wisconsin state legislature and incorporated in February 1871. A plaque was dedicated in 1955 by the State Historical Society of Wisconsin and affixed to the Hotel Menasha.

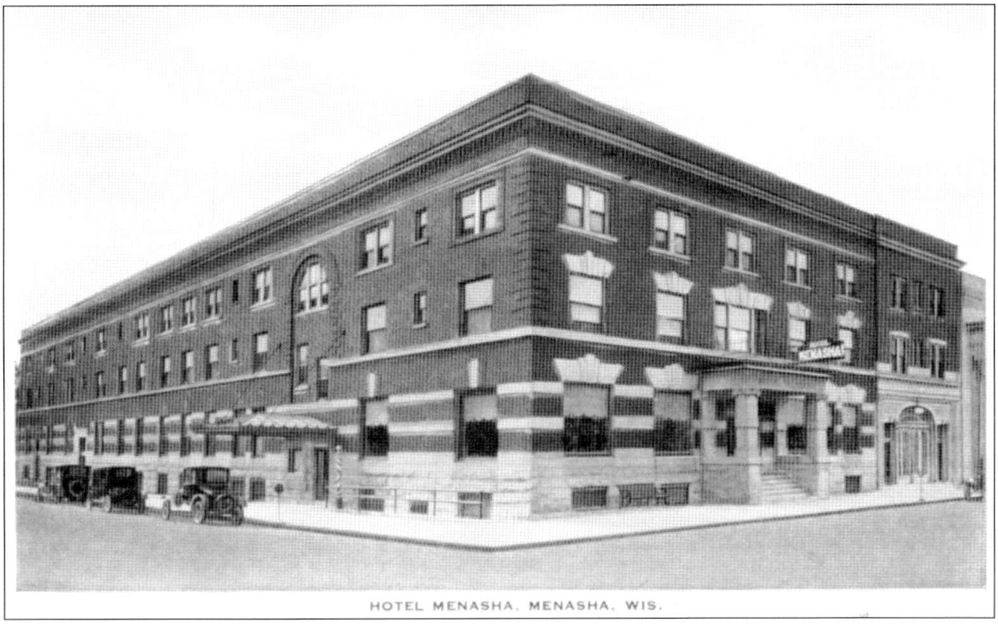

HOTEL MENASHA, MENASHA, WIS.

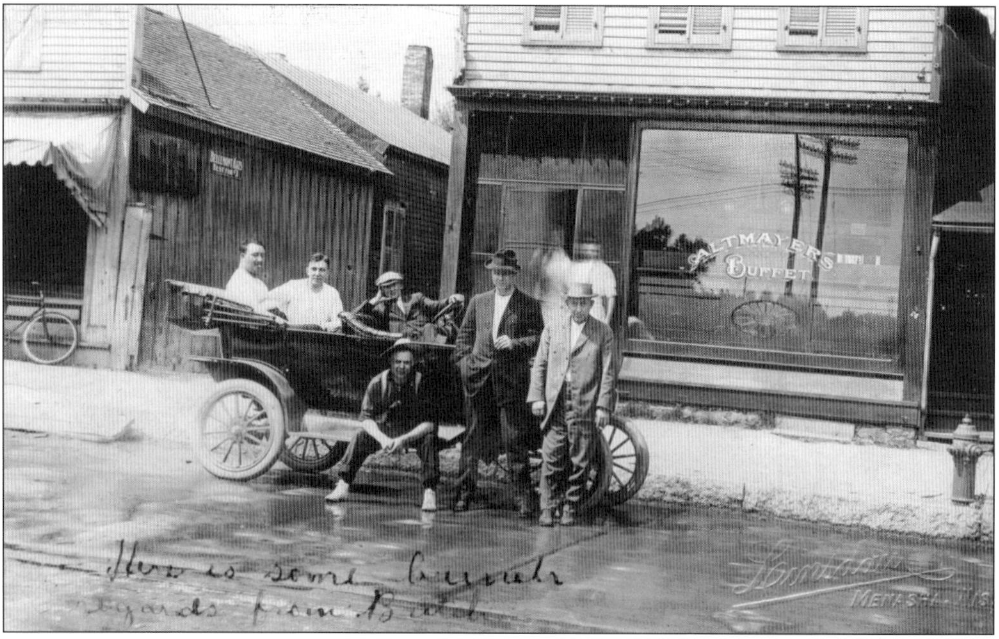

This postcard dates from 1913. George Altmayer's buffet was on the north side of Main Street, just a few doors down from the corner of Main and Racine Streets. By 1920, Altmayer had moved his establishment to the south side of Main Street in the Tuchscherer's shoe store block, directly across from the Fox River House. By then, it was called College Inn, and by 1924, it was no longer in business.

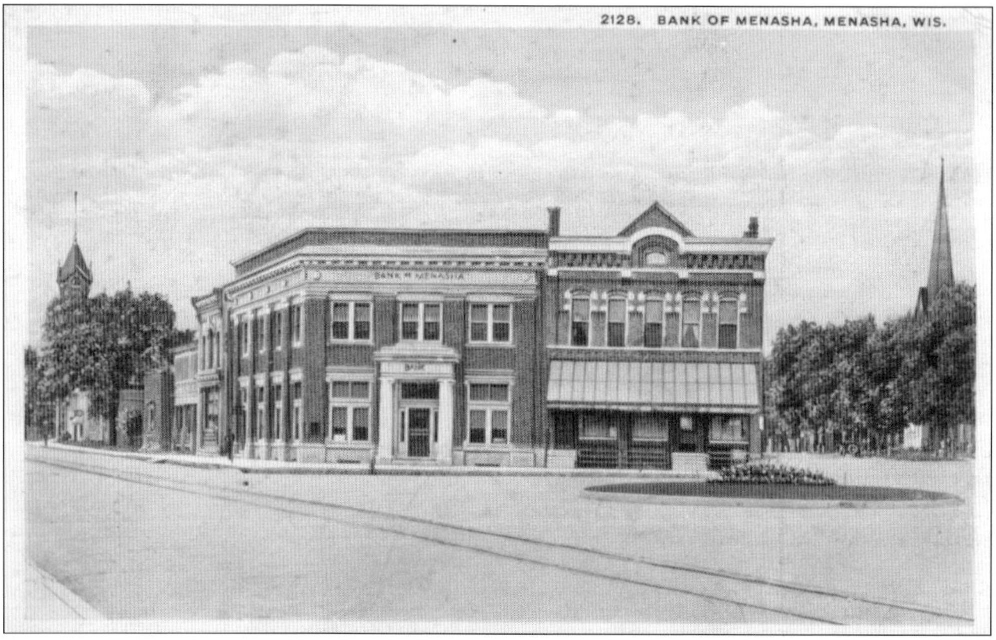

The Bank of Menasha was founded in 1870 by Henry Hewitt as the National Bank of Menasha. Hewitt, who was born in England in 1814, moved to Menasha in 1856 as a contractor, overseeing the excavation of the enlarged canal and the construction of the crib work in the front of the dam and the original wooden Tayco Street Bridge. He began his banking career in Neenah in 1865.

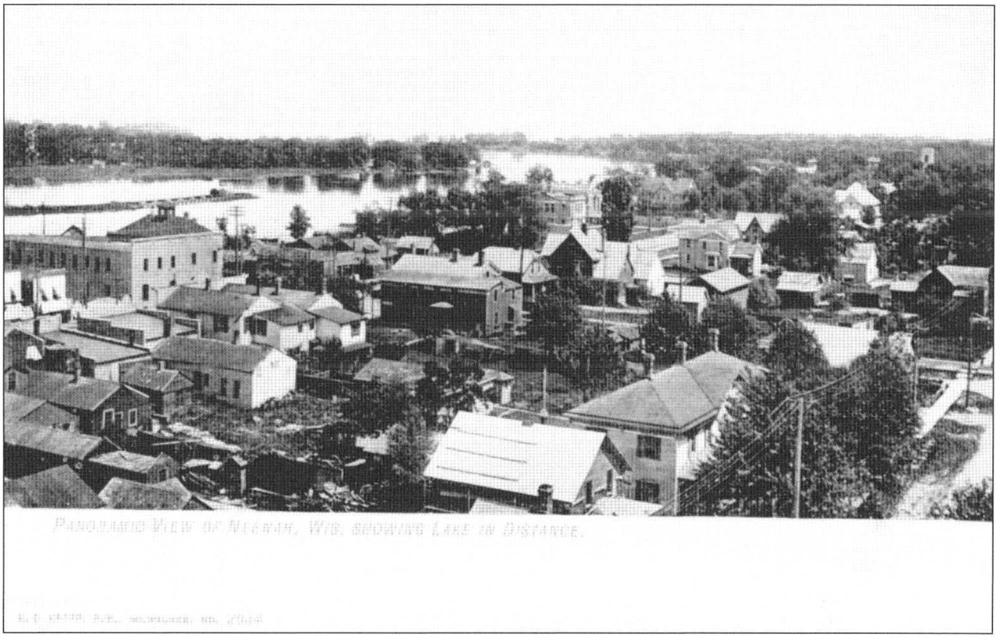

This aerial view of Neenah was likely taken from a vantage point on top of city hall around 1906. The Fox River can be seen prominently to the left flowing away from the city into Lake Winnebago. The recently completed public library makes an appearance on the south bank of the Fox in the center of the photograph.

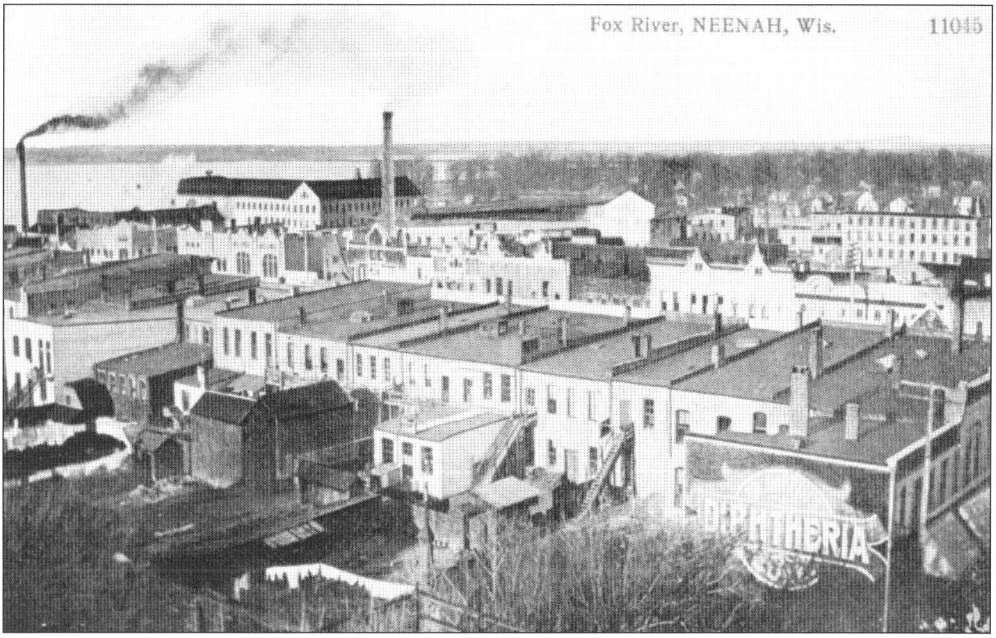

Here is a view to the northwest with Little Lake Butte des Morts in the background. Prominently shown up front is an advertisement on a building for Dr. Giffin's diphtheria preventive and cure. Dr. Leverett W. Giffin was a prominent physician in Neenah and marketed what he called the Muco Solvent, a diphtheria cure. Patent medicine was common at the time and quite popular with the buying public.

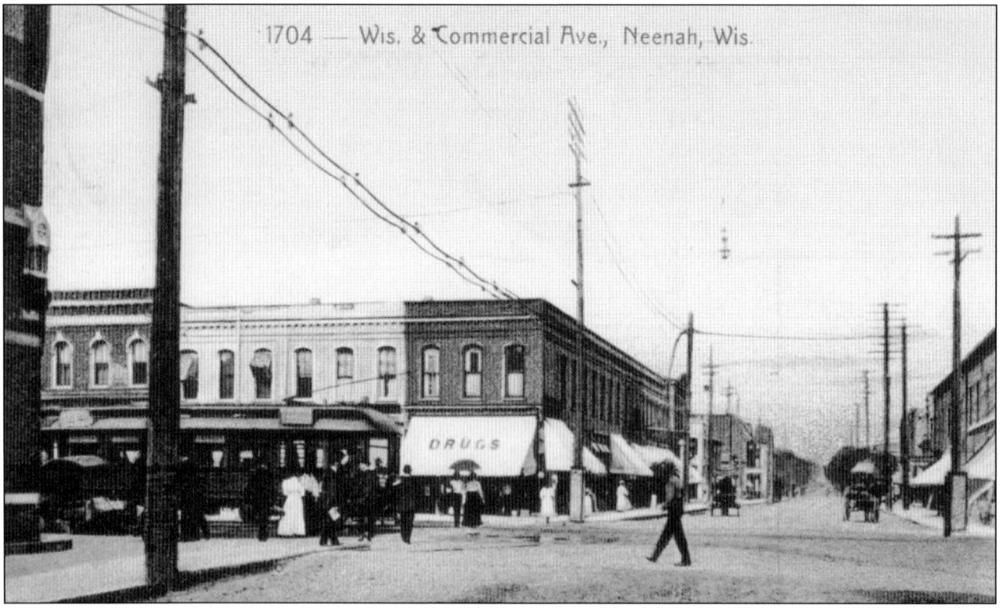

Visible to the extreme right is Anspach's Department Store, a Neenah institution since 1855. In 1910, the store suffered an extensive fire, but it was rebuilt. When it closed in 1931, it sold its inventory to Jandrey's Department Store and the building to Woolworth's. Across Commercial Street on the corner is the Barnett Pharmacy. The streetcar stopped in front of the pharmacy was likely taking passengers to Fond du Lac.

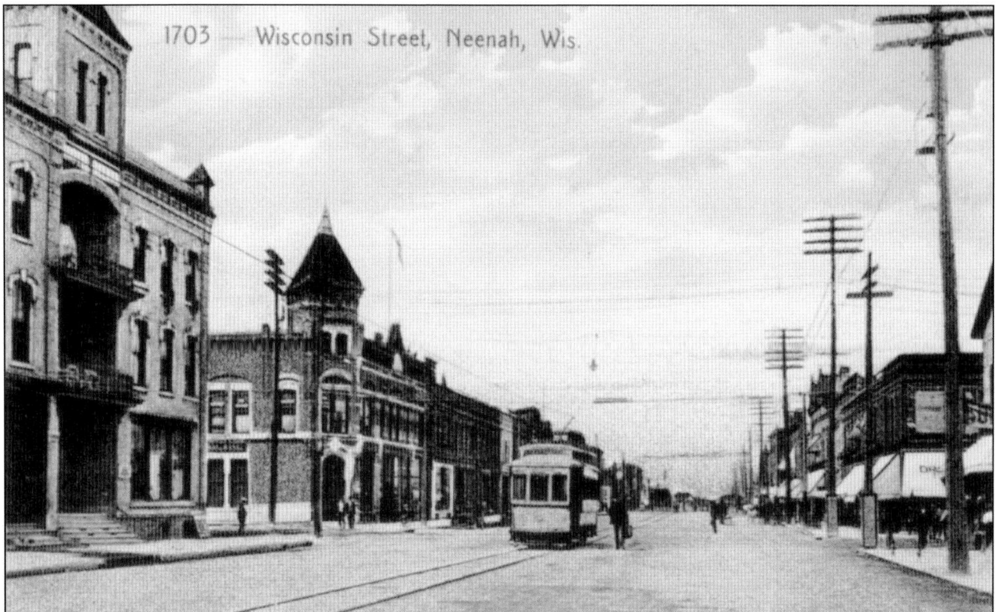

The building across from the Hotel Neenah (left) housed the First National Bank and replaced the storefronts known as the Pettibone block, which had burned in January 1883. The fire crossed Commercial Street, then known as Cedar Street, and extensively damaged the hotel, then known as the Russell House. Thankfully, no lives were lost. This building was replaced in the early 1920s by a new bank.

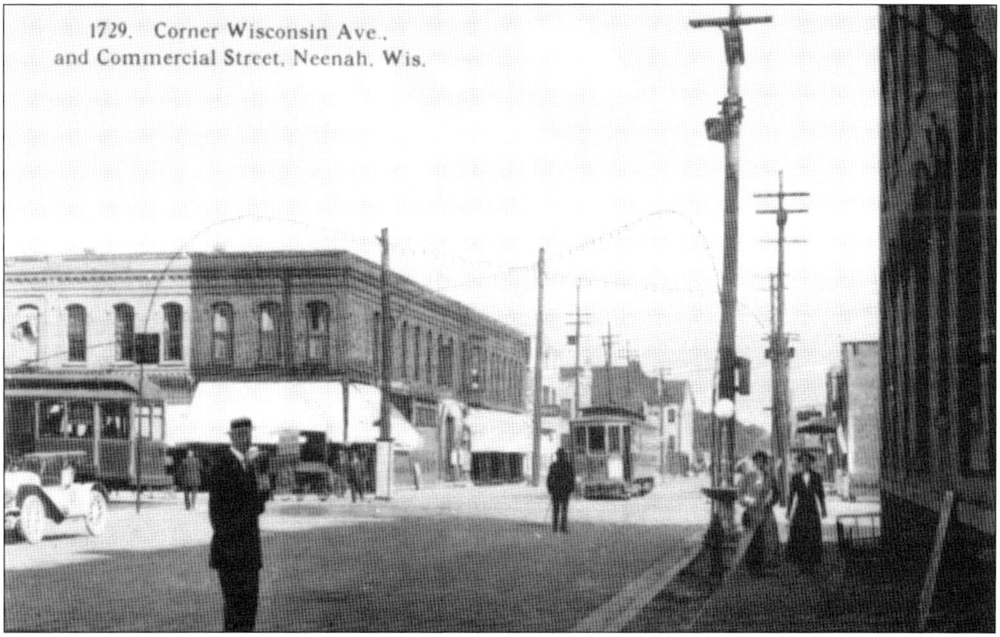

This card is representative of many that showcase a city's transportation assets—figures caught in mid-stride down a sidewalk or hailing the next available trolley. With the slow speed of automobiles of the day, or their absence, the sight of a lone figure standing in the middle of the street is not a rarity. This intersection, being the heart of downtown Neenah, justifiably gets much attention.

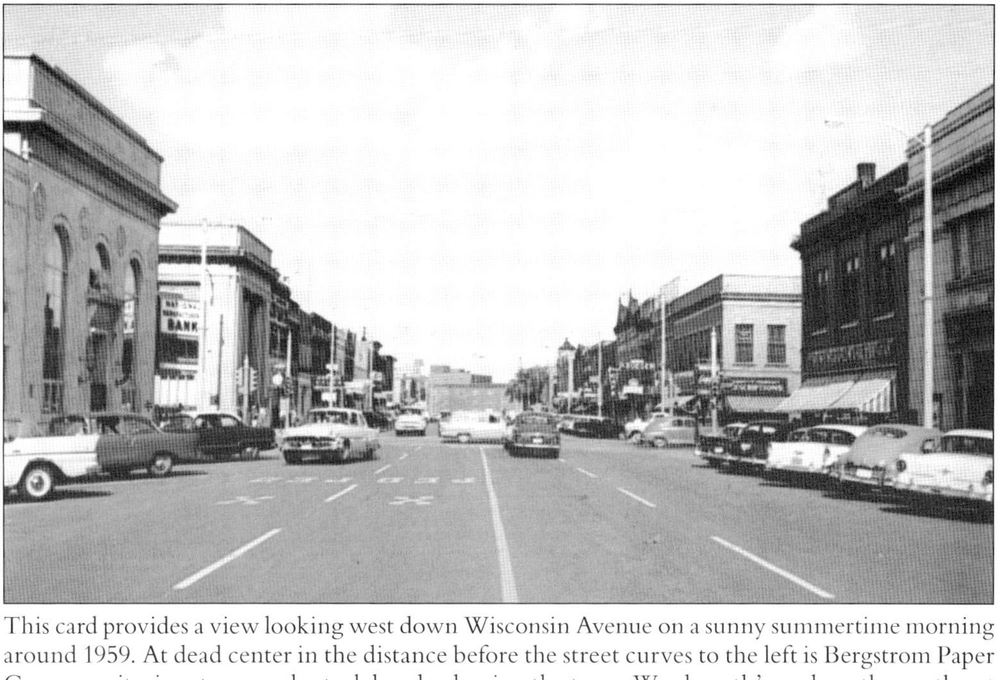

This card provides a view looking west down Wisconsin Avenue on a sunny summertime morning around 1959. At dead center in the distance before the street curves to the left is Bergstrom Paper Company, its signature smokestack barely clearing the trees. Woolworth's anchors the northeast corner of the intersection. It was the national variety store of its day, though in the next block lies its local competitor, Schultz Brothers.

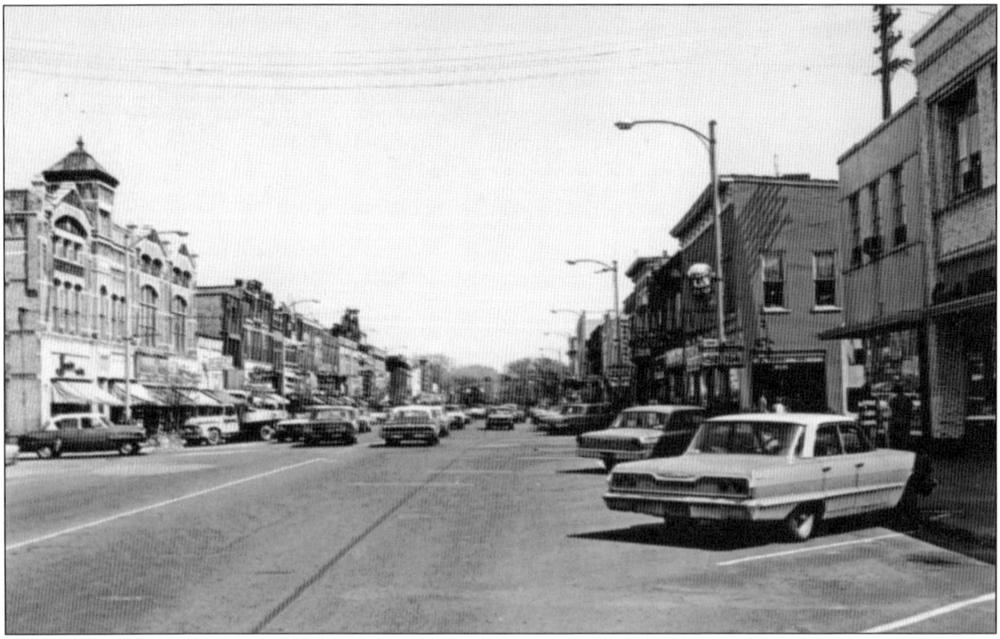

This is a view looking east down Wisconsin Avenue around 1968. Notice the A&W Root Beer sign on the lamp post, beckoning drivers on this, the terminus of State Highway 150, to make the turn right and go one block south to find sustenance in a frothy glass mug. Lots of good memories are associated with that restaurant.

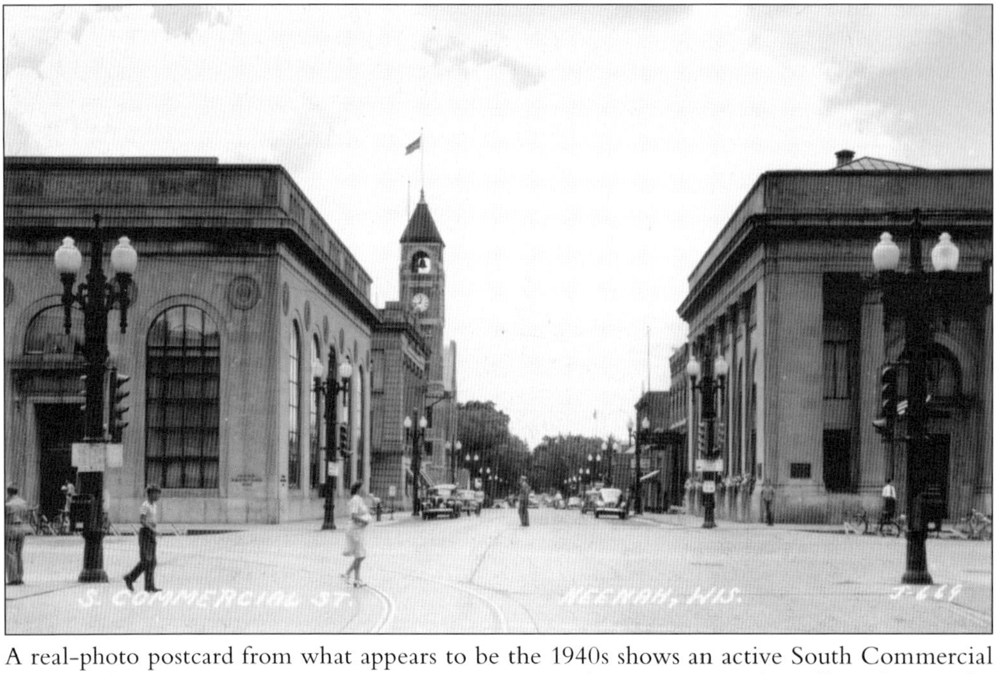

A real-photo postcard from what appears to be the 1940s shows an active South Commercial Street at the Wisconsin Avenue intersection. Notice the streetcar tracks still evident in the pavement, even though no streetcar had gone through this intersection since 1927. Judging from what appears to be a serviceman near the lamp post, this might be during or shortly after World War II.

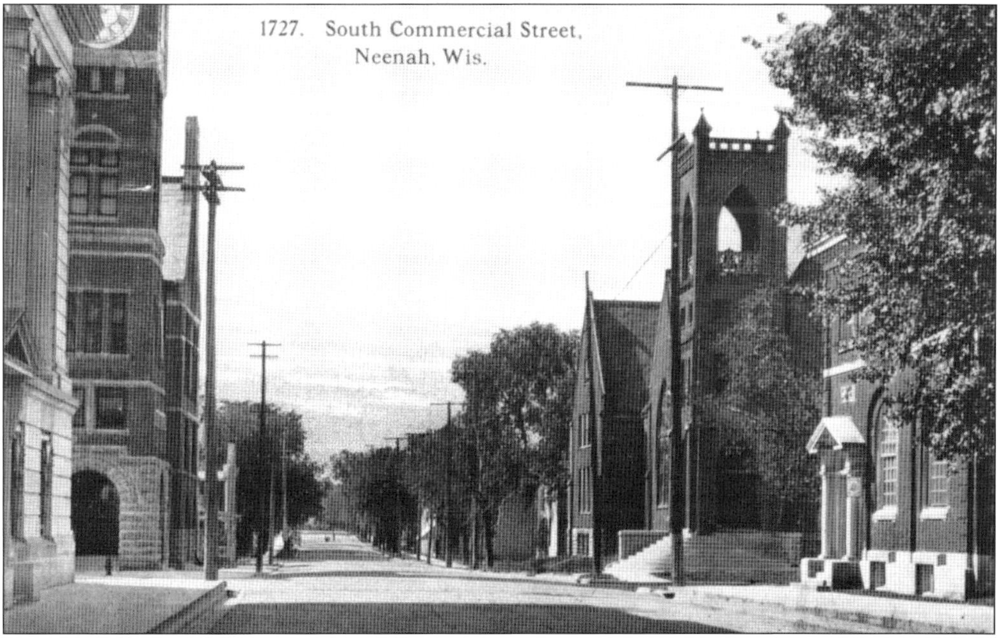

This 1914 postcard portrays a peaceful idyll on South Commercial Street. On the left is the Equitable Fraternal Union building, followed by city hall with its distinctive clock tower. Directly across the street is the First Methodist Church. Compared to the retail and banking hustle and bustle of Wisconsin Avenue, this looks rather placid.

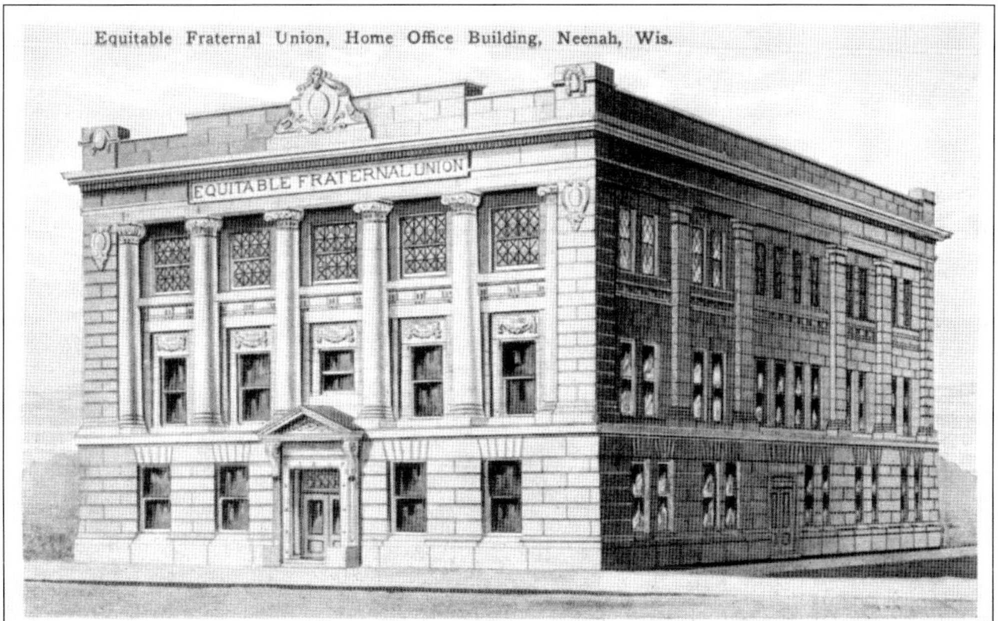

The Equitable Fraternal Union, formed in 1897, was a life insurance company that merged with Fraternal Reserve Association in Oshkosh in 1930 and several other insurance plans over subsequent years. This postcard shows the home office building on South Commercial Street that was dedicated in 1909. In 2016, this building, designed by Oshkosh's William Waters, was listed in the National Register of Historic Places.

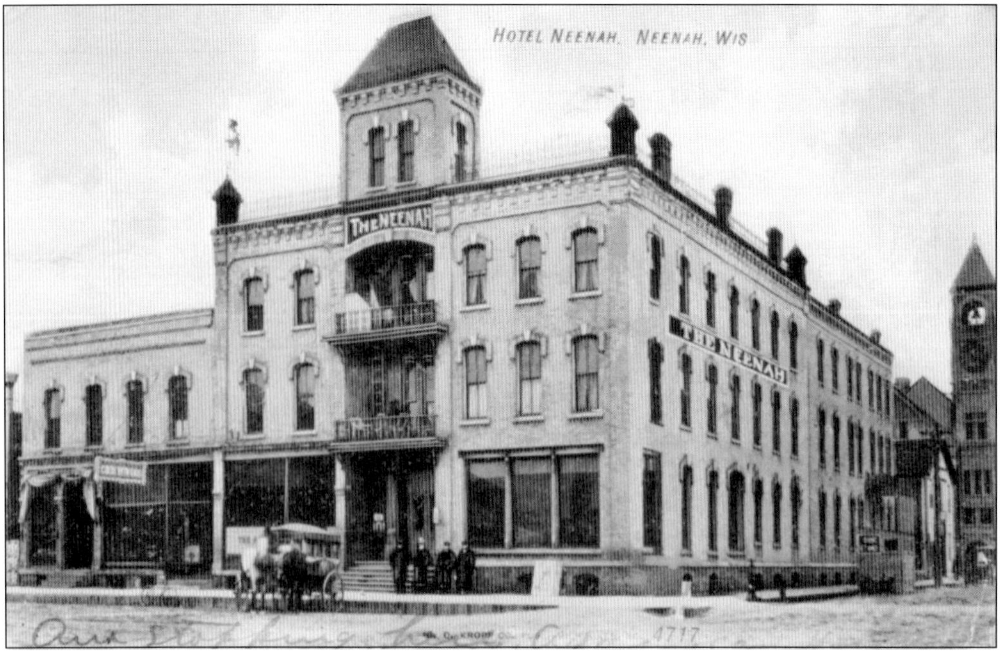

Neenah enjoyed hotel accommodations in the heart of downtown at this corner of Wisconsin Avenue and South Commercial Street, beginning in 1854 with the old Weeden Hotel. Beginning its life as the Russell House in 1875, this facility suffered a devastating fire in January 1883 but was rebuilt to the standards pictured here. The hotel lasted until 1922, when the National Manufacturers Bank purchased the site.

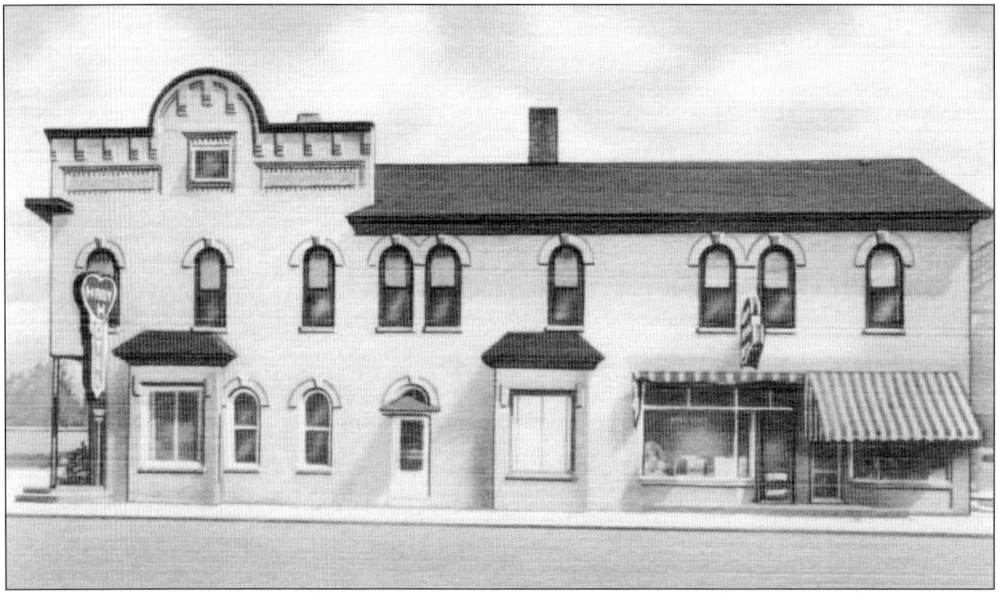

This linen postcard portrays the Hart Hotel, which was on North Commercial Street, across the street from the Chicago & North Western Railway depot. The back of this postcard uses the motto "Excellence Without Extravagance" and lists the hotel as being on US Route 114 "in the heart of the beautiful Fox River Valley, on Lake Winnebago." In keeping with the time of its printing, appeal to the vacationer was paramount.

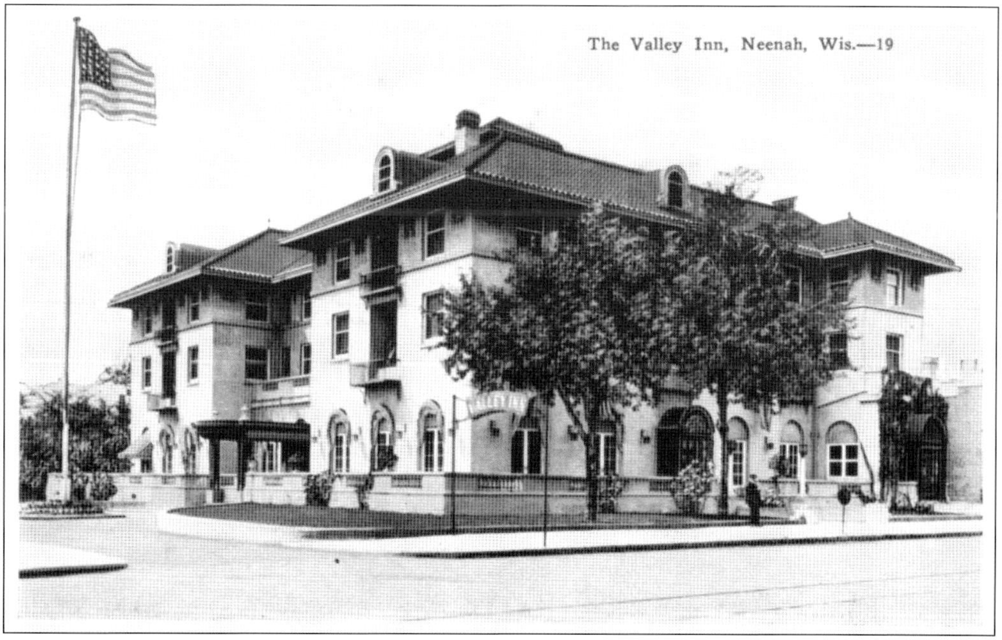

Built in 1916, the Valley Inn was Neenah's answer to the call for a "modern" hotel and was designed by local notable George Edwin Bergstrom, who later designed the Pentagon. It is said that the hotel's architectural design reflected Bergstrom's California influences, as he had relocated to Southern California after college and practiced architecture there. Sadly, the facility was razed and another hotel built on the site in the late 1960s. The photochrome card below, from the late 1950s, lists the hotel on the back as "The Aristocrat of the Valley" and touts its "Food of Distinction."

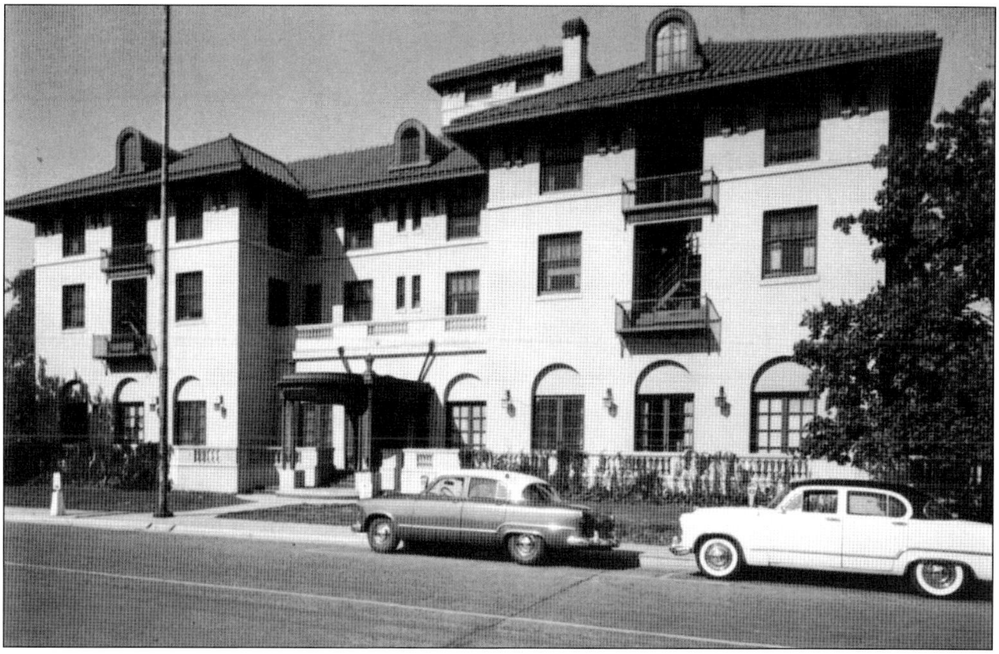

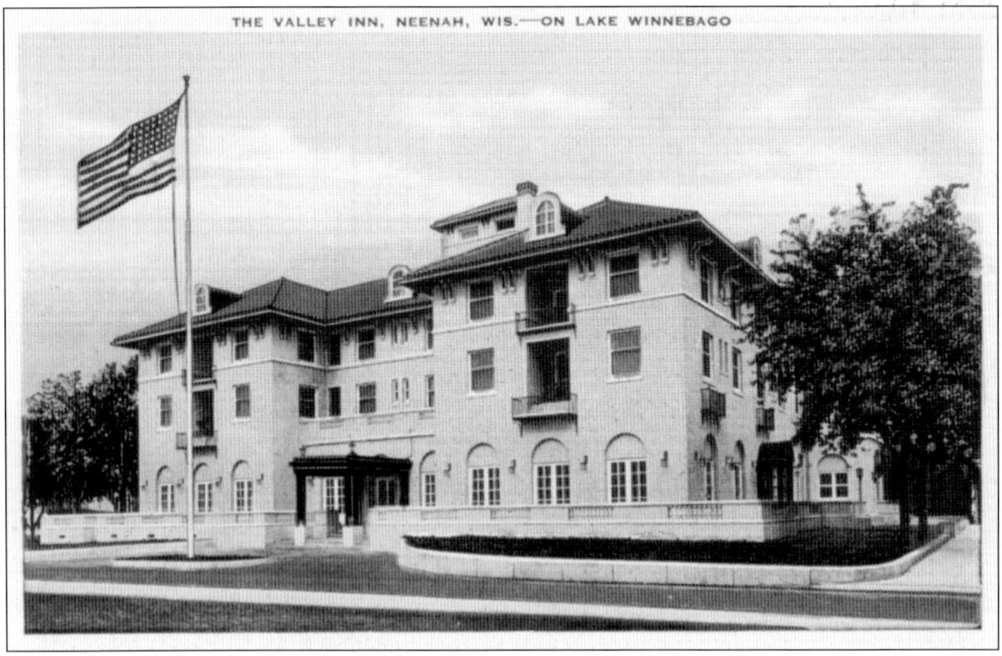

When it was time to name a location for the Valley Inn, locals were said to have been polled extensively as to their ideas. Needless to say, the retailers along Wisconsin Avenue were overjoyed to welcome a hotel in their midst. Some proposed locating the hotel on Lake Shore Avenue overlooking Lake Winnebago or at another location on South Park Avenue near the water plant. They argued that such a location would be attractive to summer tourists. This might have been a good idea, because a cursory review of these postcards' text implies the Valley Inn is actually on Lake Winnebago. The creative punctuation gives that impression, when the truth is that it is Neenah that is located on Lake Winnebago—advertising, indeed.

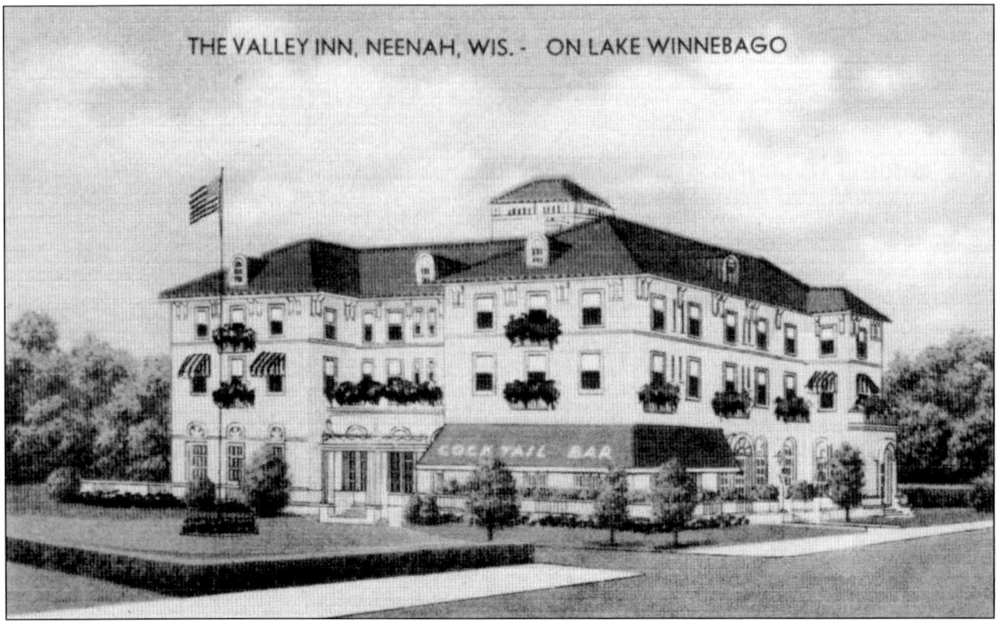

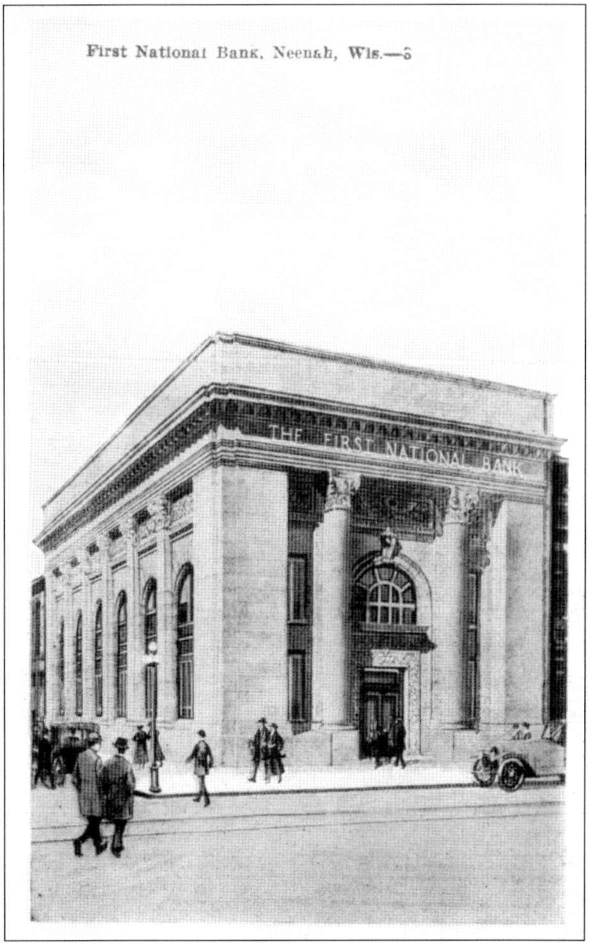

The First National Bank of Neenah began life in 1861 as the Bank of Neenah with Robert Shiells as its first president. It was a private bank at its inception, but in 1865, it applied for a charter as a national bank and then was known as the National Bank of Neenah. The First National moniker was added in 1905. Henry Hewitt, of Bank of Menasha fame, was its second president. The bank pictured at right dates from January 1921. It operated from its familiar site at the southwest corner of Wisconsin Avenue and Commercial Street, even when that structure was razed for the more modern facility pictured below, which opened in May 1964.

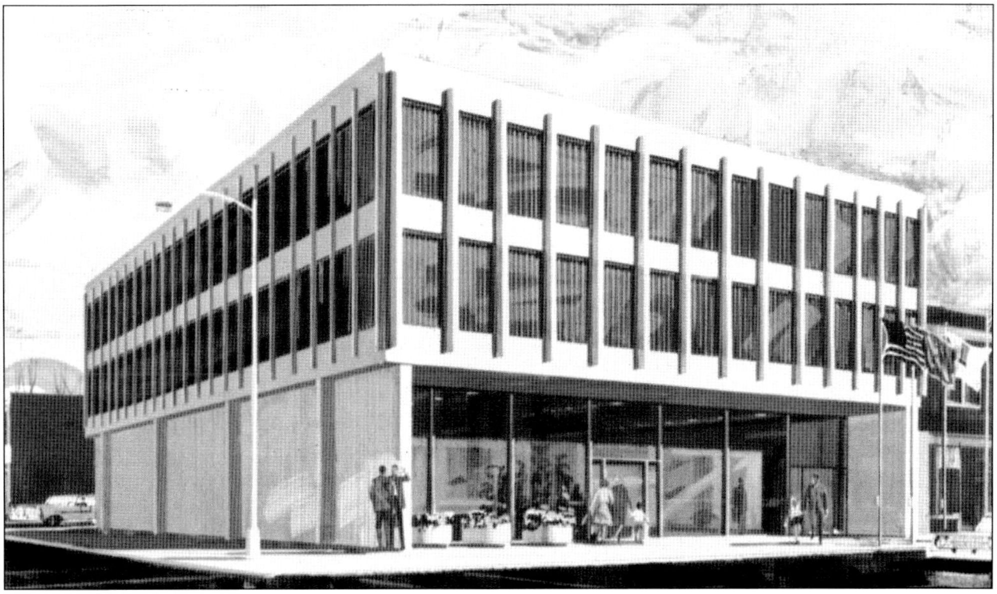

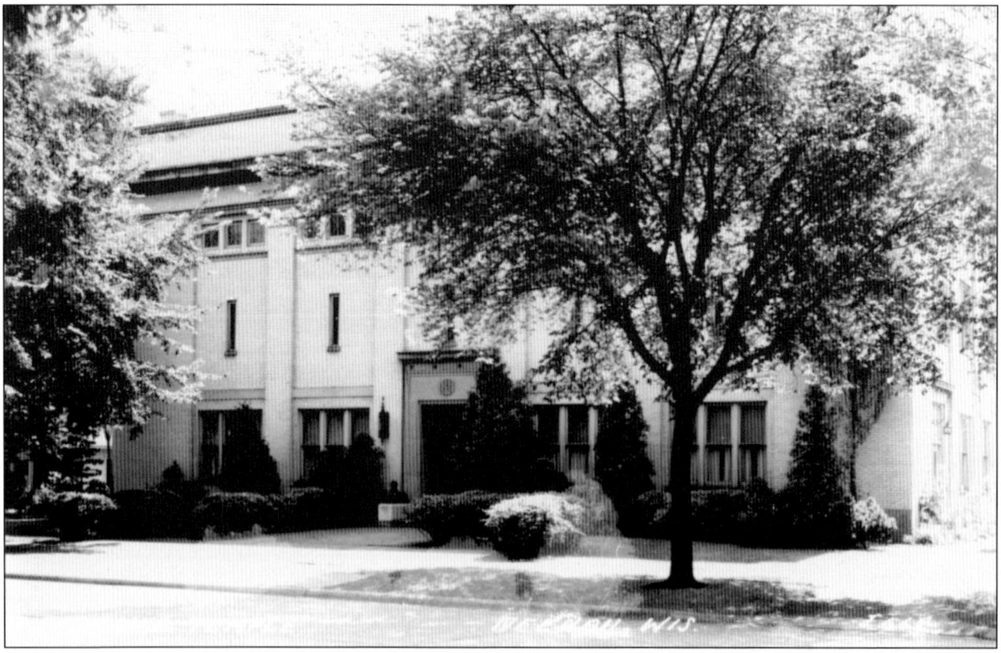

This real-photo card shows the Masonic temple at 241 East Wisconsin Avenue, which was dedicated in 1926 and sits across Wisconsin Avenue from the Neenah Public Library. The local lodge was formed in Menasha in early 1855 and consisted of members from both towns. Today this lodge is known as Twin Cities Lodge No. 61.

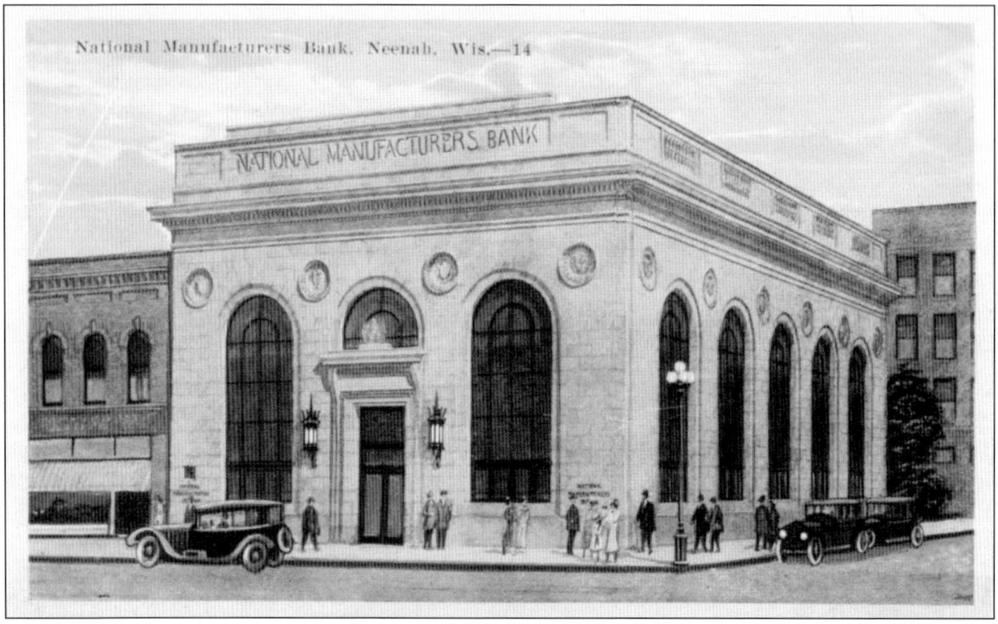

June 15, 1923, saw the grand opening of this imposing facility of the National Manufacturers Bank of Neenah. Located on the site of the former Russell House/Hotel Neenah property, the bank had been a Neenah institution since 1881 and was known then as the Manufacturers National Bank of Neenah. Its original location was at 109 West Wisconsin Avenue, the old photographic studio of C.B. Manville, later president of Johns-Manville Company.

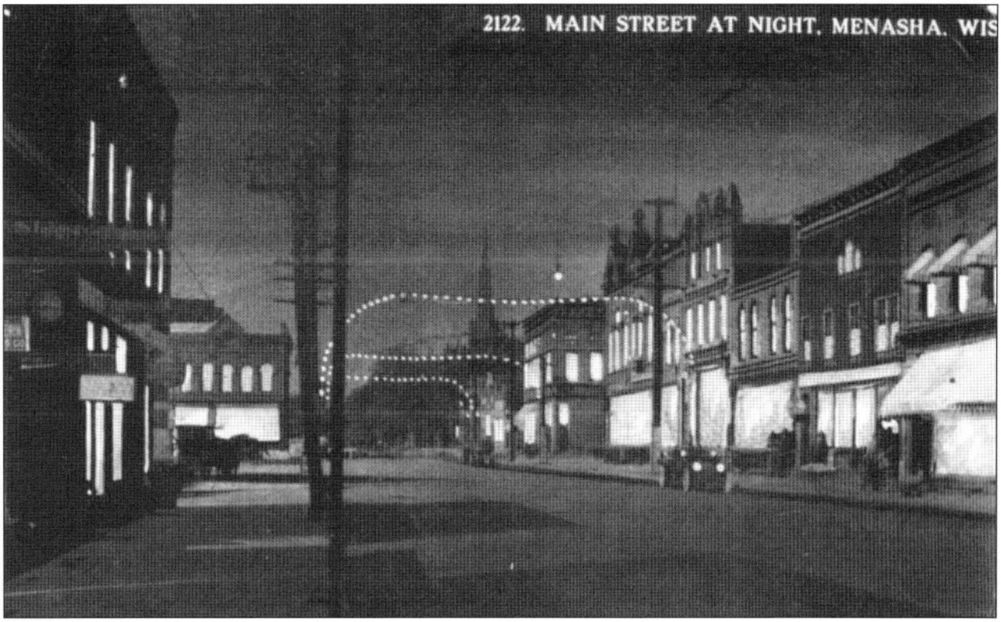

This is a pair of night-time scenes from the downtowns of both Neenah and Menasha. The view of Neenah looks up North Commercial Street toward Doty Island from the vantage point of the city hall clock tower. Despite the hour, a number of pedestrians head toward Wisconsin Avenue. The Menasha view takes in a quieter Main Street, looking west as an automobile is parked near a business with a sidewalk display in evidence. Farther up the street, a horse-drawn carriage awaits a passenger in front of the Hotel Menasha. The clock above the Wells Fargo office shows the time as 8:20.

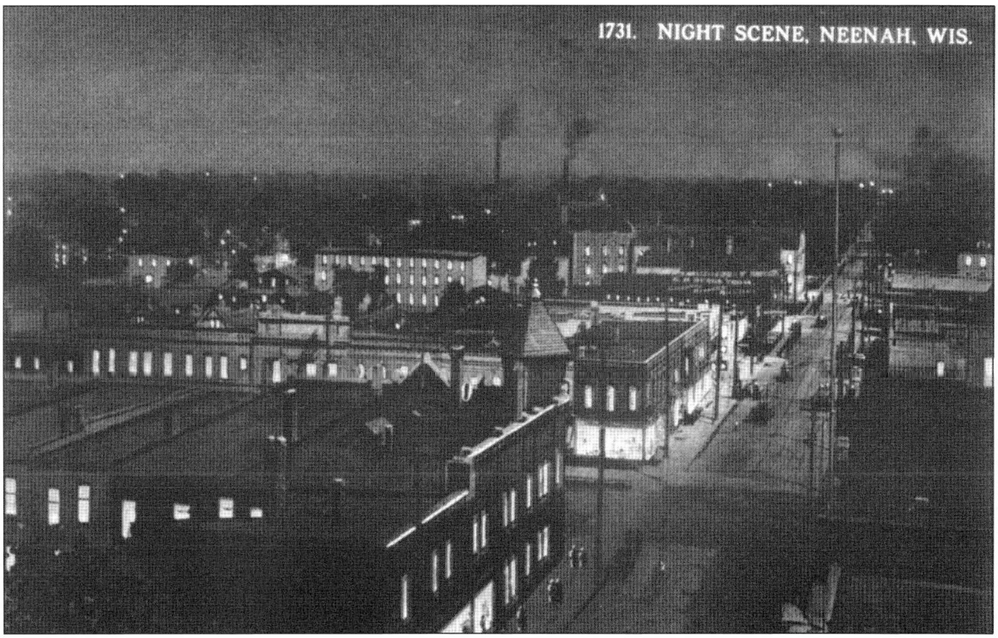

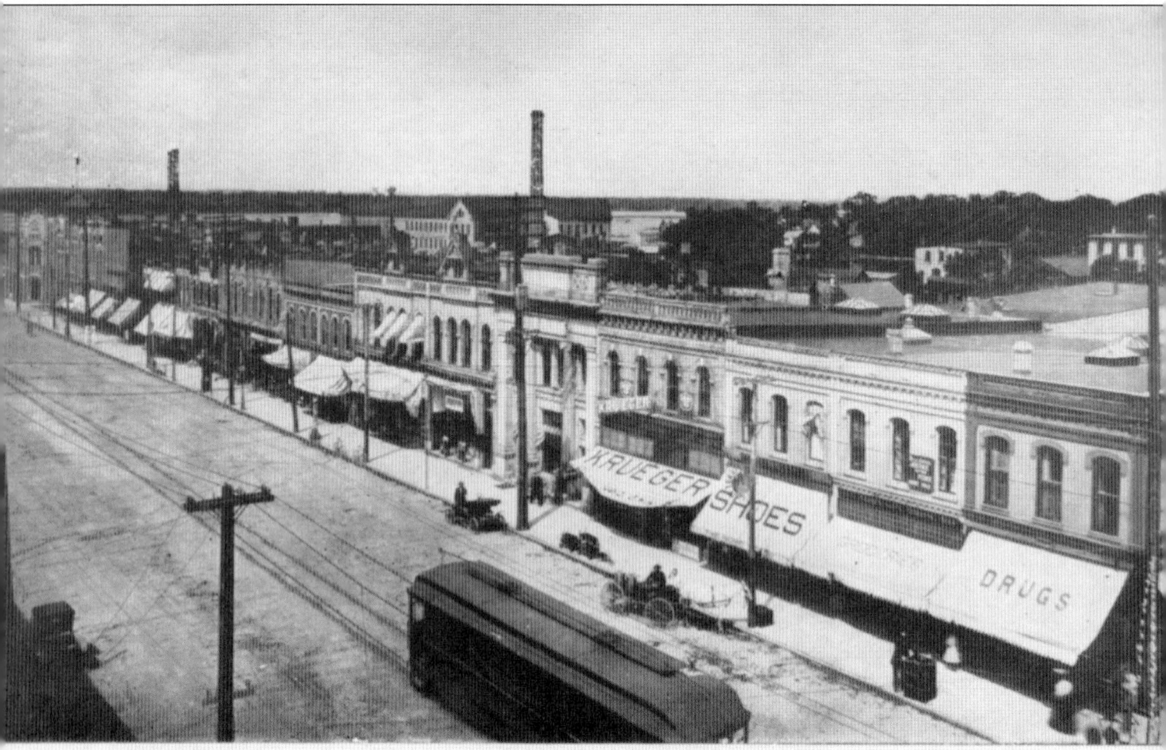

North Side of Wisconsin Avenue, looking West, Neenah, Wis.

Looking west on Wisconsin Avenue, the prominent storefronts of some local merchants are seen with extensive awnings. Krueger is a hardware store still in business in Neenah to this day. William Krueger, who founded the company one year after the Civil War, was born in Mecklenburg, Germany, in 1830 and came to Wisconsin at 21 years of age. He engaged in farming until 1866, then came to Neenah from the town of Clayton. Krueger partnered with W.P. Peckham to sell hardware, wood-burning stoves, dynamite, and tin, and provide blacksmithing services. In time, he bought out his partner and continued the store, bringing in his sons as time went on. The corner awning labelled "Drugs" is the Barnett Pharmacy. Maurice Barnett, owner of the pharmacy, married William Krueger's daughter. Their son, Lt. Maurice Edward Barnett Jr., was killed at the Battle of Meuse-Argonne in 1918 during World War I.

Five

City Services

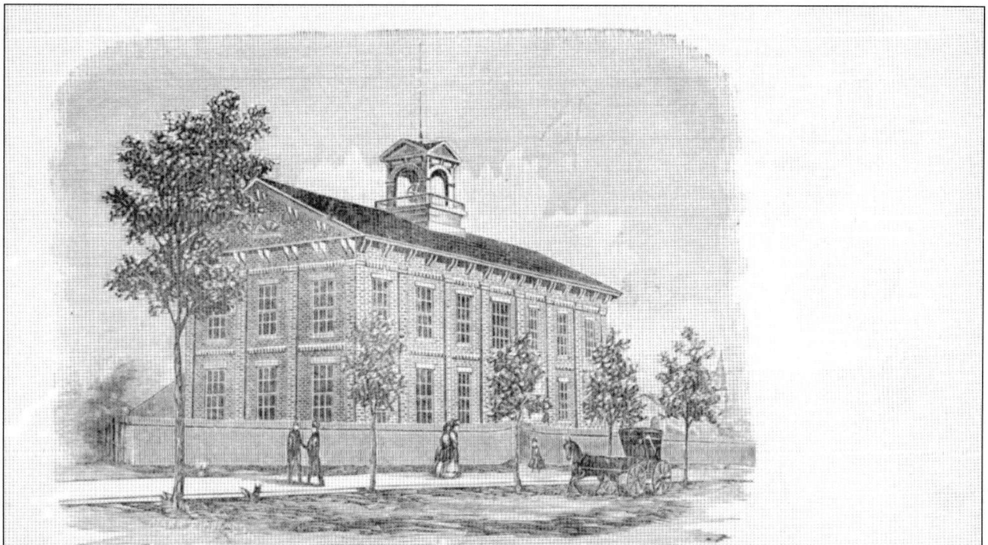

The original Menasha High School, constructed in 1871, is featured in this fanciful woodcut illustration on an 1890s-era postcard. The first high school graduating class was in 1876, and the school was on the site of the present public library at First and Racine Streets. It was known as a "union school" because it housed both primary and secondary classes.

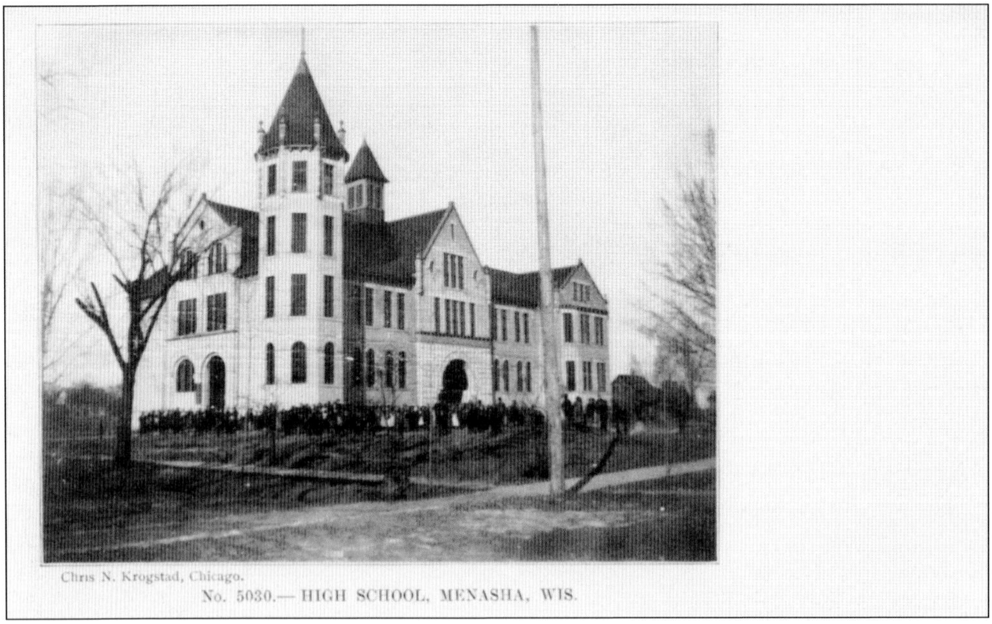

In September 1895, the board of education passed a resolution for a new high school to be constructed due to increased enrollment and the poor condition of the existing high school. Costs were not to exceed $25,000. Work began at the close of the school year, in June 1896. The completed school had eight grade rooms, separate cloak rooms for boys and girls, a large assembly room, and three recitation rooms. Over time, additions and new innovations were added to the existing high school. In June 1918, a barracks building was added to aid in expanding the manual training department. That same year also saw the addition of a school nurse. In 1920, a north wing added 14 classrooms. To Menasha's delight, a band was organized in the late 1920s that took the national marching band championship in 1931.

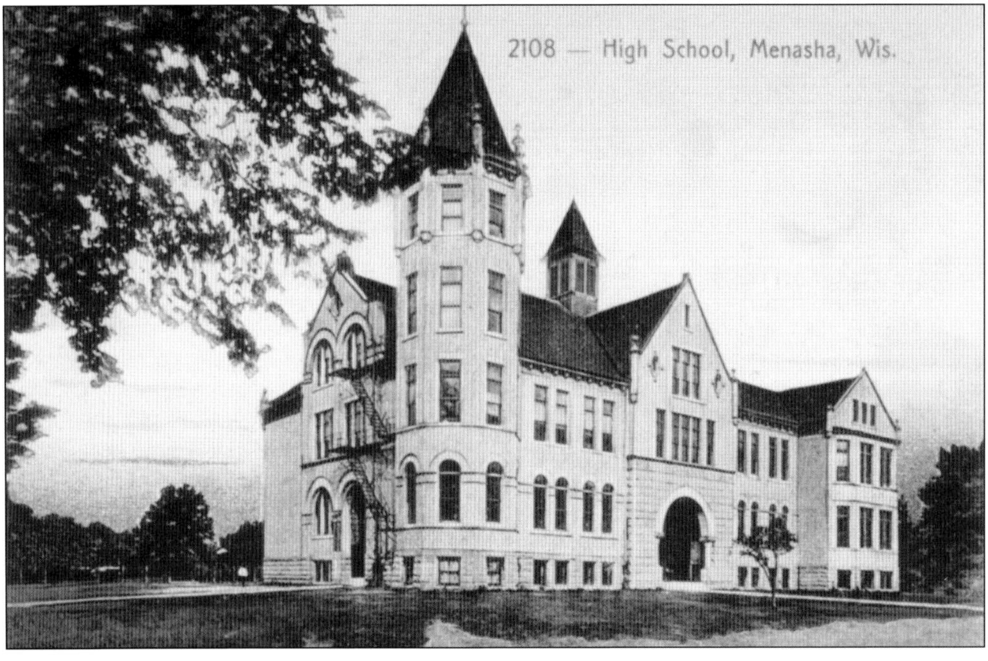

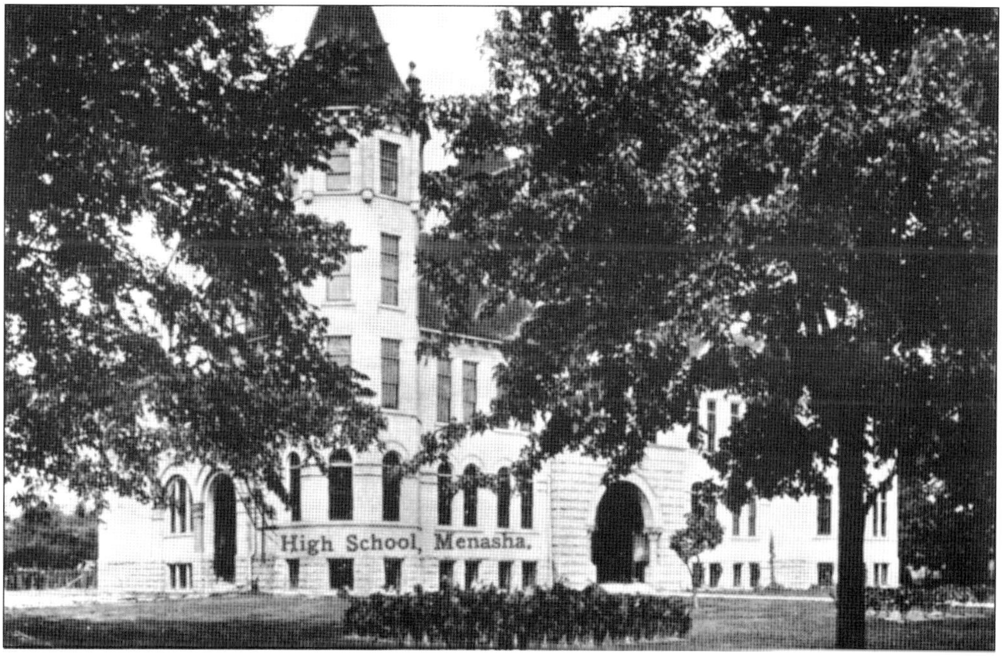

On March 21, 1936, the old Menasha High School was destroyed by fire. Only the outside walls remained intact. The cause of the fire was never officially determined, though it was generally believed to have started in the print shop. For the next two years, classes met out of necessity in various public buildings, including the public library, Germania Hall, the fire station, and the Memorial Building. Two years later, a new Georgian Colonial structure on Seventh Street was dedicated. Out of this tragedy came a historic feat: with all the material for the yearbook destroyed in the fire, the *Nicolet* editors started over from scratch. As a result, theirs became the first high school yearbook in Wisconsin to be printed by its own students.

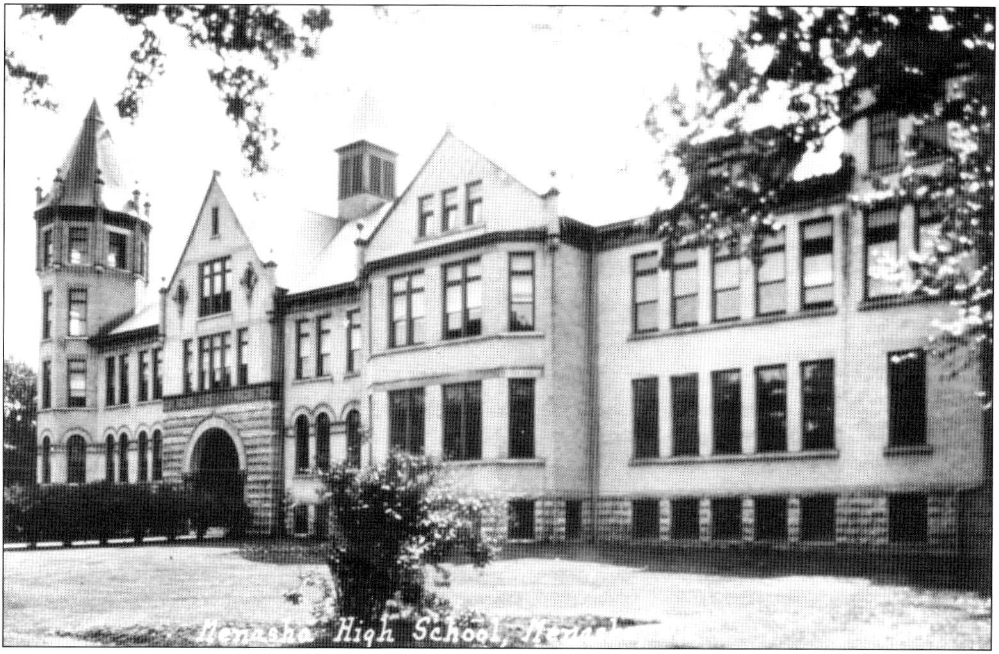

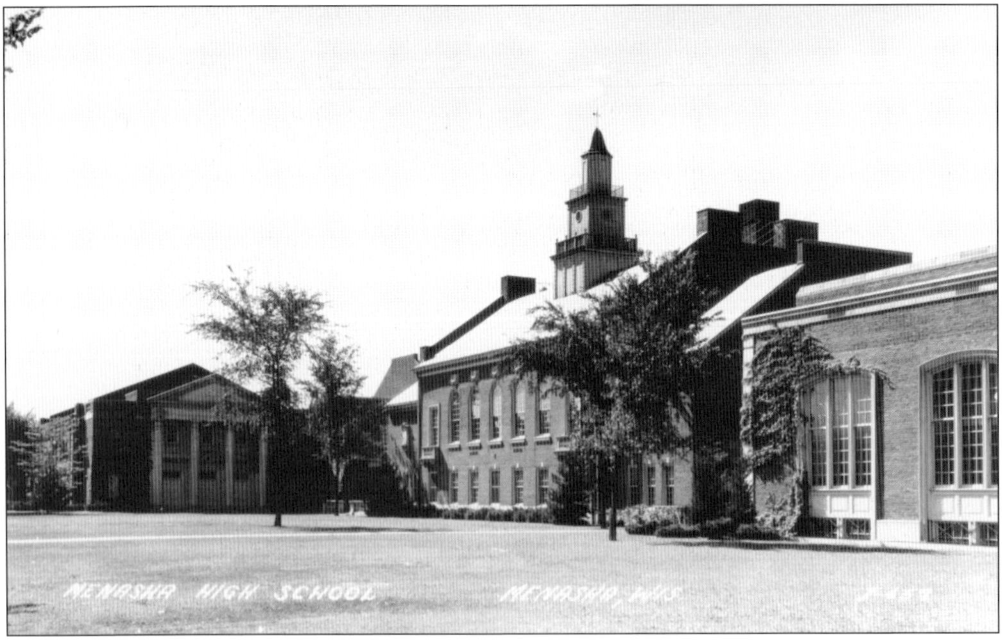

The image above is a real-photo postcard of the new high school, completed in 1937, which began classroom use in January 1938. The new $700,000 building was unique for its time in that it housed not only junior and senior high school classes under one roof but also vocational school classes. The new school provided a completely equipped gymnasium, a theater, a swimming pool, and facilities where students could learn printing and the manual arts. Graduation ceremonies for the 71 seniors in the first class took place on June 2, 1938. Below is a 1958 postcard view of Menasha High School. At this point, the school was about 20 years old.

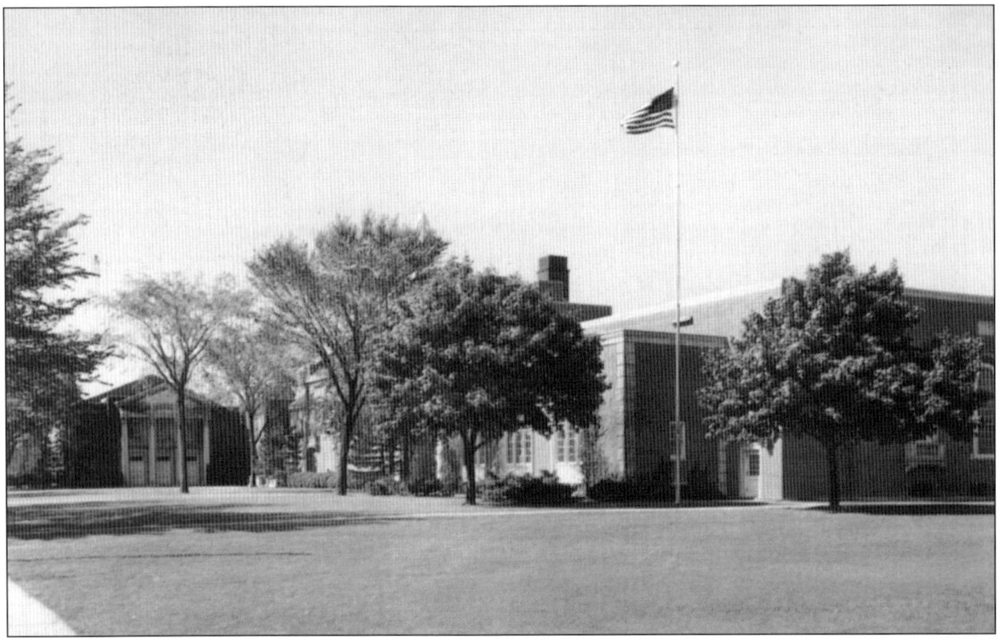

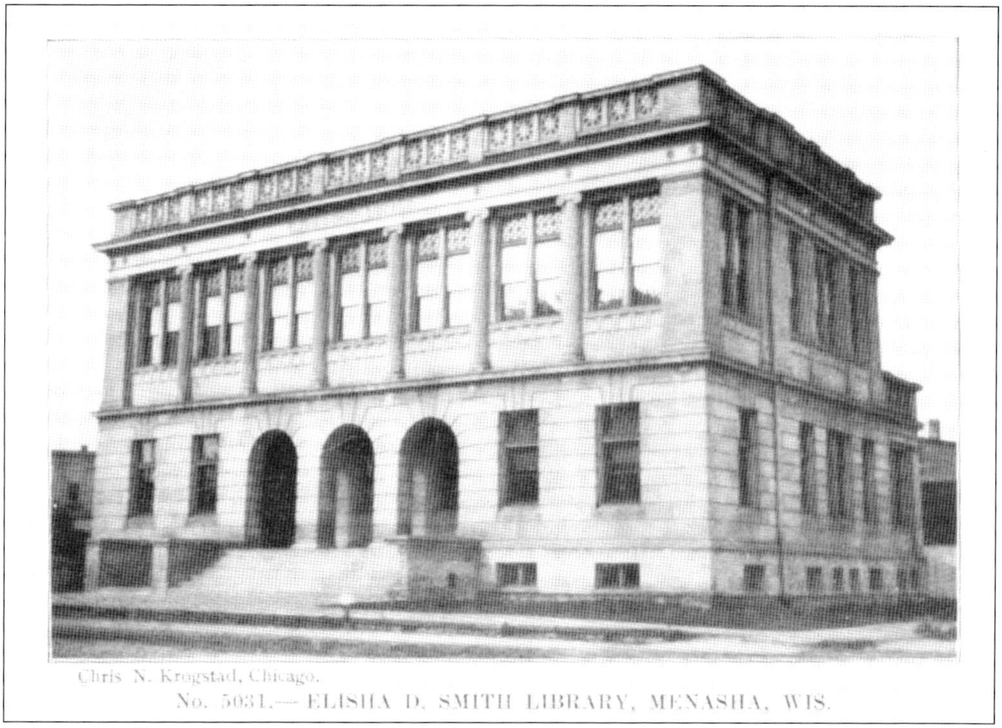

The first Menasha Public Library opened in upstairs rooms in the Tuchscherer and Schlegal department store at the corner of Chute and Milwaukee Streets in 1896. Lucy Lee Pleasants (sister-in-law of George Banta, founder of the Banta Corporation) pushed for establishing the library and became its first librarian, holding the position until her retirement in 1919. According to her, in the first month of operation, "there were given out at the Menasha Library 1,172 books: of these, 110 were German, 62 were Polish, 42 history and biography, 42 literature, 5 natural science, 2 social science and 2 useful arts. The rest were fiction."

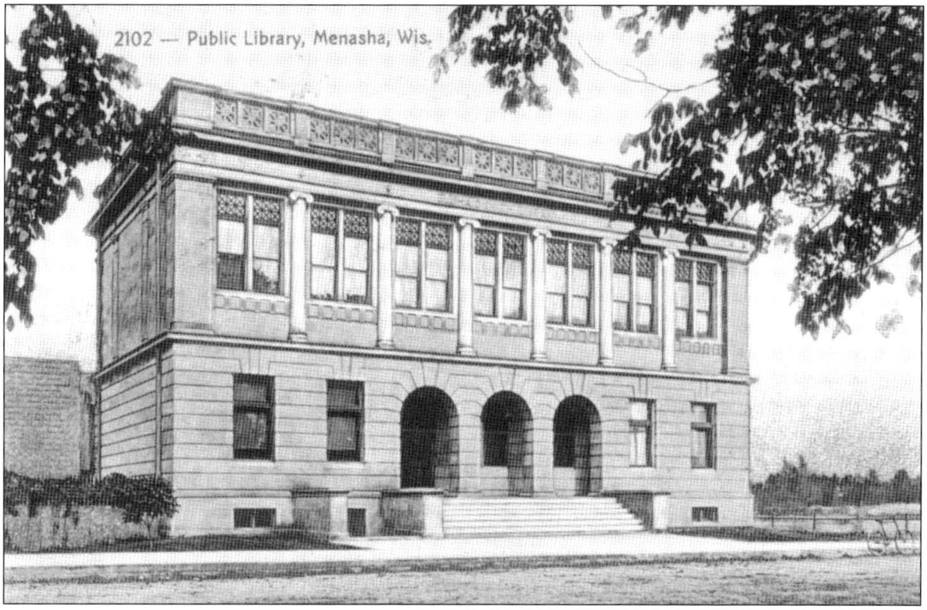

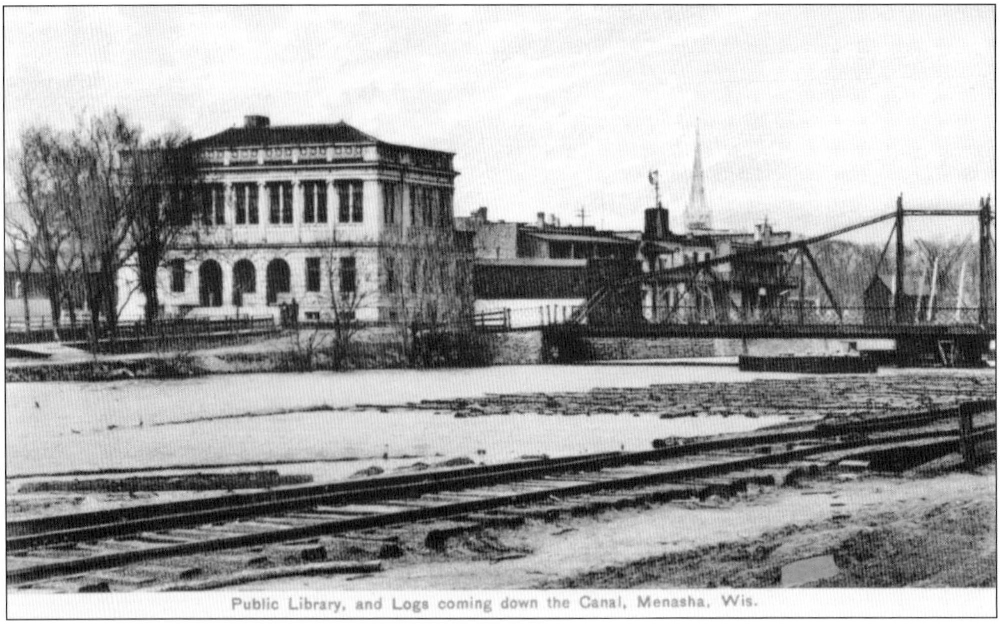

In 1898, Elisha D. Smith, founder of Menasha Wooden Ware, donated the land and money to build a library on Mill Street. The library was named the Elisha D. Smith Public Library after he passed away in 1899. This dramatic panorama of downtown showcases the library and the logs undoubtedly destined for his wood products plant.

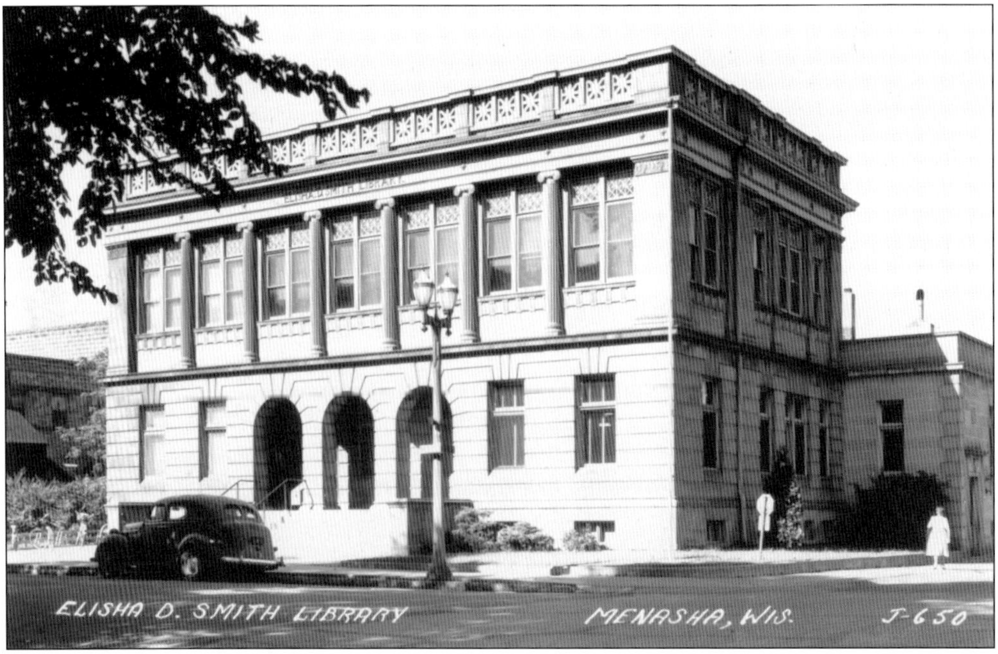

This real-photo card from 1951 shows the building on Mill Street that was used until 1969, when a new building was constructed at 440 First Street. The Elisha D. Smith Library was described in an August 1984 National Register of Historic Places inventory nomination form as a "large two-story stone library from the Neo-Classic period of construction." In the rear of the building is the children's library, added in 1930.

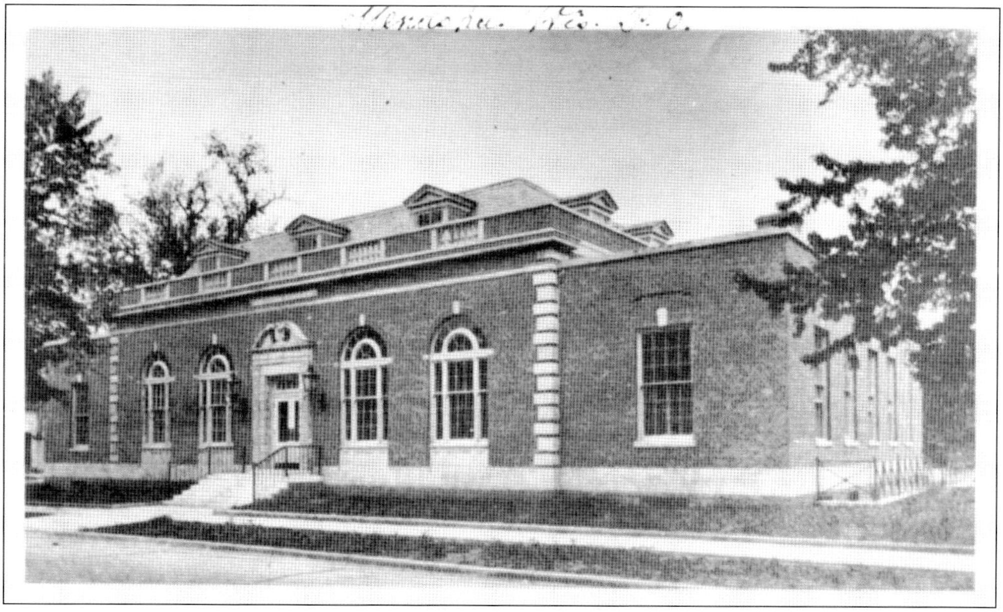

The Menasha Post Office was constructed at the intersection of Broad and Racine Streets and opened for business in 1933. An example of work from the Public Works Administration during the Great Depression, it was built in the Colonial style. In the 1930s, the federal government built over 1,100 post offices, and many of them are now listed in the National Register of Historic Places, including this one.

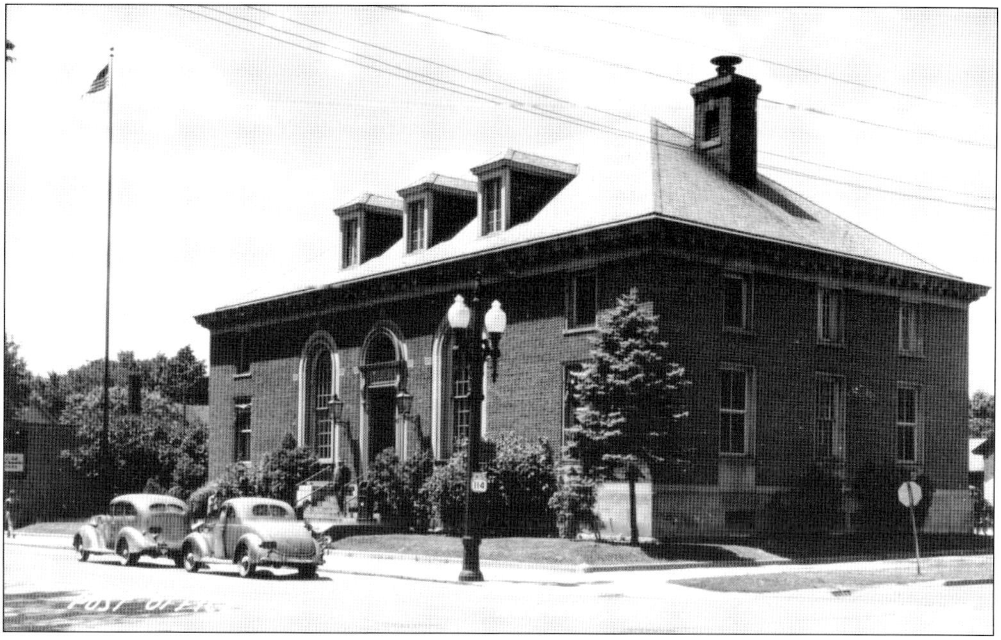

The former Neenah Post Office was built at the intersection of South Commercial Street and Columbian Avenue in 1917 and dedicated in 1918. It has been termed a two-story Colonial Revival post office. A larger facility was constructed at 130 West Franklin Street around 1966; this building became a disco and restaurant in the 1970s. Saved from the wrecking ball, the facility houses a number of businesses today.

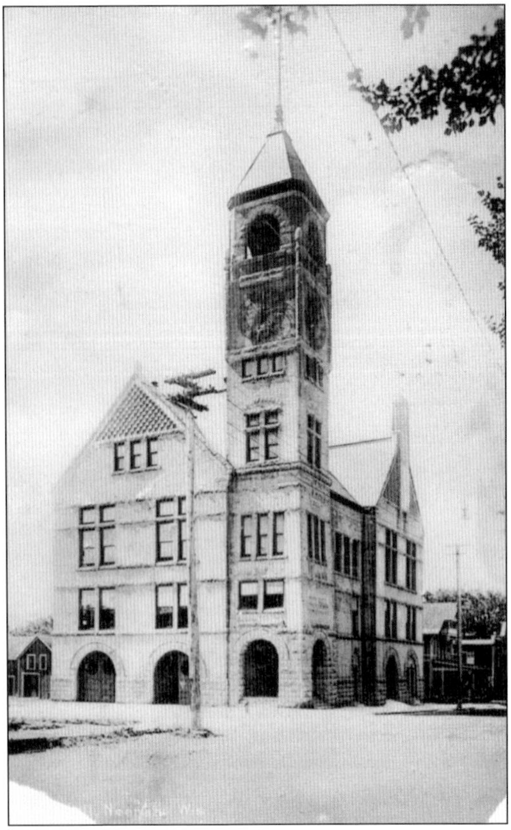

The old Neenah city hall was erected on South Commercial Street in 1888 and 1889, designed by famed Oshkosh architect William Waters. Originally, all city offices were housed in the building, including the police and fire departments. The bell in the tower was used to summon teamsters to the firehouse to pull the boiler to the fire. In advance of the public library being built, the second floor even housed the city's library. In 1972, city hall was vacated, and there were plans to tear it down, but this news instigated a city movement to save the building. All but the clock tower was razed in 1975. The 110-foot-tall clock tower was dedicated in the nation's bicentennial year of 1976 to the citizens of Neenah.

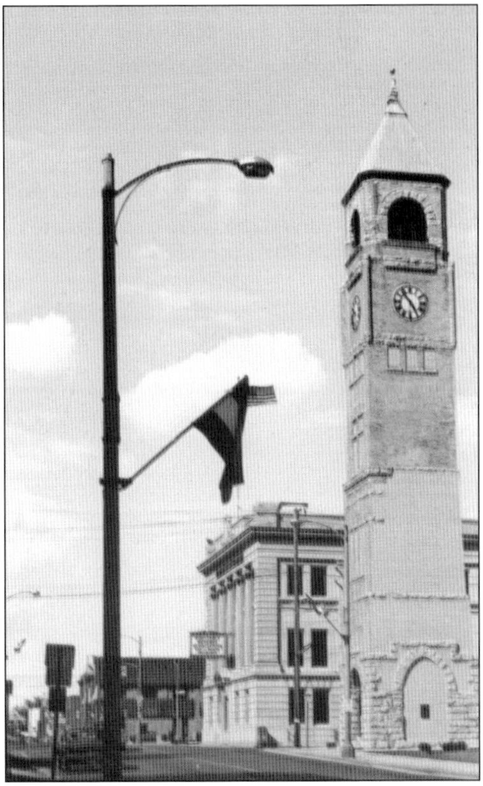

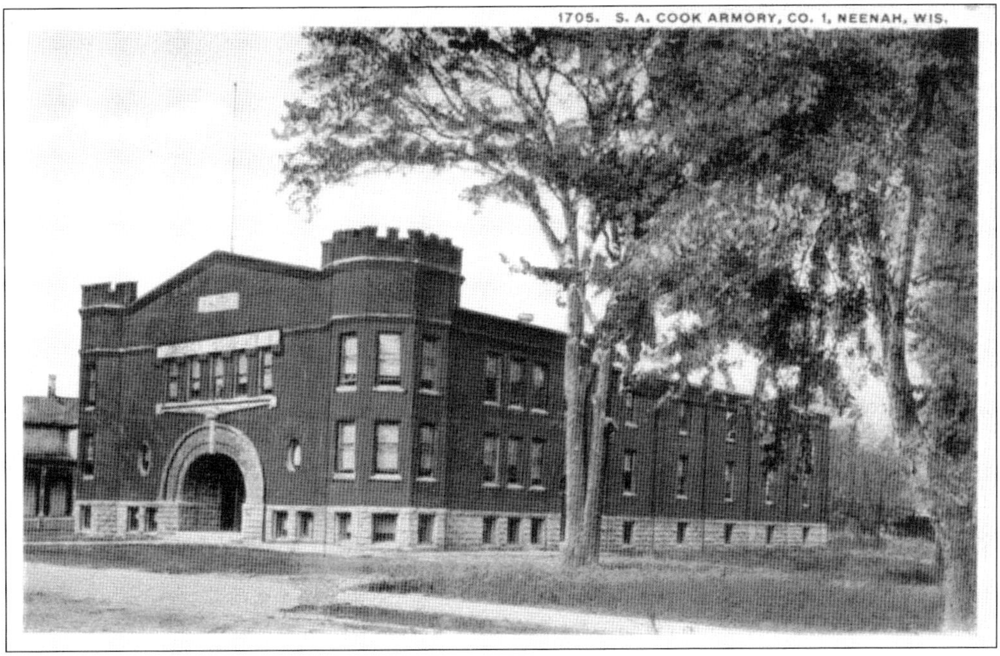

This armory was built in 1906 and was designed to straddle the borders of Neenah and Menasha as closely as possible near Nicolet Boulevard, because Company I of the Wisconsin National Guard recruited its soldiers from both cities. It was built by S.A. Cook, a Civil War veteran, mayor, assemblyman, and congressman, and gifted by him to the Twin Cities. At a cost of $25,000, this facility provided a drill floor measuring 67 by 87 feet, a basement with a rifle range, bowling alleys, and baths. The second floor was reserved for the use of two local organizations, the local Grand Army of the Republic post and the Women's Relief Corps of the Twin Cities.

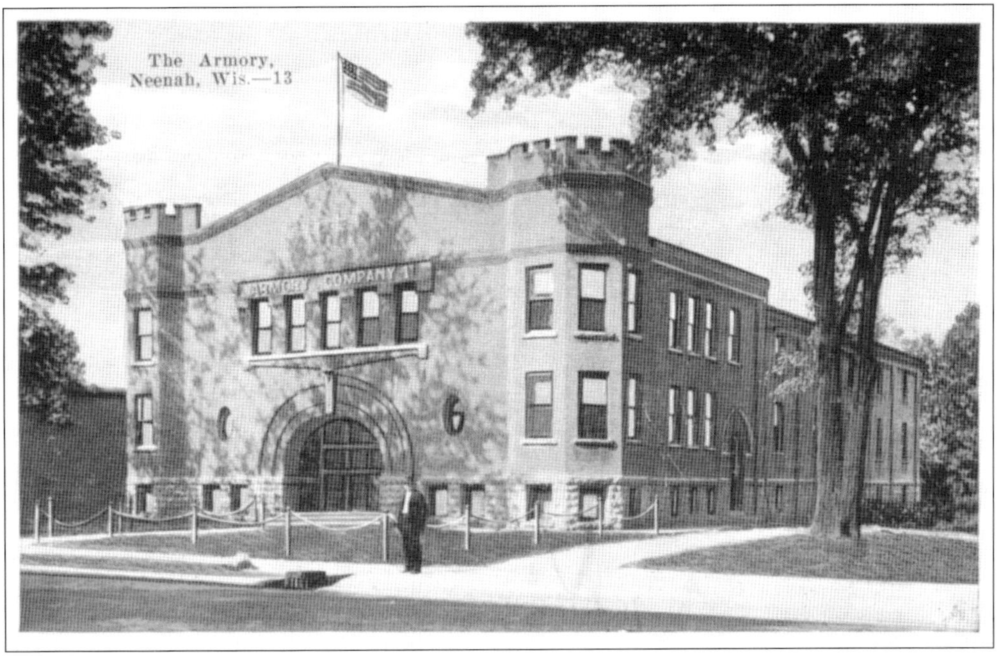

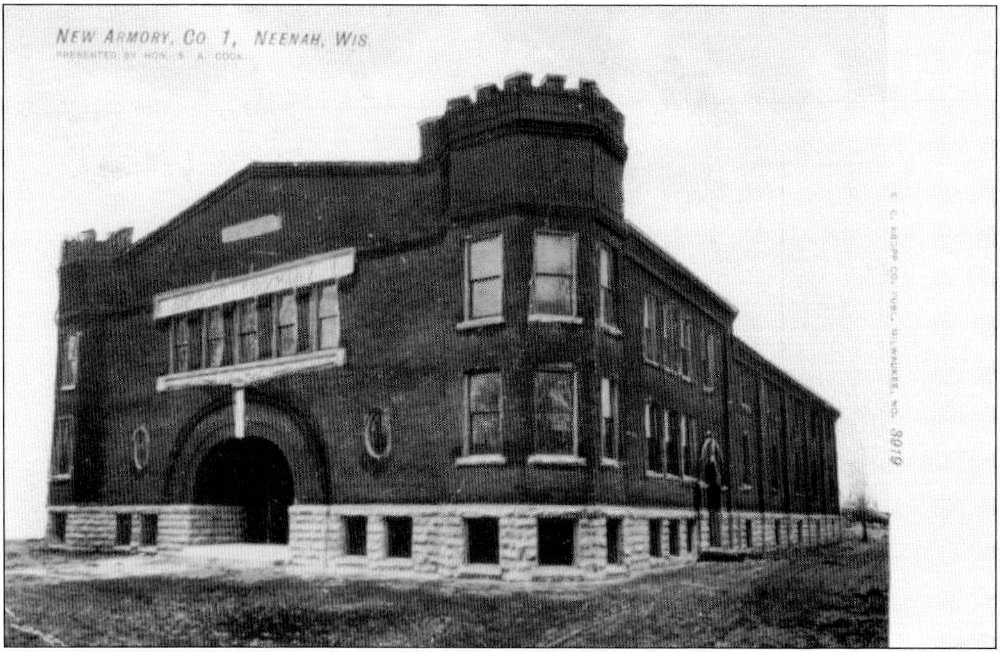

The summer of 1969 saw the troops vacate the armory as they were reassigned to a National Guard unit in Appleton. Though there was some talk of turning it into a youth center for Neenah-Menasha, the facility was purchased for commercial use. In 1970, borrowing from the English Tudor exterior, the building was renamed the Castle and was divided into several unique shops—a ski shop, a candle and incense shop, women's clothing shops, a shoe store, and a jewelry store, among others. There was a drawbridge and moat, castle-themed shops, and a "round table" café. This building saw its demise in 1988 and has since been replaced by a warehouse.

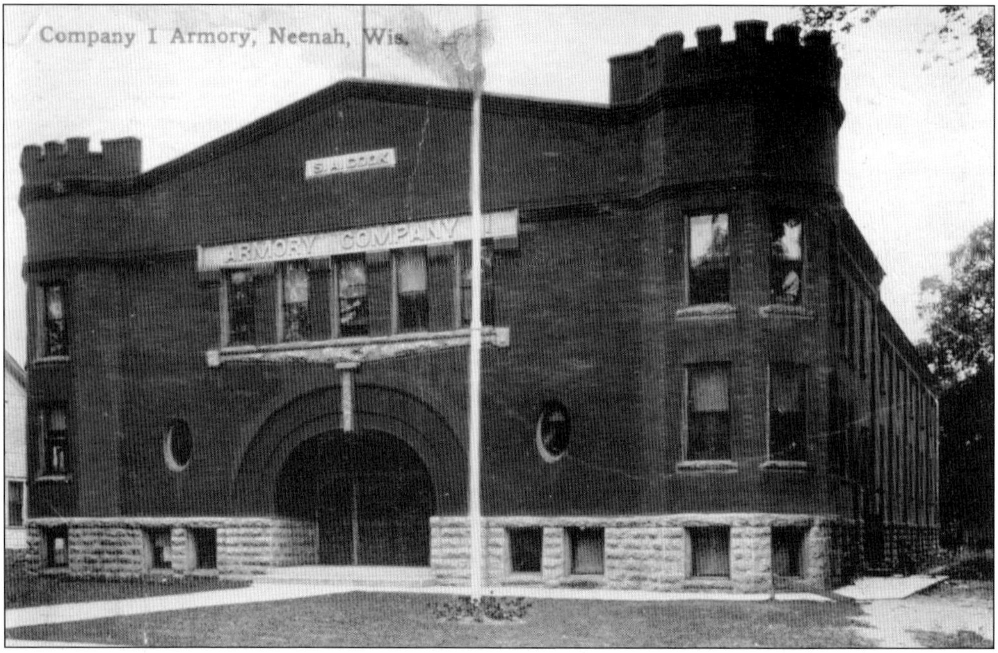

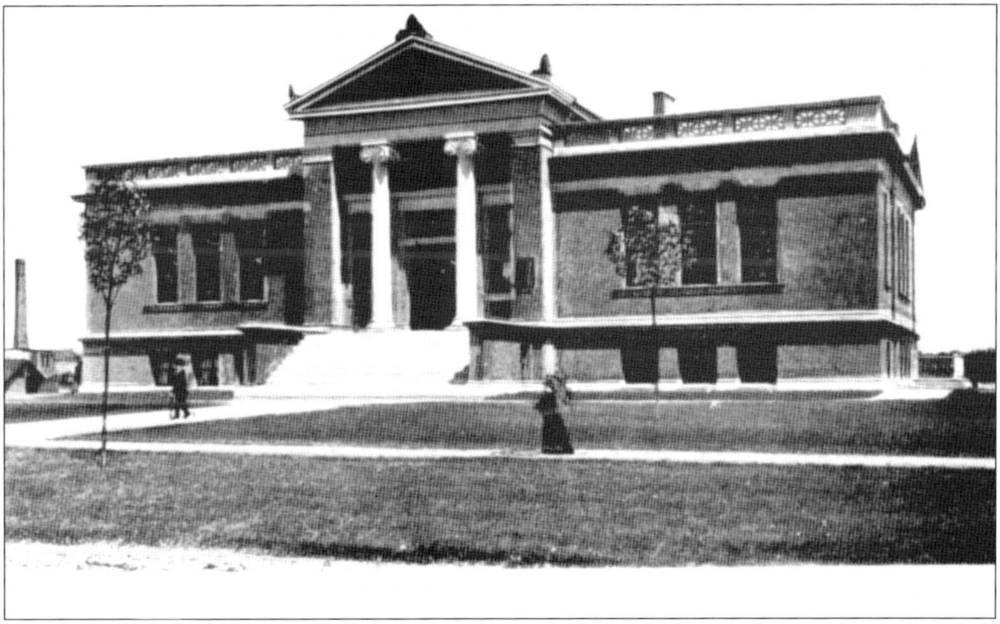

The Neenah Public Library began its life as an adjunct to city hall in the 1880s. The Neenah Library Association was organized in 1882 to raise funds to establish a public library. The money raised was turned over to the city, and the library was housed in city hall from 1883 until the formal library building could be constructed. Louise Lachmann was the first librarian. In time, the city hall location became too cramped, and a new location was needed. A donation of land, coupled with monetary donations from Theda Clark Peters and Andrew Carnegie, led to the library's construction at a cost of $28,000. It opened in 1904.

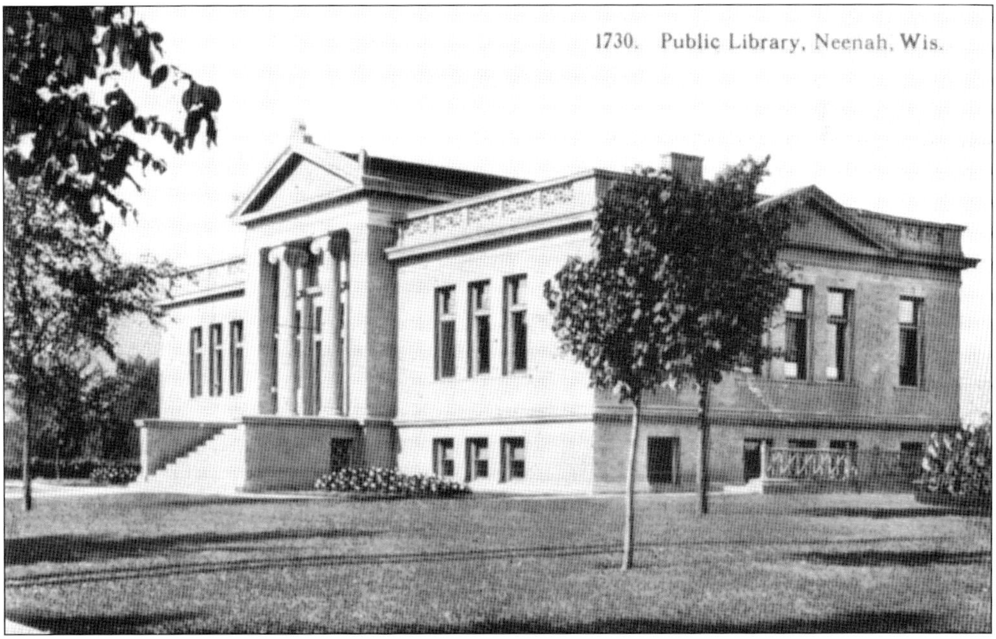

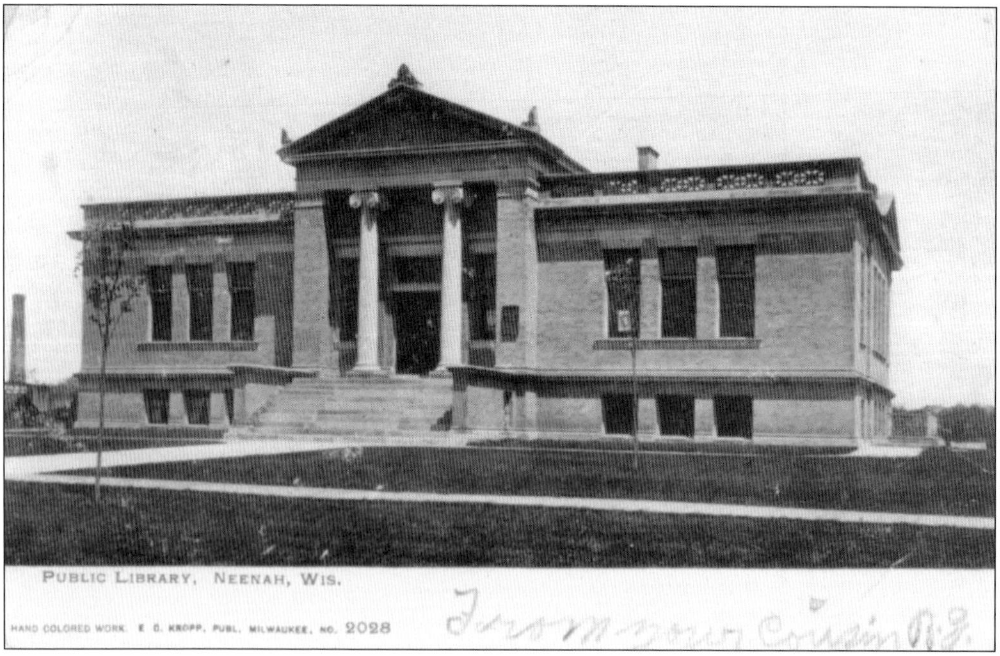

The Neenah Public Library was one of 64 public libraries in the state of Wisconsin to be partially funded by Andrew Carnegie. A total of 2,509 Carnegie libraries were built between 1883 and 1929, some belonging to public and university library systems, including Beloit College and Lawrence University in Wisconsin. In time, this library outgrew its space and required more. To preserve the old library building, a plan was designed in 1964 to construct a building around and attached to the old building to increase total floor space. This lasted until the late 1990s, when it became obvious that a brand-new facility must be built. By 2000, the old library was history.

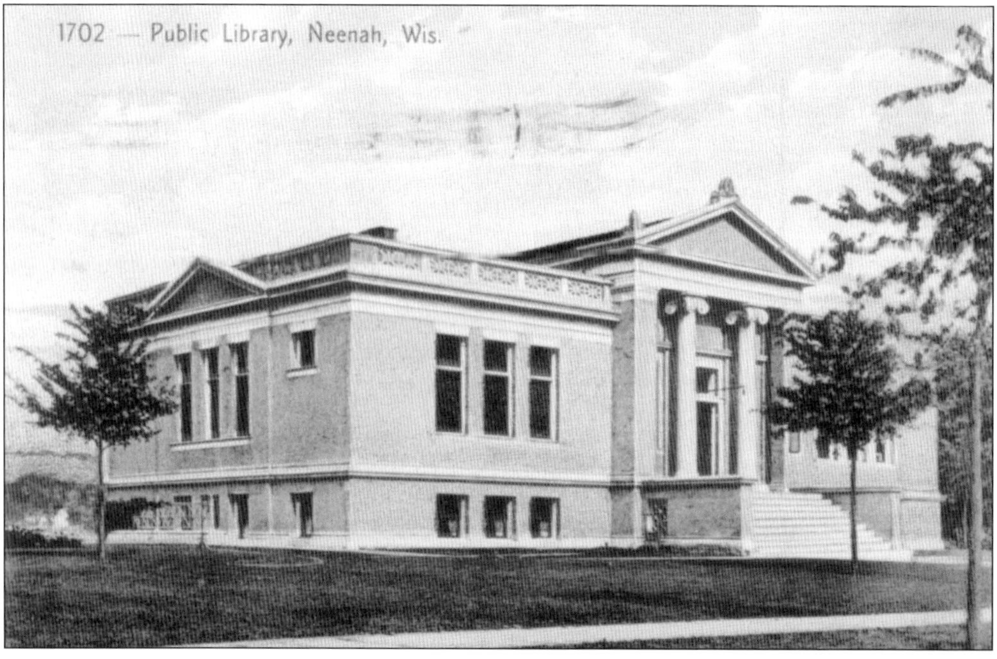

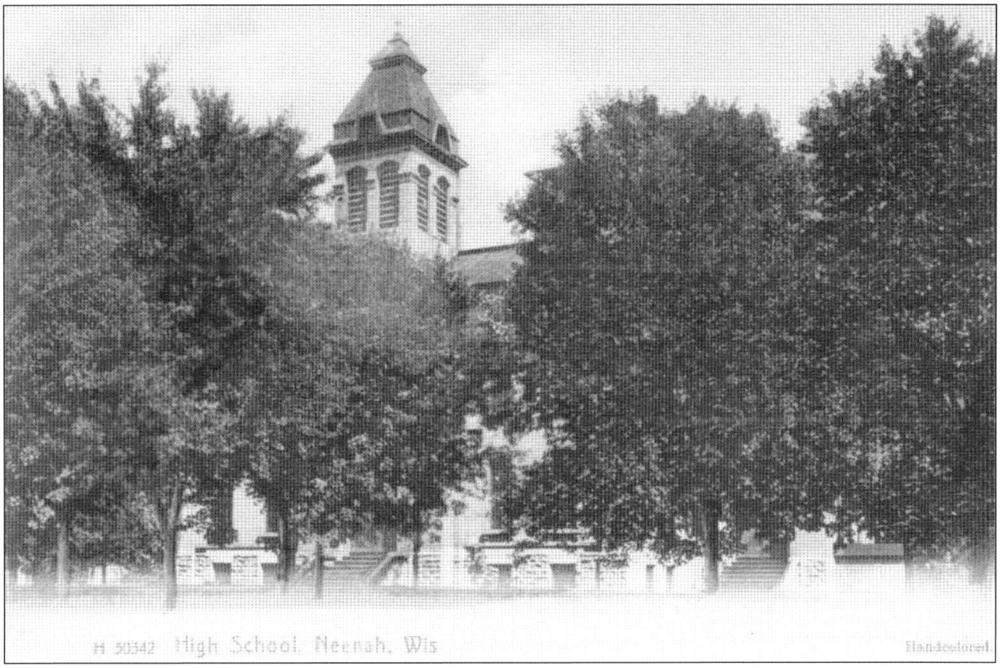

Pictured here around 1900 is Neenah High School. The first Neenah High graduation was held in 1877 with a class of nine. In 1879, the original structures on the Walnut Street site were removed, and the school pictured here was erected. This school housed grades one through eight, with three rooms on the second floor for the high school.

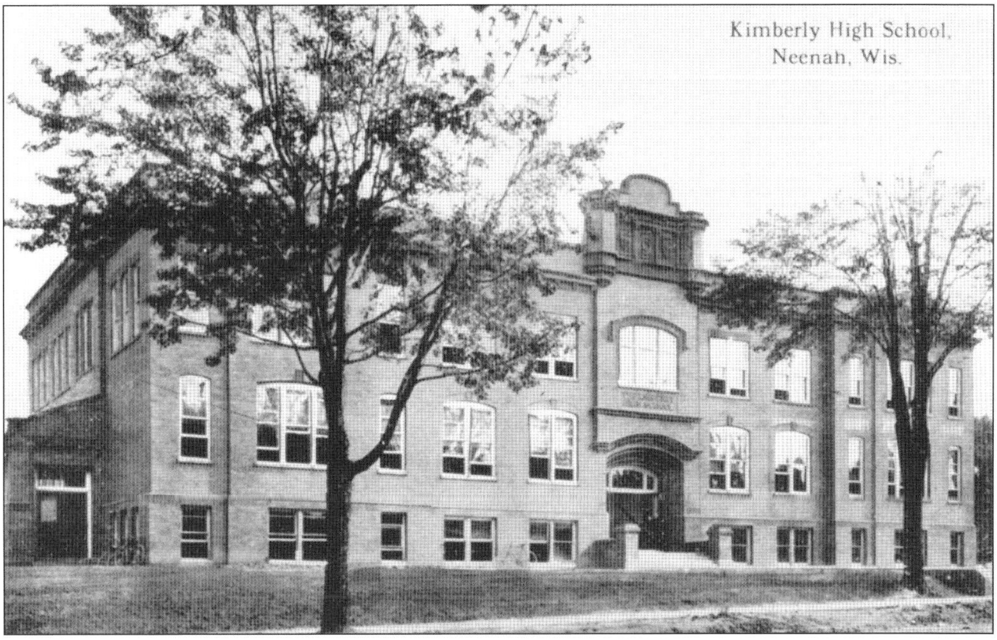

As the existing high school was becoming crowded, it was decided in 1906 to erect a separate building to house the high school and vocational school students, who were attending the First Ward School. The end result was the Kimberly School on South Commercial Street, pictured here in 1917. By 1929, this was supplanted by yet another school.

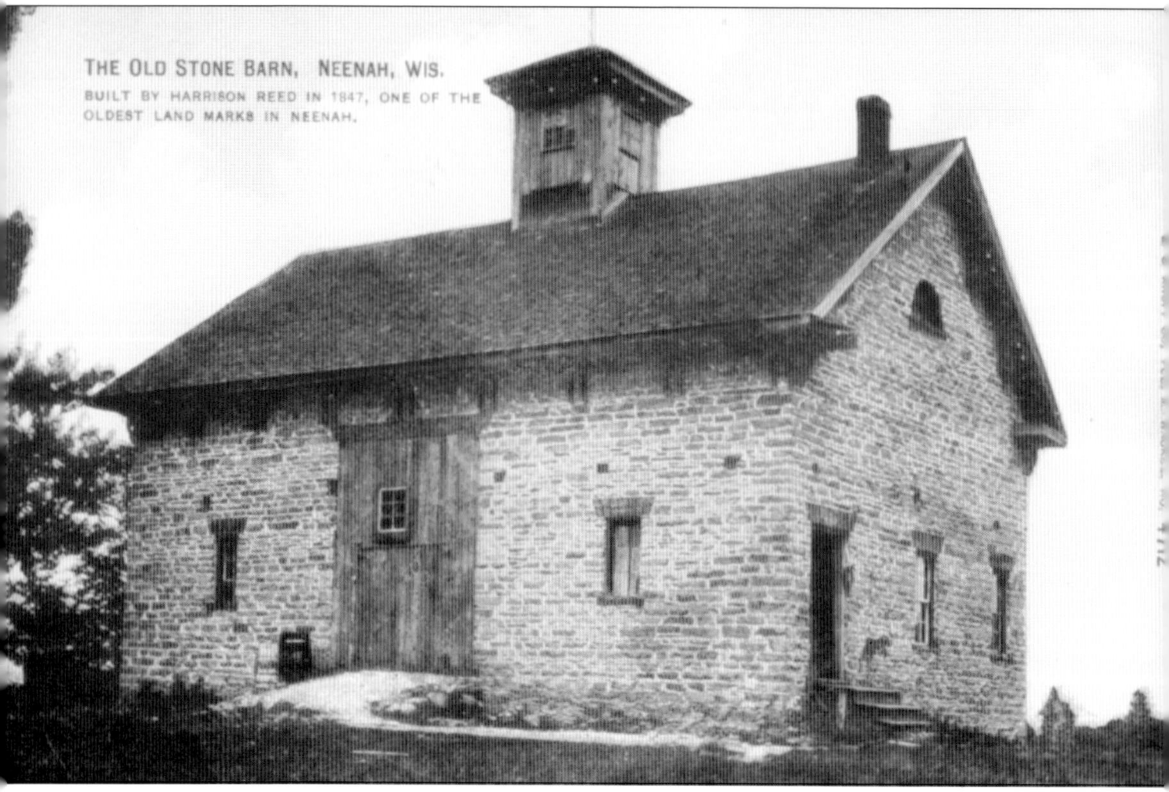

This postcard shows the "old stone barn," said to have been built by former newspaper editor and founding father of Neenah Harrison Reed in 1847, one year after his purchase of 562 acres of land in Winnebago Rapids. This barn was purportedly at one time one of if not the oldest landmark in Neenah. Located on what is now South Park Avenue, this structure eventually became a residence, but not before a legendary history that, unfortunately, cannot be completely verified. Originally built to house cattle with rooms above to house workers, stories abound about its history as a tavern, a wayside stop for stagecoach passengers, a livery for a company that cut ice from Lake Winnebago, and even a period of time when it was a pesthouse, a lodging suitable for diphtheria and smallpox patients.

Six

Places of Worship

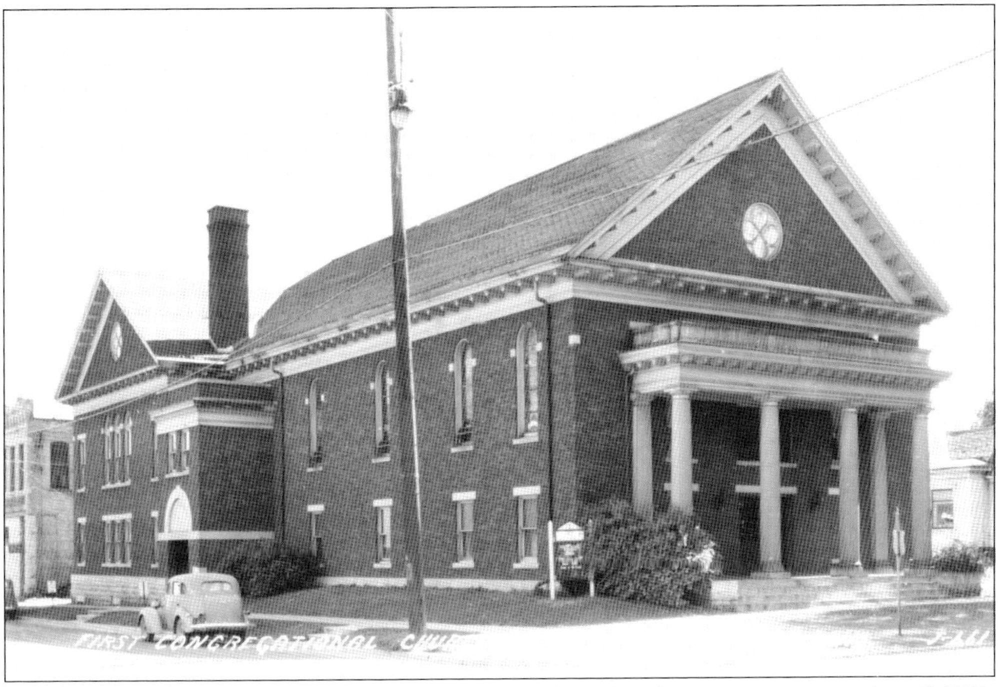

Organized in February 1851, the First Congregationalist Church was not constructed until 1858. The congregation believed that the area where the church was built at Second and Appleton Streets would become the center of town. When it became apparent that this was not happening, the congregation sold the church to St. Mary's and built at Broad and Milwaukee Streets. The First Congregational Church is historically significant as the oldest congregation in Menasha.

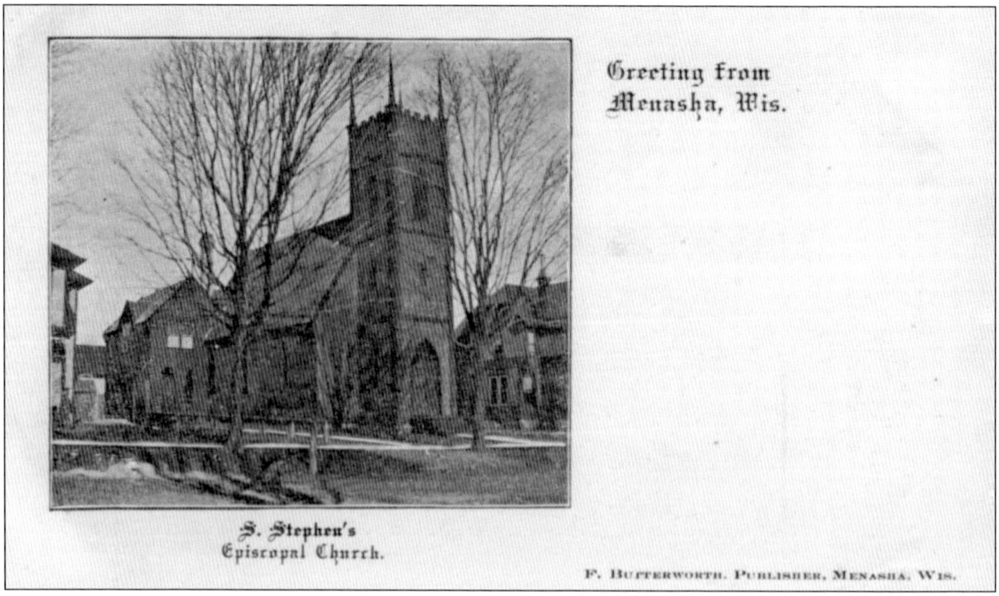

St. Stephen's, as shown above, was one of the forerunners of the eventual St. Thomas Episcopal Church on Washington Street in Menasha. This church was located on First Street near Appleton Street until 1888, when it was moved to 408 Broad Street. Unification with the Trinity Episcopal Church in Neenah had been talked about for years and finally occurred in 1915. The location for the new combined St. Thomas Church, seen below, was chosen as it was near the Neenah-Menasha border. In 1961, fire destroyed the western third of the church building. In 1963, a new addition was dedicated that integrated the old sanctuary and nave, giving a modern appearance.

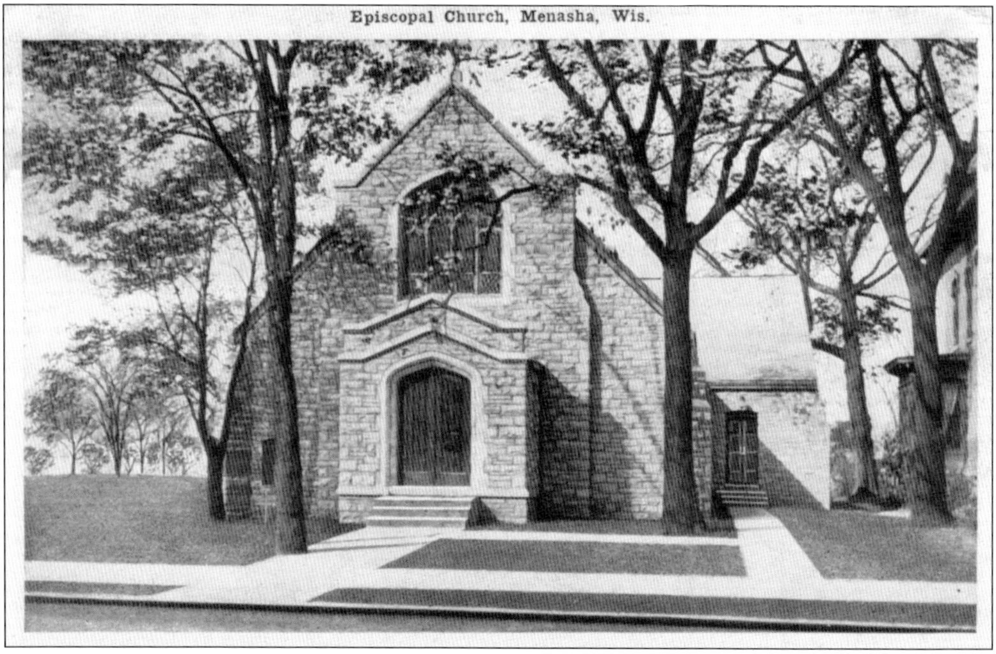

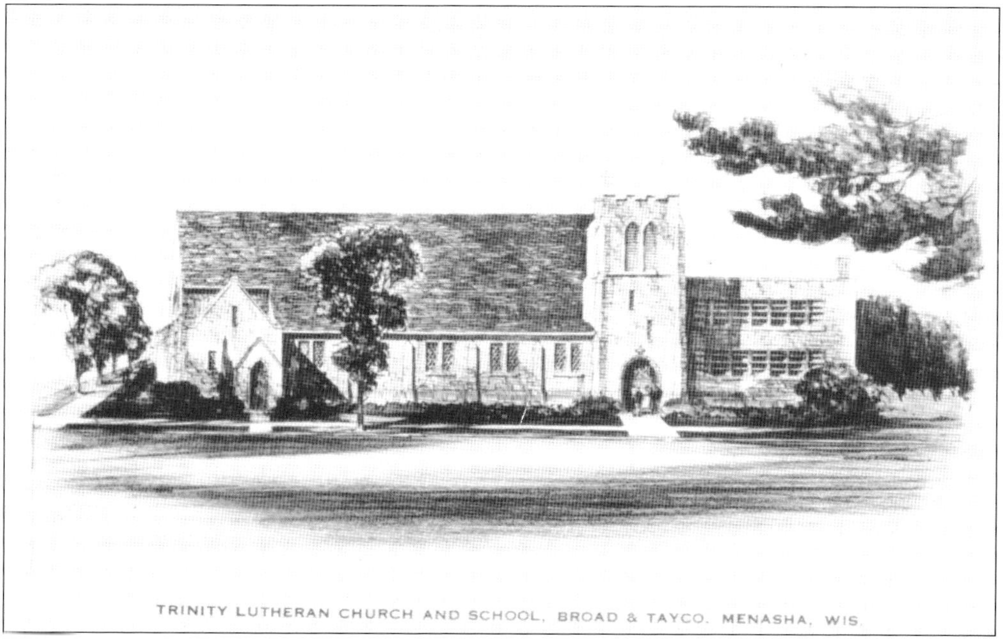

Trinity Lutheran Church was founded in 1857 to serve the growing German population in the Twin Cities. Originally planned for the northwest corner of Naymut Street and Nicolet Boulevard, the church was ultimately constructed on the south side of Chute Street between Tayco and Milwaukee Streets in 1863. In 1890, the church purchased the W.P. Hewitt residence on Broad Street. The home itself was used as a parsonage and school, while the rest of the property became the site of a new church, completed in 1893. Trinity Lutheran Church added a parish hall and a new parsonage to its grounds in 1917. Trinity Lutheran School served the congregation as an elementary school and community hall until the construction of the Broad Street church in 1957, after which the school was sold to the Knights of Columbus.

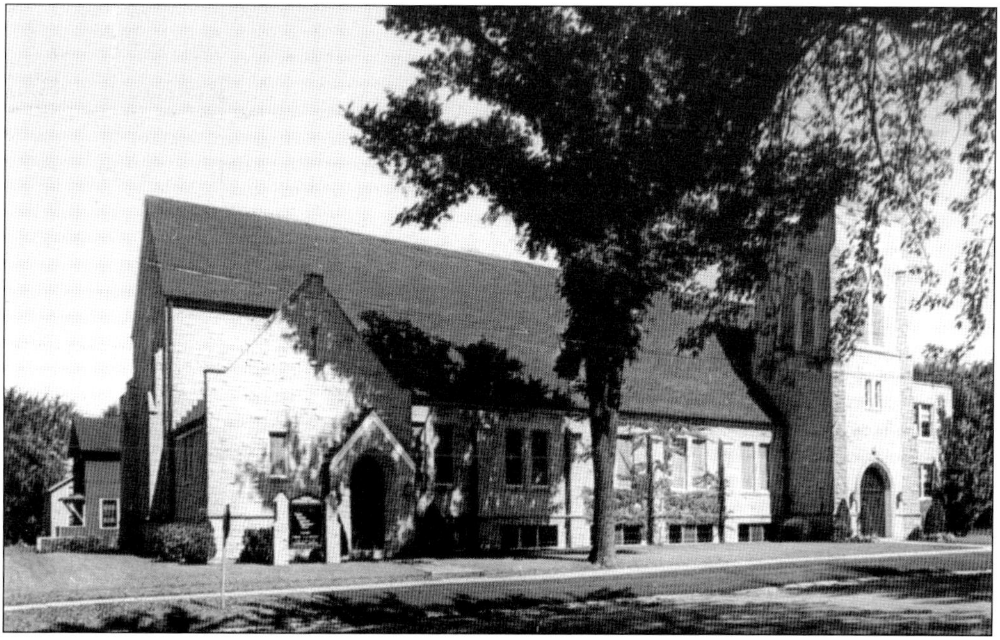

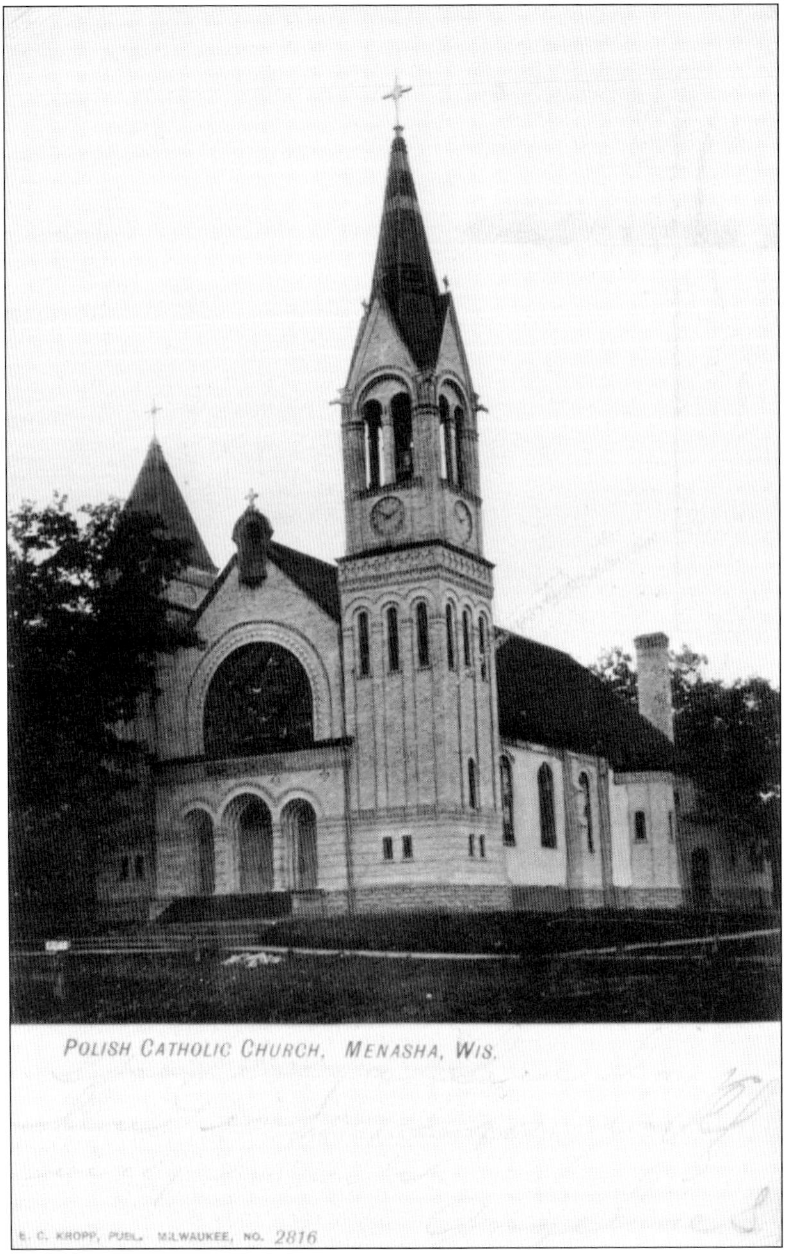

On February 25, 1888, seventy-five Polish Catholic families broke away from the German Catholic congregation at St. Mary's. The result was the formation of St. John's Polish Catholic Church and School in what was referred to as the "Polander Settlement." The church building pictured here was erected in 1900 on the corner of Fifth and DePere Streets. The cost of the church was $16,000, and the building is an example of Romanesque Revival architecture. Over time, though, the church's structure changed. A new entrance was created, and the church's twin spires were leveled off. The St. John Grade School educated parish children for well over 100 years. However, the school closed its doors in June 2002 due to finances and lack of students. St. John is now a linked parish with St. Mary's and is served by the latter's pastor. Despite all these changes, 2013 marked the 125th anniversary of St. John's Parish.

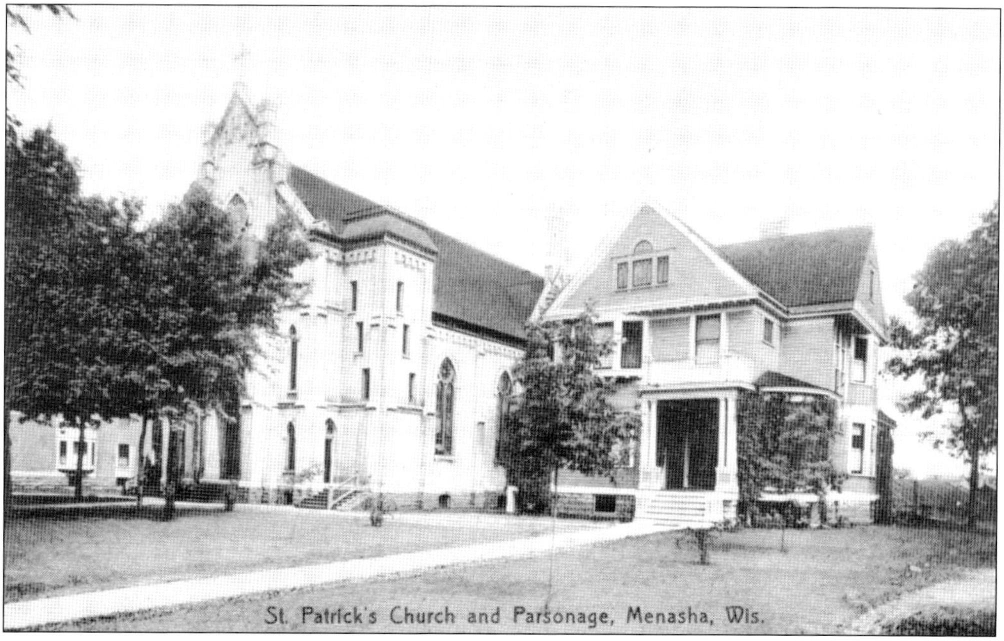

In 1849, twenty-five Irish families who worked on the Fox River dam and canal erected a log church on this site. Two years later, a wood-frame church was erected, and in 1857, it was dedicated to St. Charles Borromeo. In 1868, a brick school was added. In March 1882, fire destroyed the wooden church. The brick church shown here was built the following year and dedicated to St. Patrick.

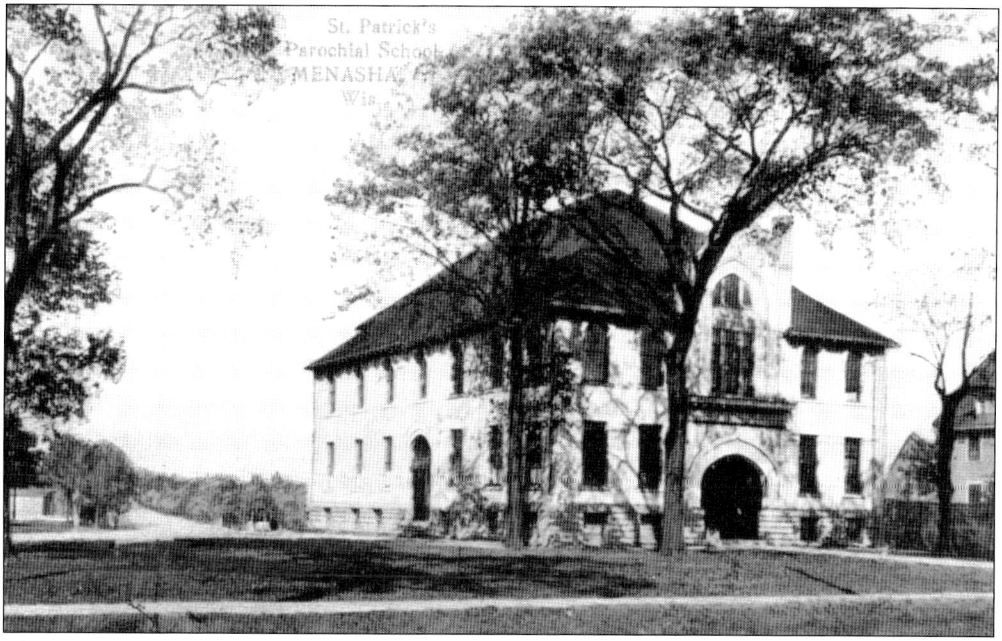

This 1910 postcard shows St. Patrick's Grade School on Nicolet Boulevard, or "the Avenue" as it was called until the 1906 dedication of the Nicolet Monument in Smith Park. Also shown is the largely undeveloped Washington Street heading towards the horizon and into Menasha proper. This school building, the parish's second, lasted until June 1940.

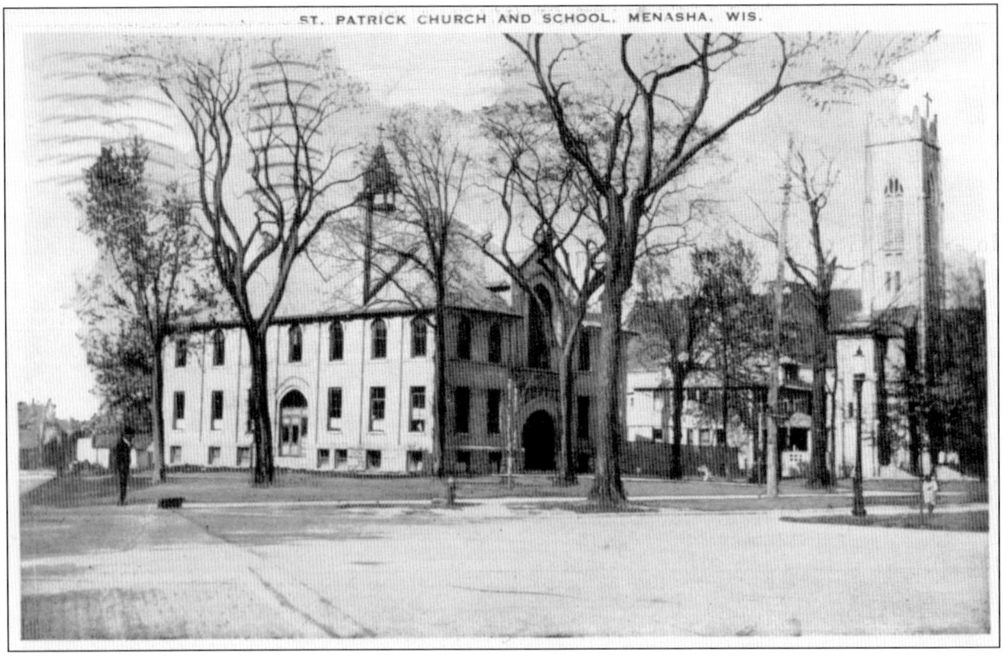

This postcard dates from 1934 and shows a tranquil Nicolet Boulevard in front of St. Patrick's campus. This is shortly after the era when manufacturers of picture postcards began putting a white border around the illustrations to save the costs of ink. That era lasted roughly from 1915 to 1930. Notice the additional development along Washington Street compared to the previous view from 25 years earlier.

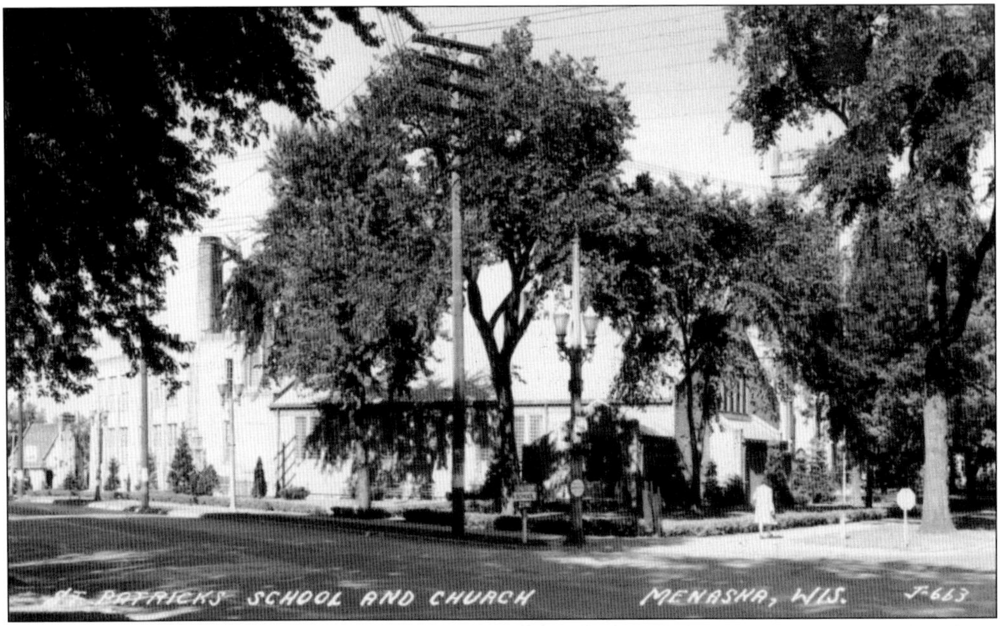

In 1941, a new school was built. This lasted until 1986, when the grade school was closed. In 1989, the school reopened as Seton Catholic Middle School with the reorganization of the Twin Cities' Catholic school system. When a new middle school adjacent to St. Mary Catholic High School was built in 2016, this building was made redundant. It has since been razed.

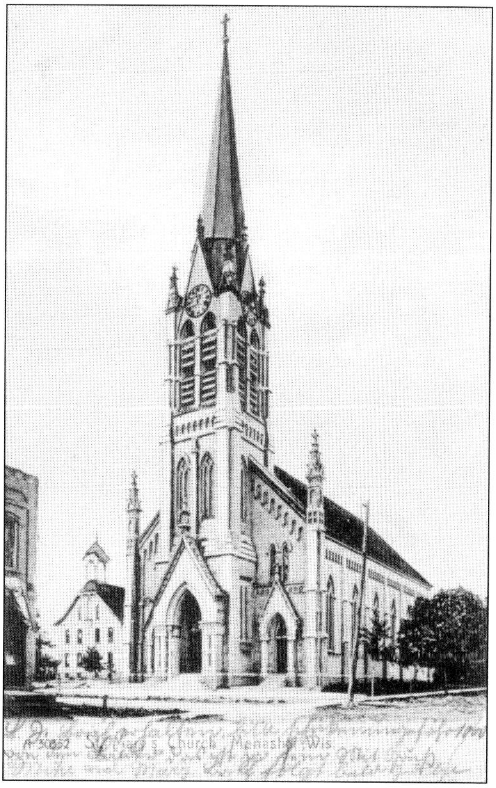

St. Mary's Catholic Church has defined Menasha's skyline for well over 130 years. In 1867, the German-speaking Catholics of Menasha separated from St. Charles Borromeo (now St. Patrick's) and organized a parish of their own—St. Mary's. On Ash Wednesday 1883, fire destroyed the first St. Mary's, devastating the parish. But somehow, within three days, the pastor rallied his parishioners to provide $14,000 toward a new church, and in November of the same year, a new church was dedicated. A classic example of German Gothic architecture, it seats 1,000, and its spire rises to nearly 200 feet. St. Mary's was the first Catholic school in the Diocese of Green Bay when it was built in 1868. In 1928, a Catholic high school was built that serves the Twin Cities to this day, though it has since relocated to Neenah.

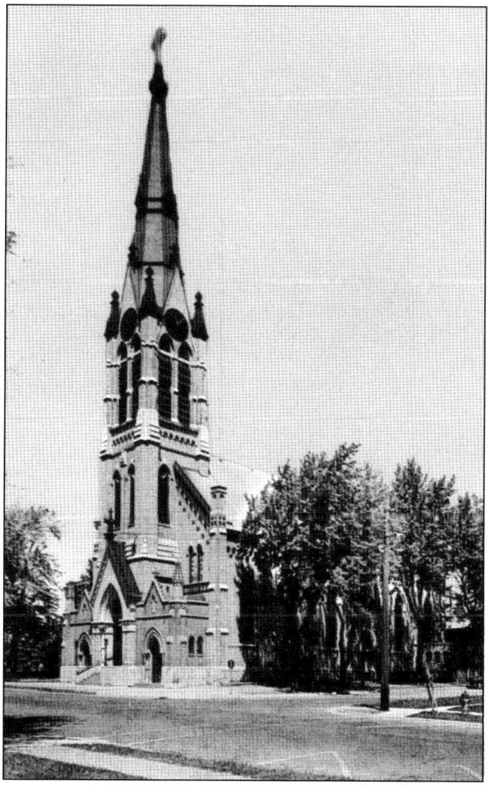

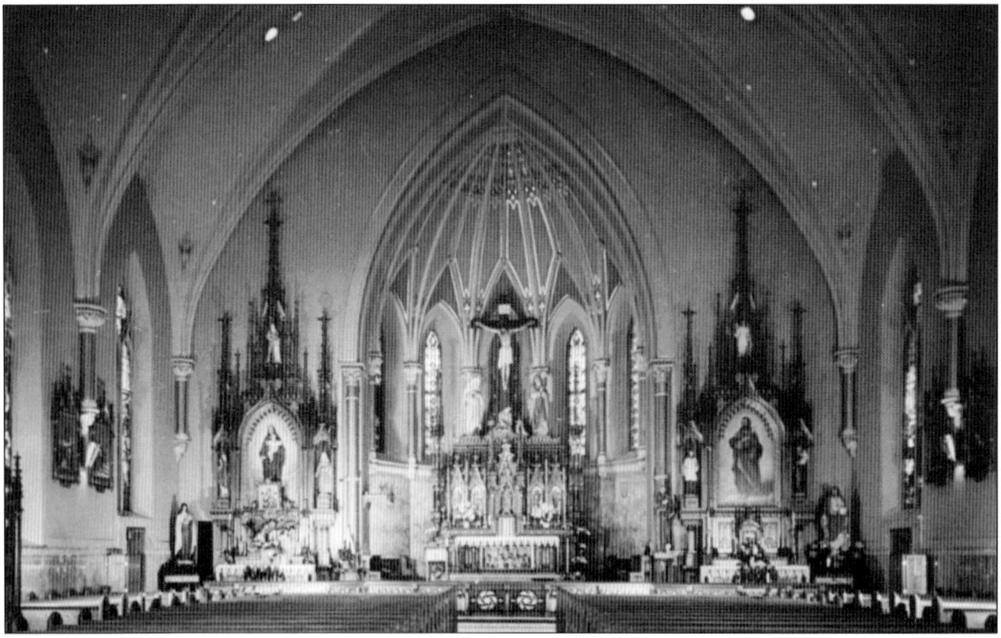

This postcard from 1958 shows the beautiful interior of St. Mary's Church. To the left is the altar to the Virgin Mary, and to the right is the altar to St. Joseph. The Gothic Revival structure's interior features elaborate stained-glass windows and paintings on the walls depicting the stations of the cross. The stained glass was designed by the Tyrol Art Glass Company of Innsbruck, Austria.

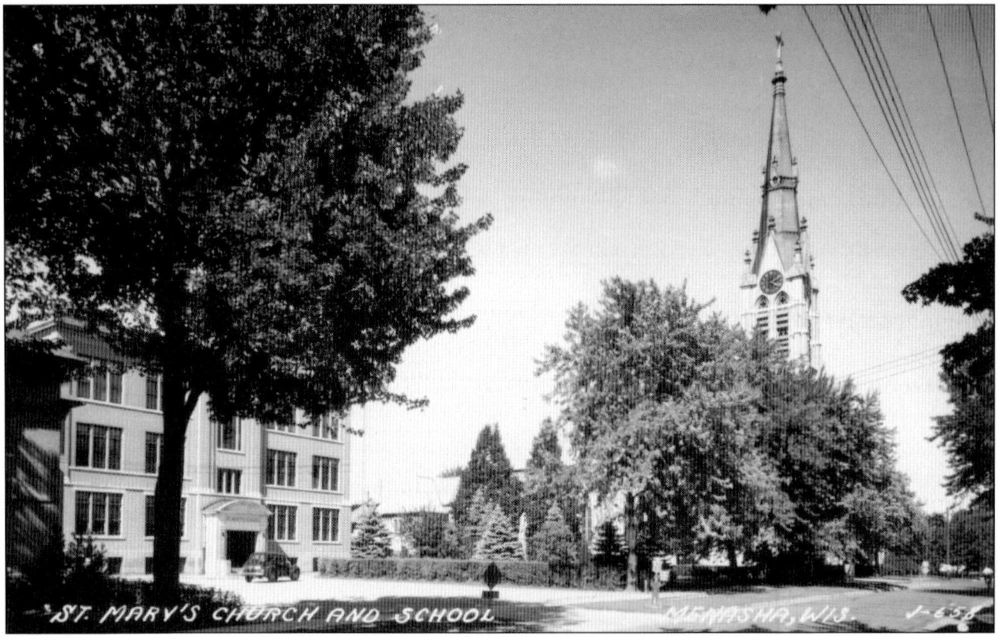

This postcard view is from the 1940s, before two crucial additions to the school. In 1952, a school building was built to house the grade school. In 1962, another addition was built on the grassy area filled by the trees to the left of the church. With this facility, the school received modern classrooms to house grades five through eight as well as a state-of-the-art library and audio-visual room.

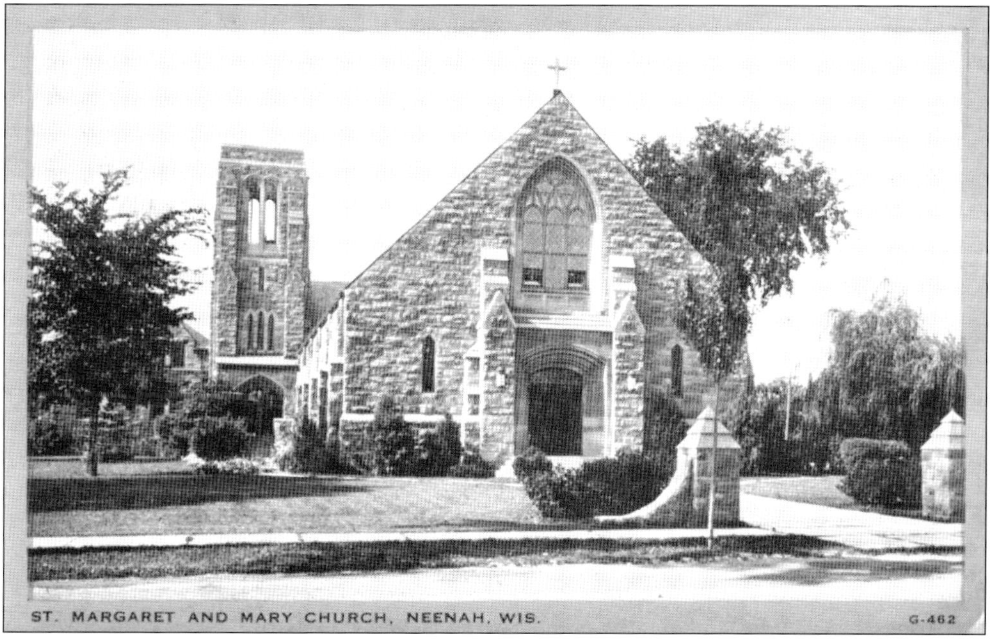

St. Margaret Mary was born from a 1932 letter from the Diocese of Green Bay calling for a new parish to serve Neenah's Catholics. In 1933, the beautiful new church for the St. Margaret Mary congregation was completed at the corner of Division and Reed Streets. The first mass was celebrated in the new church on Easter Sunday of that year. Prior to the completion of St. Margaret Mary Church, Neenah Catholics were served by St. Patrick's Church and School. Since that time, Catholic residents of the Doty Island side of Neenah have remained with the St. Patrick's congregation, while St. Margaret Mary claims the rest of Neenah, along with another Catholic parish, St. Gabriel. During the early 1950s, an extensive building program was launched, resulting in a parochial grade school, convent, and gymnasium.

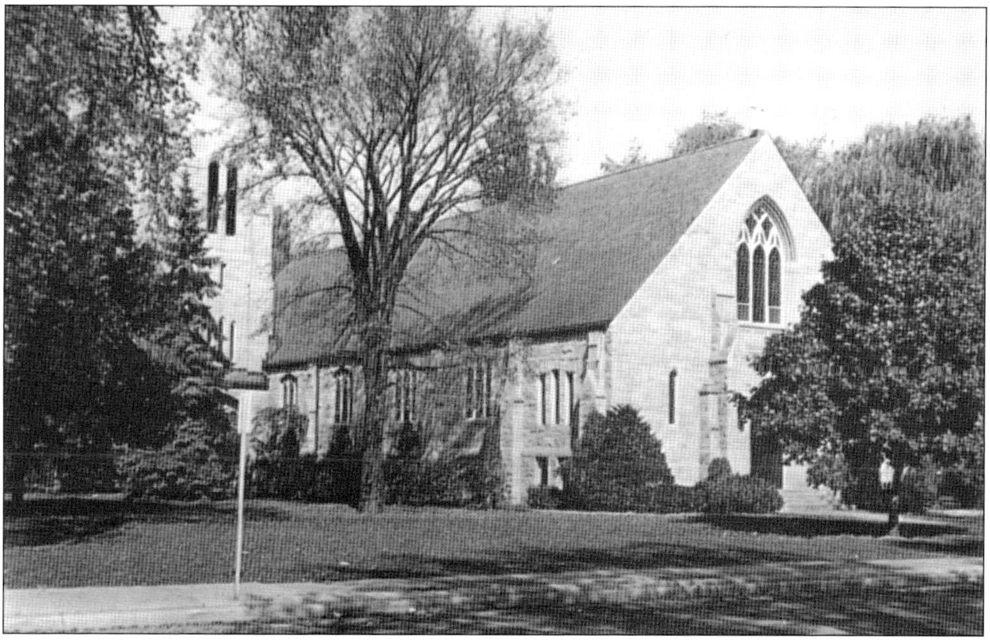

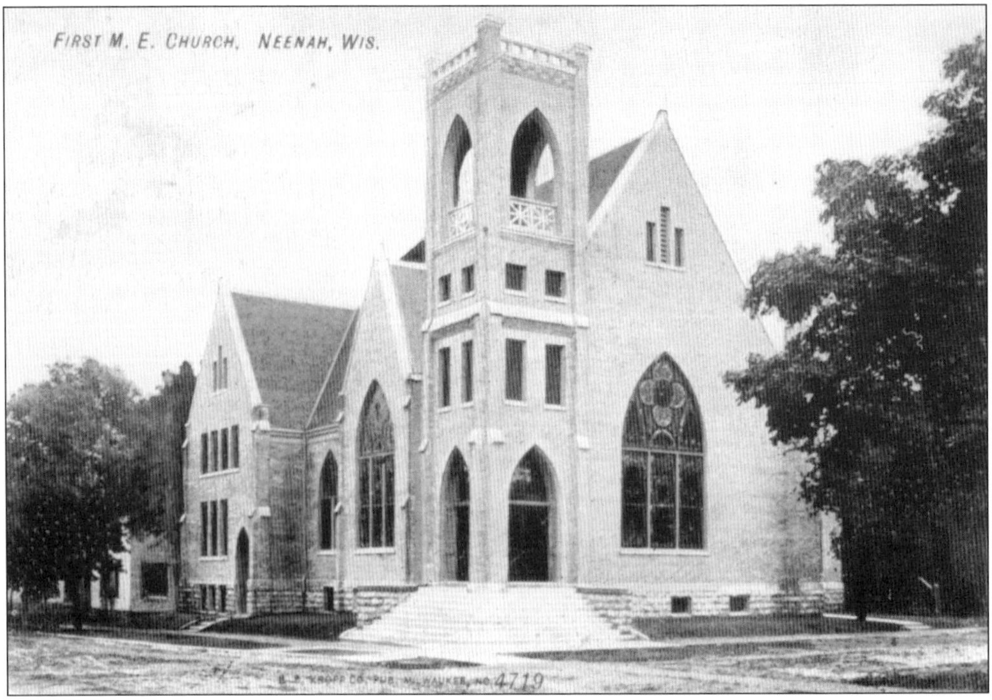

Seen above is the First Methodist Church on the corner of Doty Avenue and Commercial Street, which served Neenah from 1906 to 1937, when a devastating fire gutted the building. Prior to this period, the church had been on Wisconsin Avenue since 1874 in an old Presbyterian church. The church had its roots in the area's earliest days, when the Rev. O.P. Clinton, a Congregationalist minister, held services in his home in Menasha. From this group came three different churches: the Congregational church in 1847, the Presbyterian church in 1848, and the Methodist church, also in 1848. Below is the replacement church, which was dedicated in 1939.

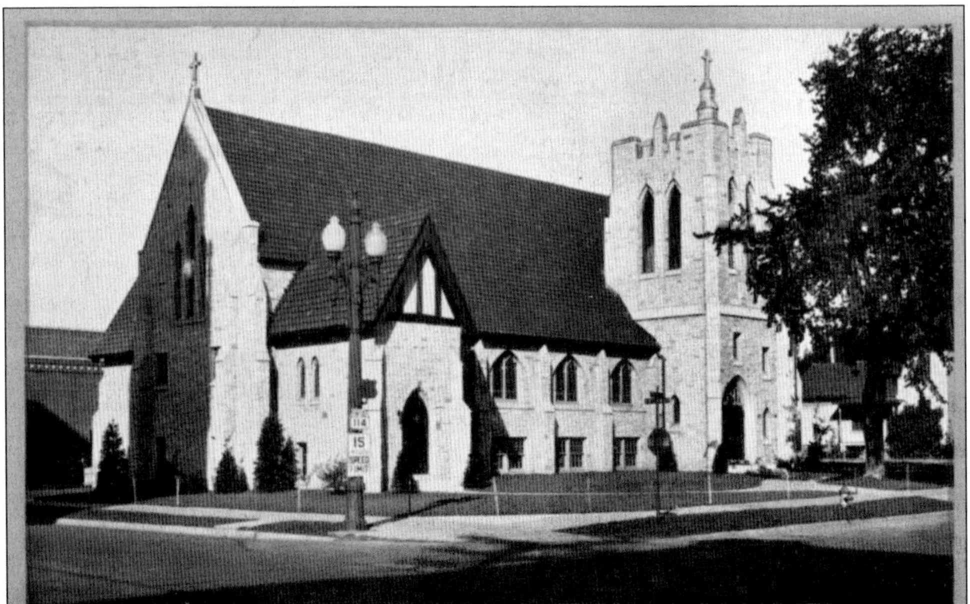

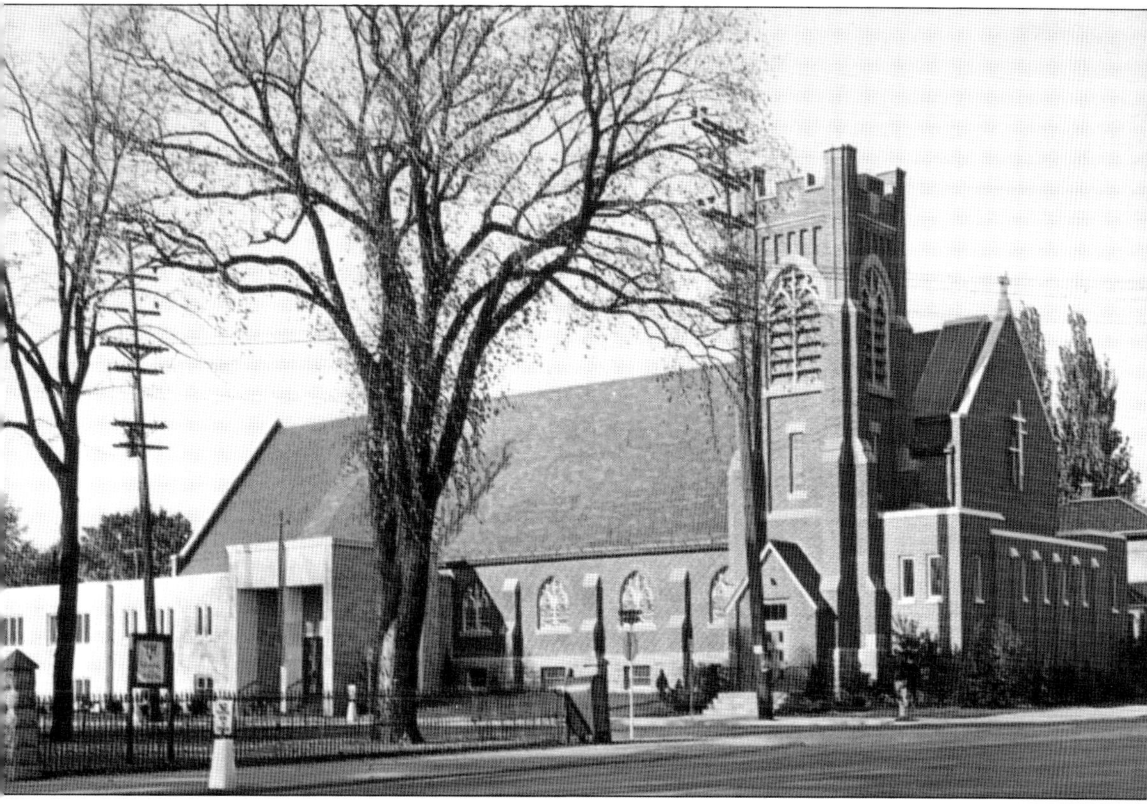

St. Paul's Lutheran Church, a member of the Evangelical Lutheran Church in America, was founded in 1912 as the first Lutheran church in Neenah to offer services in the English language. Up to that time, there were five Evangelical Lutheran congregations in the Neenah-Menasha area, but none conducted worship services in English. A missionary pastor from Oshkosh, the Rev. William C. Stump, came to Neenah in the spring of 1912, and arrangements were made for services to be held in a small chapel owned by the Norwegian Lutherans at Bond and High Streets. The church was organized on September 22, 1912. This small chapel was purchased in 1913, and services were held here regularly. A rapidly growing congregation called for large quarters. The present location on the corner of North Commercial and West North Water Streets was obtained in 1914. St. Paul's Evangelical Lutheran Church was dedicated on May 21, 1916.

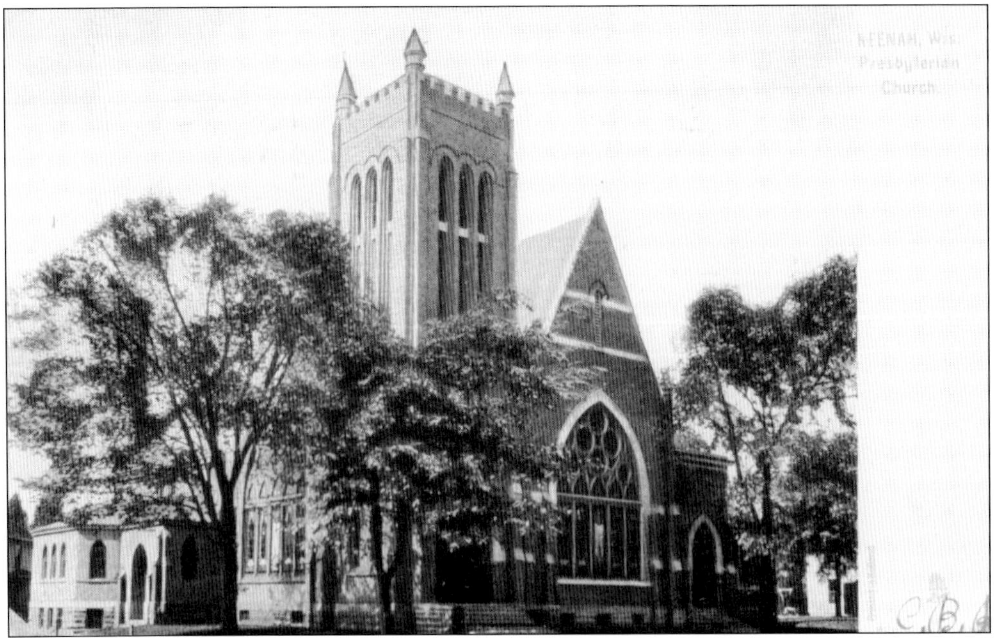

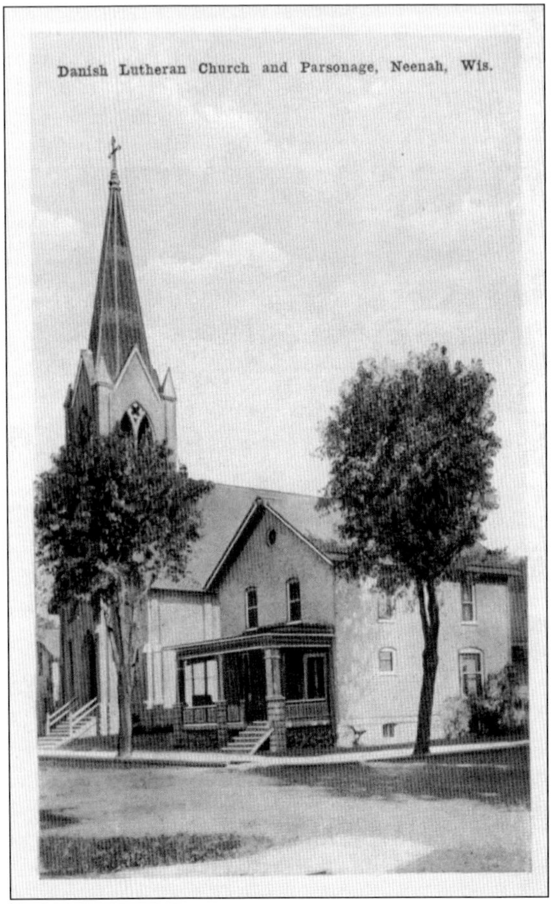

The First Presbyterian Church was organized with a membership of 20 in 1848, in Neenah's earliest days, when it was still known as Winnebago Rapids. The first meeting of the newly formed church was in a large room over the store of Yale & Jones, which stood on the site of Shattuck Park.

Our Savior's Lutheran Church on South Commercial Street is the successor to the old Danish Lutheran Church pictured here. One of the church's significant pastors was the Rev. Jens Jersild, who came to America in 1885. He also brought knitting equipment to supplement his church salary in support of his family of 10. Jersild Knitting lasted nearly 100 years in Neenah, making beautiful sweaters and jackets.

Seven

Around Neenah

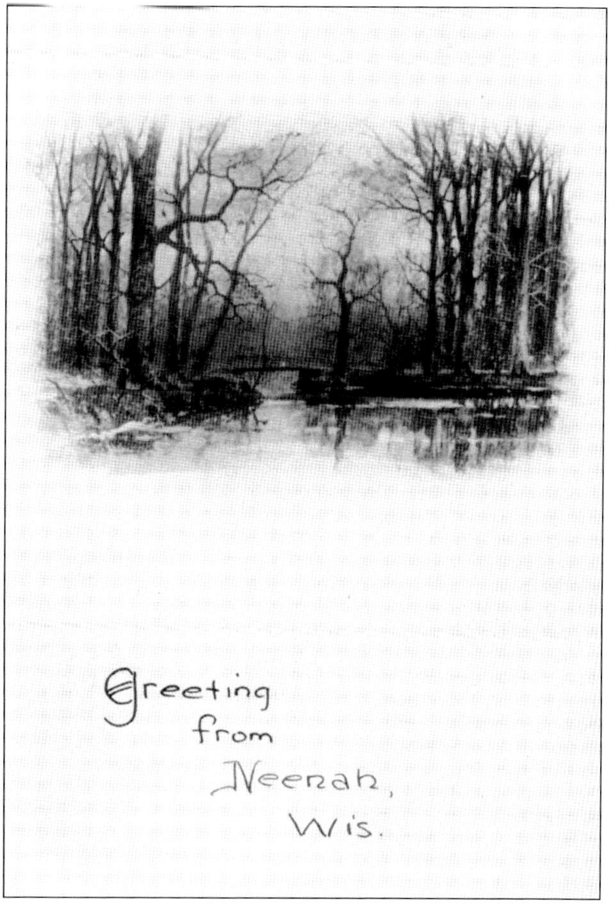

This watercolor of a woodsy park image with a scenic bridge, while reminiscent of Neenah's Doty Park, is suspected to be a standard illustration where the publisher could insert any town's name. Still, it is an elegant form of the "Greetings from" genre, which soon enough would encompass the more famous "big letter" cards that generally shouted to the viewer.

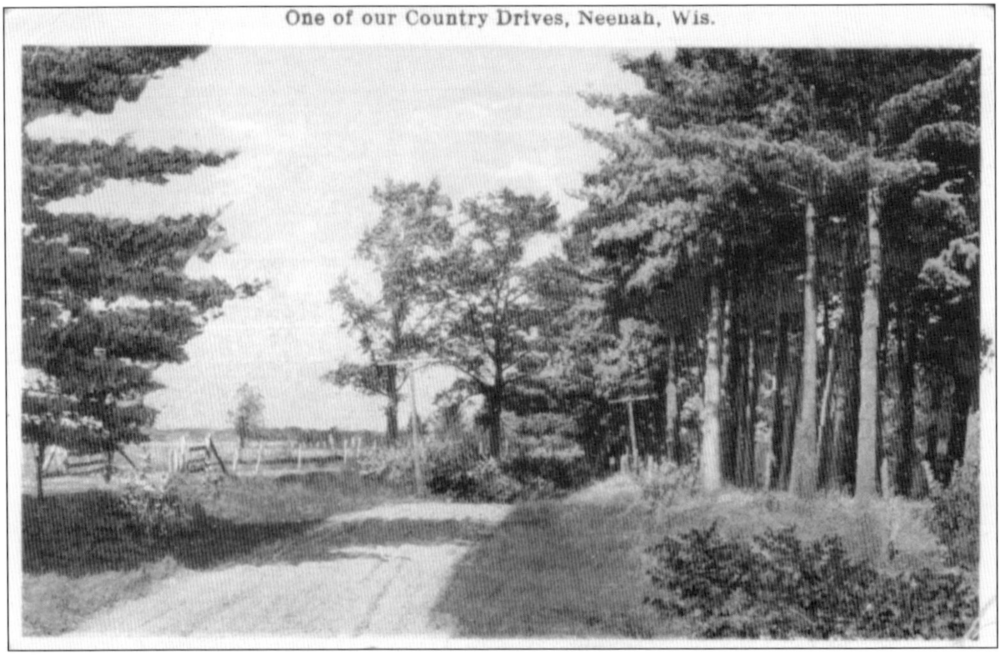

These two post–World War I white border cards emphasize the outdoorsy qualities of Neenah, including the rustic nature of the woods while also showcasing water fun with boating and fishing. Of course, without any outstanding landmarks, these two are as generic as they come, and again, they could serve as a jack-of-all-trades for card publishers. In fact, the card below labels this as one in a series of "small lake scenes—10 subjects." Sometimes, for the sake of ease, a simple pretty scene would do if one was just looking for a medium to write upon while avoiding the mundane qualities of plain government cards.

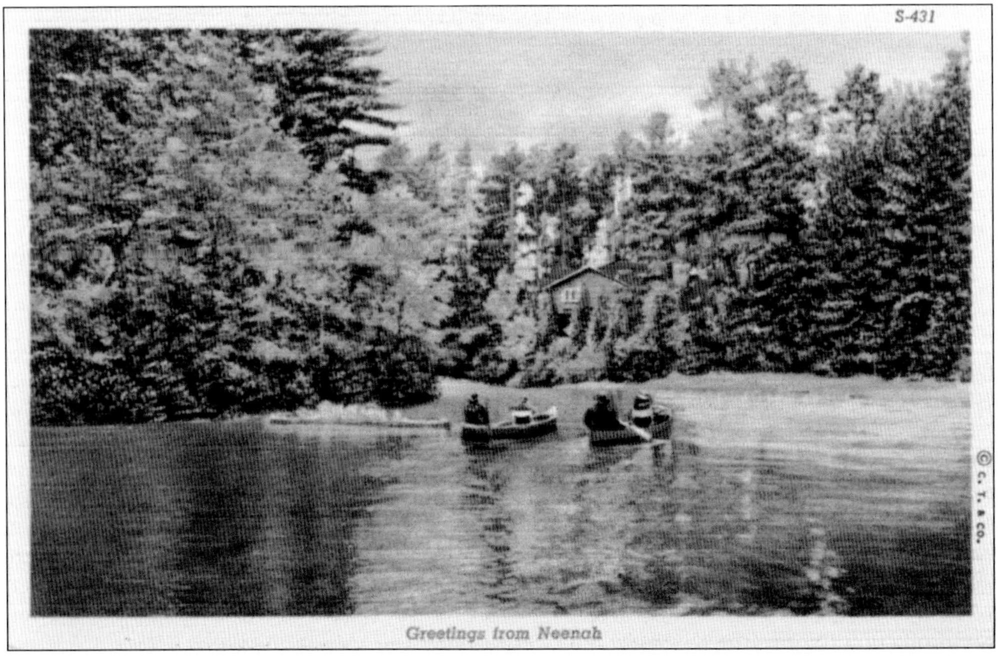

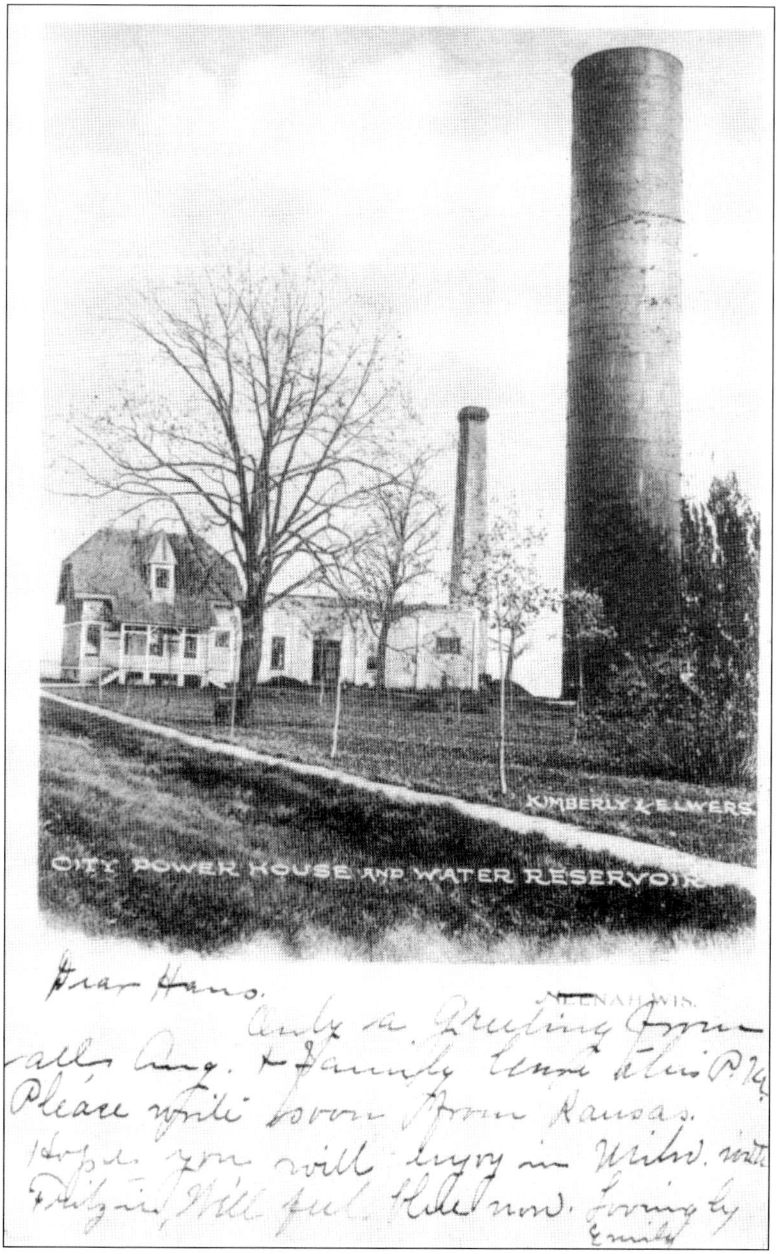

From 1905 comes this rendering of the Neenah powerhouse and water reservoir. The 1880s and 1890s brought public interest in a community water supply. Up to then, water was only thought to be purest if it came from deep wells. The Neenah Water Utility was established in the early 1900s and originally consisted of a simple well water supply to meet this demand. Although this was a short-term solution, the minerals in the water made it less than ideal for home use, so an improved source of water was sought out. This led to the construction of a water filtration plant on South Park Avenue. In the photograph, the large object to the right is a stand pipe, which stored water and generated pressure. It was constructed at a height sufficient to pressurize a water supply system for the distribution of potable water and to provide emergency water storage for fire protection. Notice the Kimberly & Elwers name featured prominently.

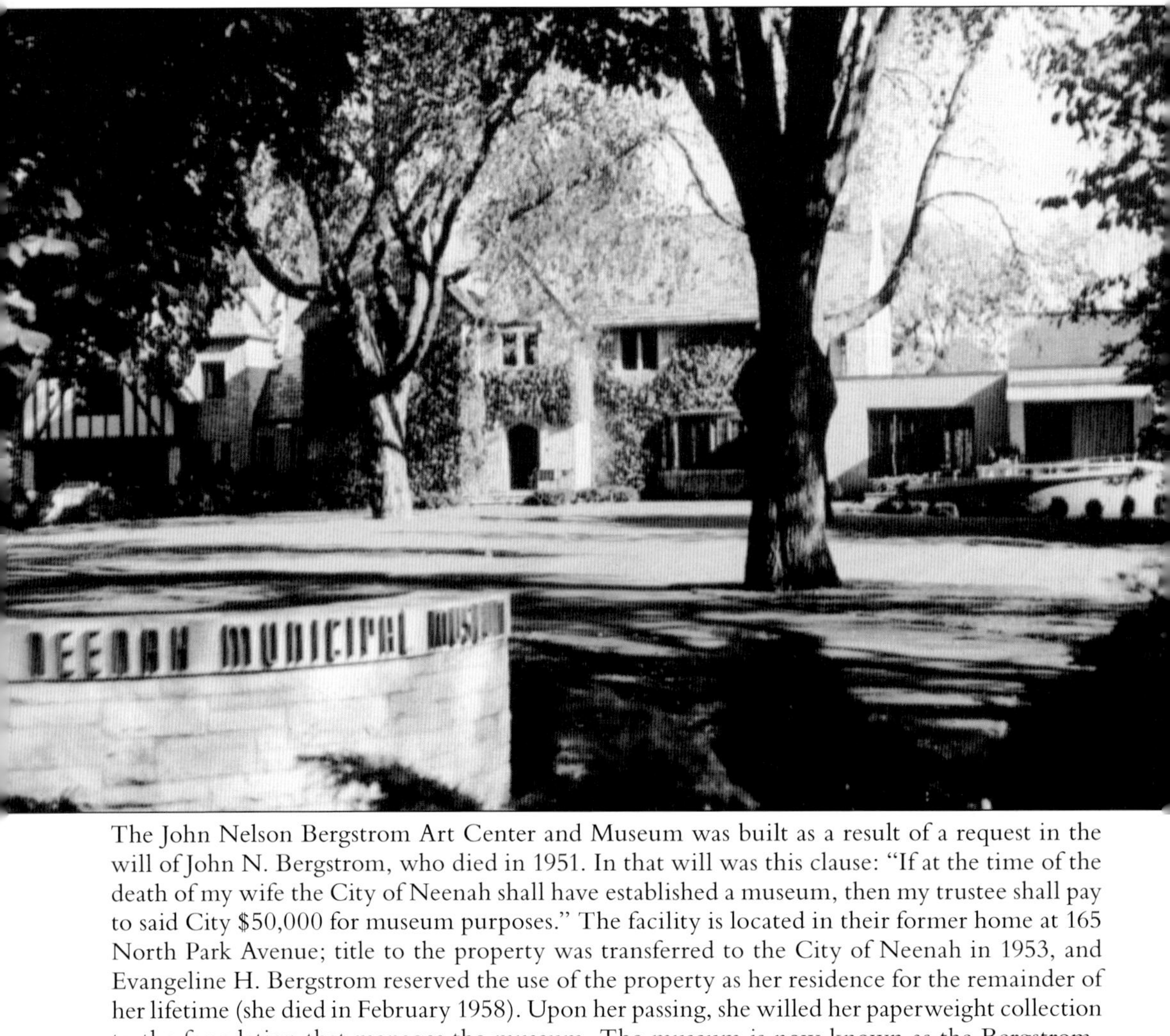

The John Nelson Bergstrom Art Center and Museum was built as a result of a request in the will of John N. Bergstrom, who died in 1951. In that will was this clause: "If at the time of the death of my wife the City of Neenah shall have established a museum, then my trustee shall pay to said City $50,000 for museum purposes." The facility is located in their former home at 165 North Park Avenue; title to the property was transferred to the City of Neenah in 1953, and Evangeline H. Bergstrom reserved the use of the property as her residence for the remainder of her lifetime (she died in February 1958). Upon her passing, she willed her paperweight collection to the foundation that manages the museum. The museum is now known as the Bergstrom-Mahler Museum of Glass and celebrates more than just paperweights.

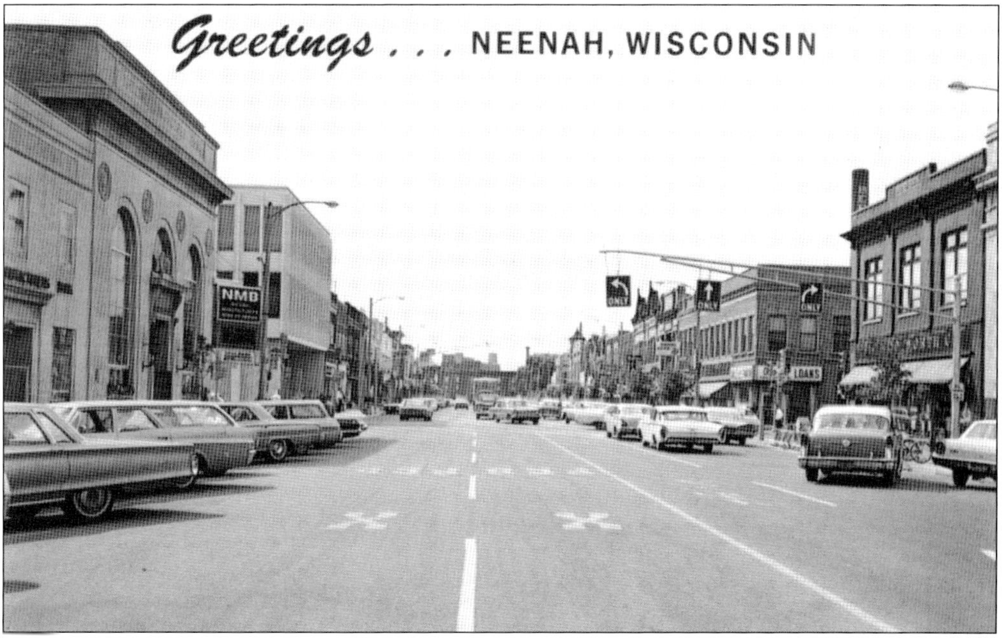

These Greetings from Neenah, Wisconsin, postcards are of the photochrome variety and were a popular type of souvenir in the 1950s and 1960s. The postcard above dates from 1964, and the view below appears to be from the 1980s. As with most before-and-after views, one can ascertain many changes on Wisconsin Avenue, Neenah's main street. Aside from the vintage automobiles with the 1950s-era long lines and tail fins, in some cases, the most obvious change is the whitewashed buildings lining the avenue, one attempt at an urban renewal effort to give the downtown a standard look.

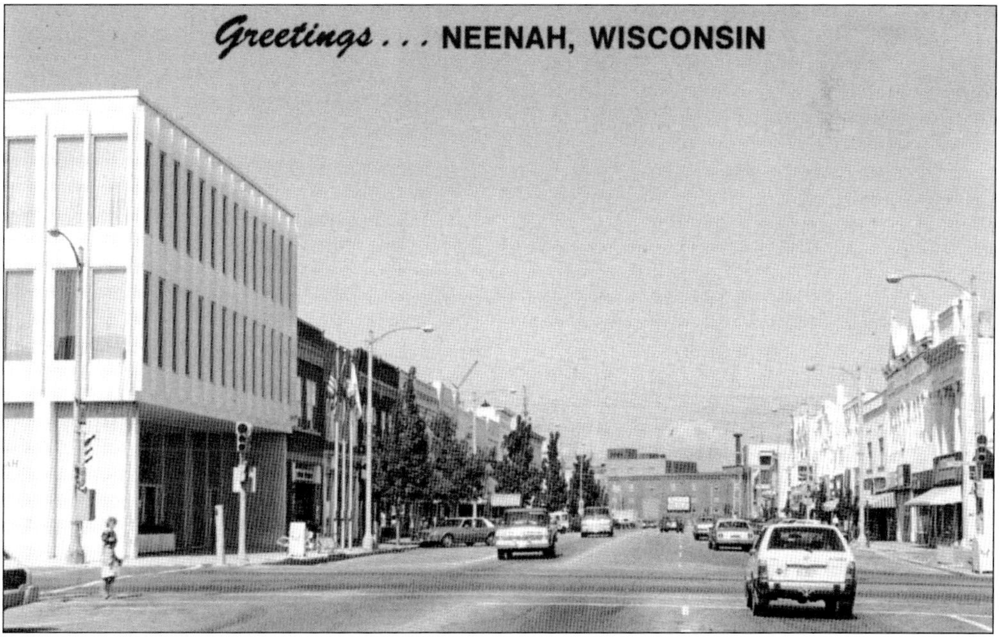

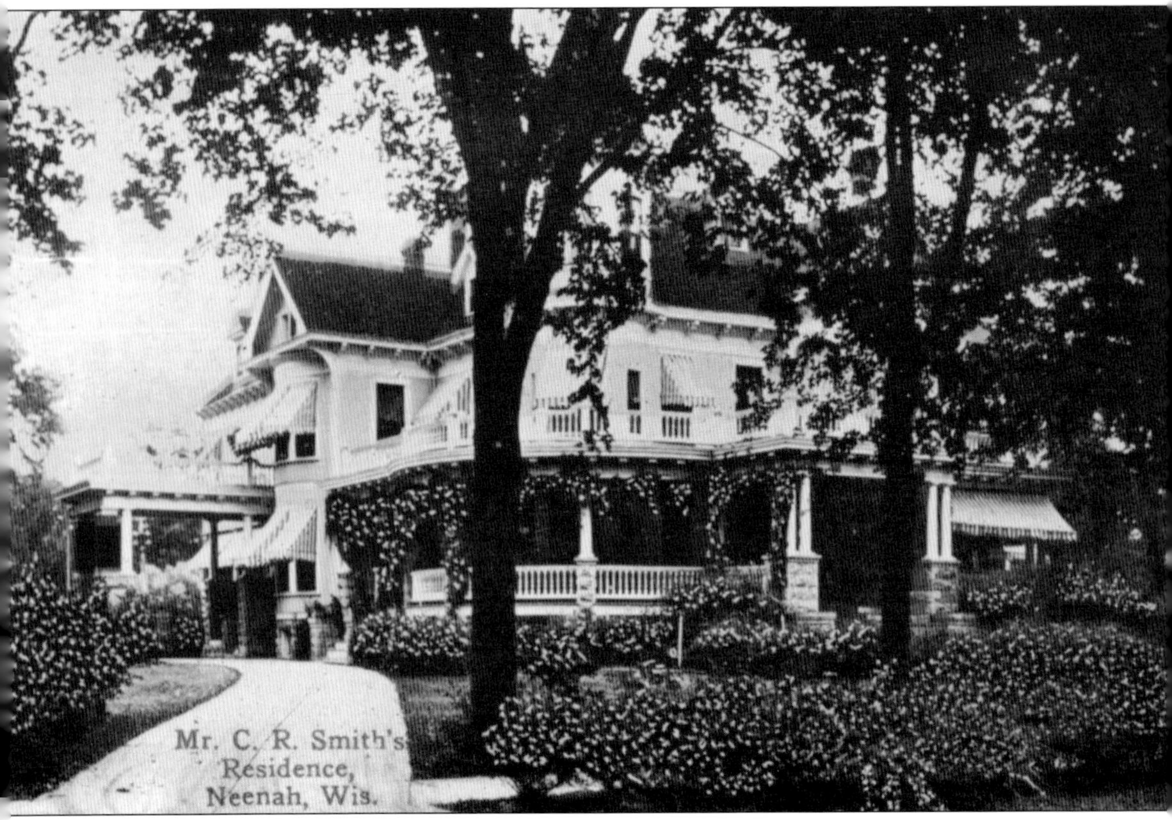

The Charles R. Smith house at 824 East Forest Avenue was described by the Wisconsin Historical Society as a "rambling altered eclectic home with Queen Anne, Italianate, and Colonial revival features" in its online Architecture and History Inventory. Charles R. Smith was the son of pioneer Menasha industrialist and city father Elisha D. Smith. Smith greatly improved Menasha Wooden Ware's fortunes. A Princeton University graduate of 1876, he took a broom handle and barrel factory he had formed by himself in Menasha and merged it with his father's existing Wooden Ware business. This made Menasha Wooden Ware the world's largest manufacturer of turned woodenware. Additionally, he became president of the First National Bank and remained in that position until his death in 1916. He was also superintendent of the Menasha school system. He helped organize the Wisconsin & Northern Railroad and renamed Warner, Wisconsin, after his second wife when Menasha Wooden Ware bought up the power site in the Flambeau River about a mile east of the village. Today, it is known as Ladysmith.

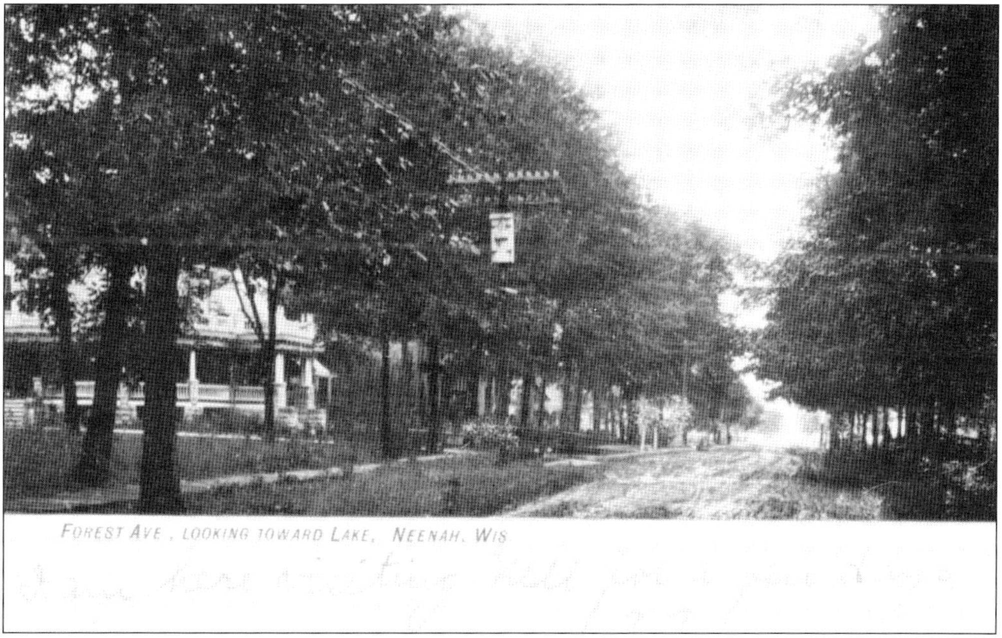

Here are two postcard views of East Forest Avenue. While it is generally known that East Wisconsin Avenue is the home of many obvious showplace mansions in Neenah, Forest Avenue was the original destination for many wealthy industrialists to build their considerable residences. Alexander Syme built a house in 1882 at what is now 910 East Forest Avenue. Syme was a partner in the Eagle Flouring Mills and an owner of barrel stave factories. When he retired to travel abroad, the home was obtained by Albert C. Gilbert, the son of Gilbert Paper founder William Gilbert. Additional mansions built on Forest Avenue include those of George A. Whiting of Menasha's Whiting Paper, the aforementioned Charles R. Smith, his brother Frank Smith, and Judge J.C. Kerwin.

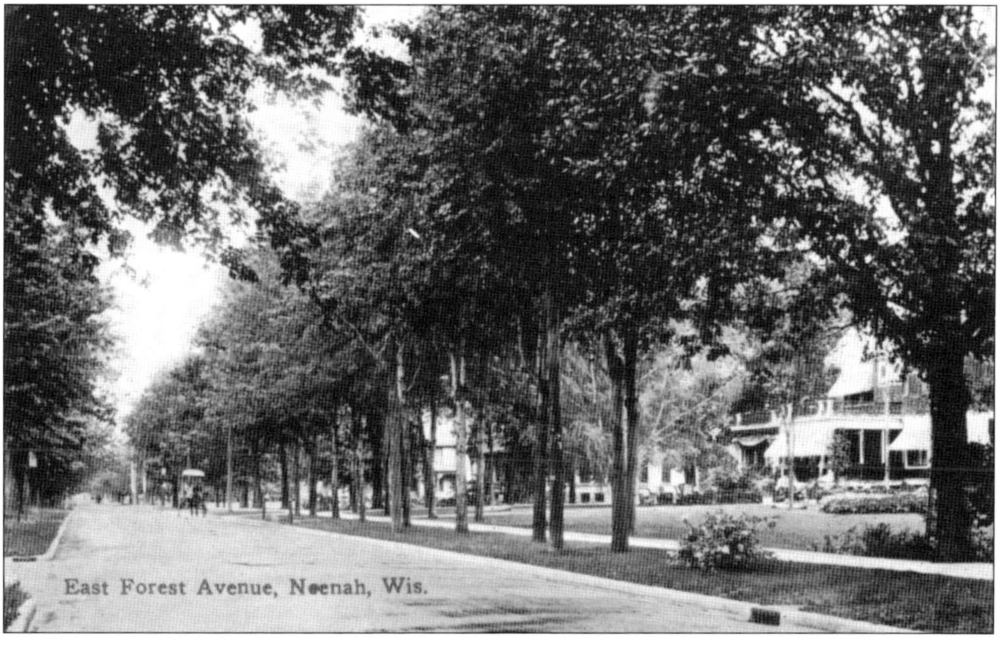

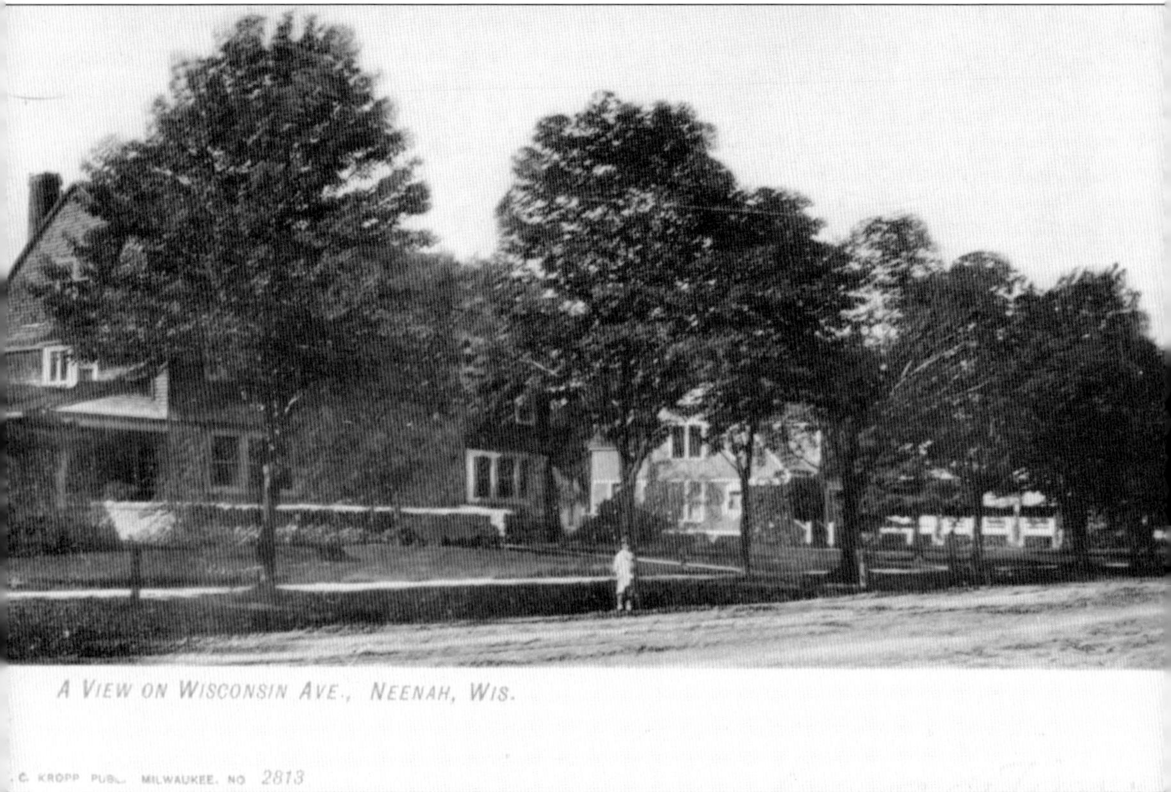

East Wisconsin Avenue was the premier destination for Neenah's industrialists to settle in the 1870s, 1880s, and 1890s. Among them was John Stevens, a flour miller who patented corrugated rollers, which became the industry standard. Largely as a result of this revolutionary roller mill process, wheat production in Wisconsin plummeted to insignificance, and the flour mills in Neenah all closed. This was due to the fact that the new process was much more well-suited to the milling of spring wheat, which could be grown cheaply on the plains and prairies of Minnesota and the Dakotas. The effect in Minnesota, as the Minneapolis mills such as Pillsbury and General Mills adopted the process, led to dramatic growth in that state. By 1889, Minnesota had become the number-one wheat-growing state in America. Stevens sold the rights to his inventions in 1893 and retired from the flour mill business.

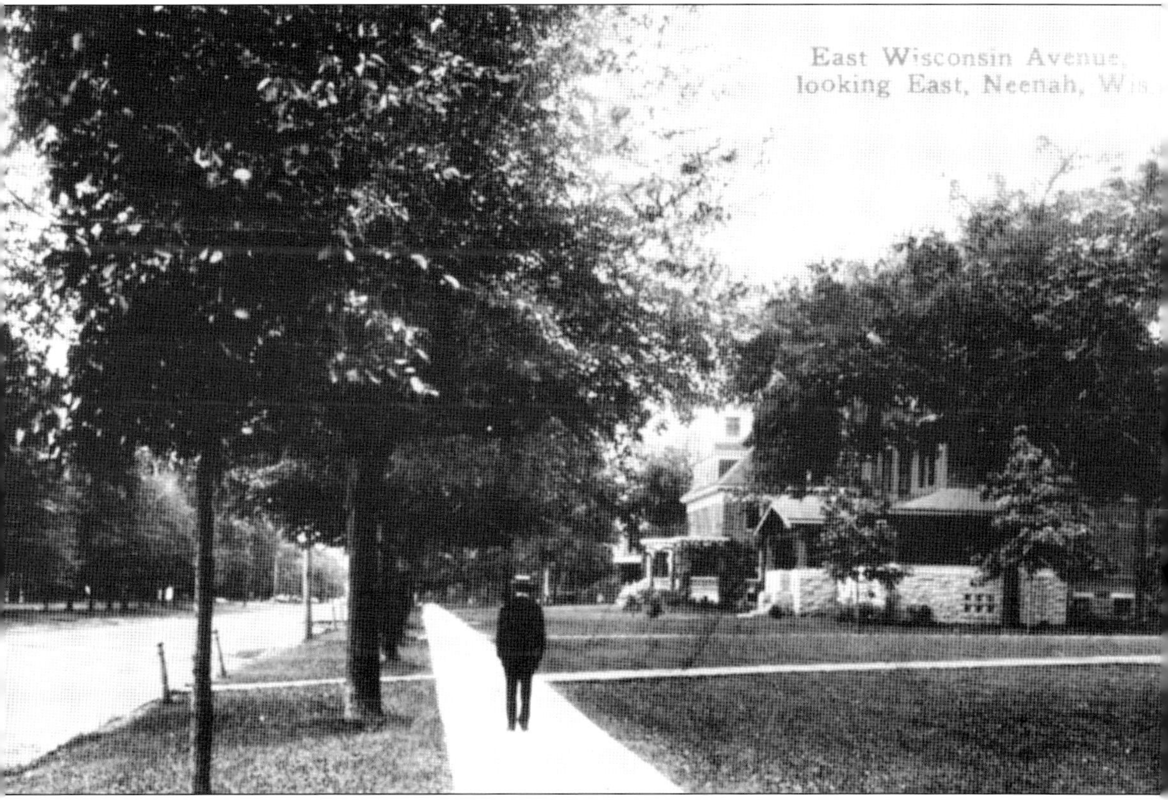

Other industrialists who settled on Wisconsin Avenue included the Kimberlys, the Clarks, the Shattucks, the Babcocks, the Sherrys, and the Bergstroms. Frank Shattuck and Havilah Babcock were two of the founding partners in the Kimberly-Clark paper company. Henry Sherry was a big lumberman, and George Bergstrom was a stove maker. The story goes that George and his brother D.W. Bergstrom did not get along in their stove making business, and they flipped a coin in 1904 to see who would keep the factory. George won the coin toss, and D.W. Bergstrom went into the papermaking business. George may have felt himself fortunate at the time, but with the advent of electricity, wood-burning stoves for cooking went the way of buggy whips and blacksmithing. This stretch of East Wisconsin Avenue was known tongue-in-cheek as "piety row," in that the Riverside Park, across the street from their mansions, did not allow alcohol and was closed on Sundays, similar to Elisha D. Smith's dictum about Menasha's Smith Park.

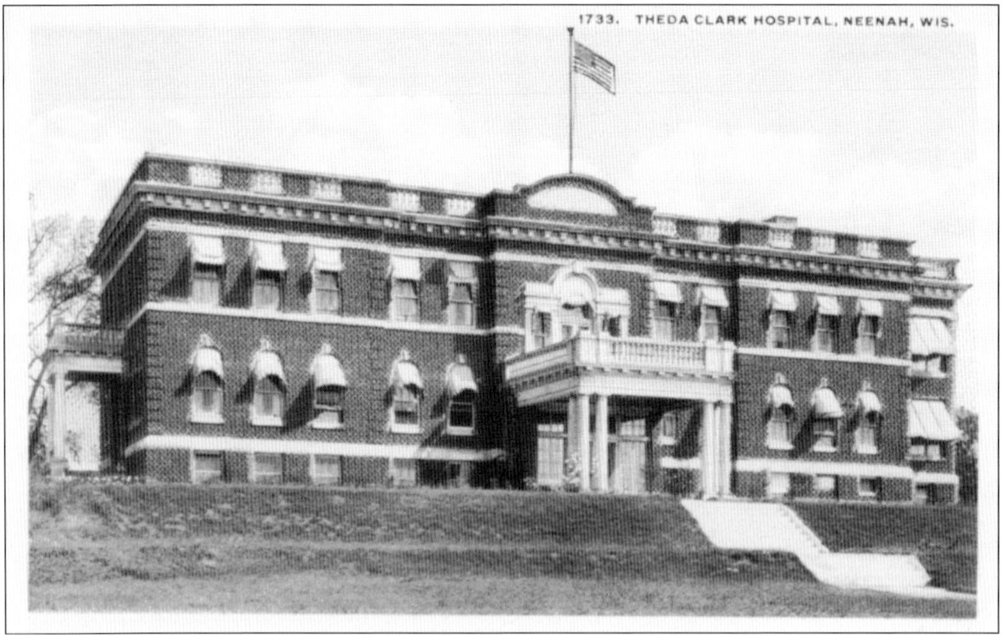

Theda Clark Peters, daughter of Kimberly-Clark founder C.B. Clark, was married in 1901 to William Cunningham Peters from Goshen, Indiana. Peters was a member of a Philadelphia wallpaper manufacturing firm and had been a newspaperman, the editor of the *Goshen Times*. Theda died in October 1903, shortly after giving birth to her daughter. Her will stated "I hereby bequeath the remaining one half of my estate to my brother Charles B. Clark—I have stated to my brother Charles B. Clark—the uses to which I wish him to apply said remaining one-half of my estate; but inasmuch as I do not wish to make public such uses, I give the estate absolutely to the said Charles B. Clark and trust entirely to his honor to apply the same to the uses which I have privately stated to him."

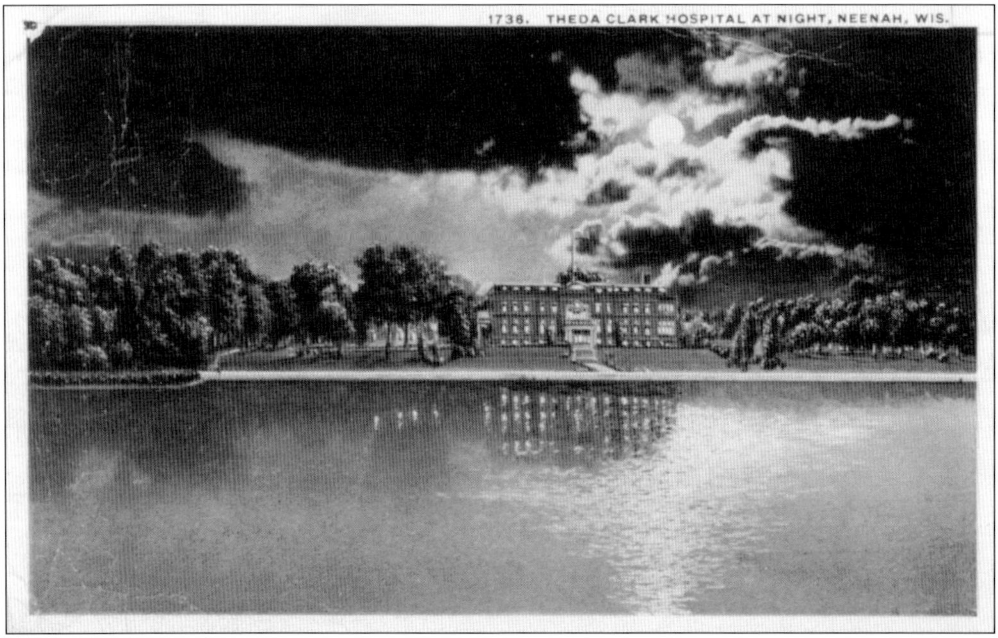

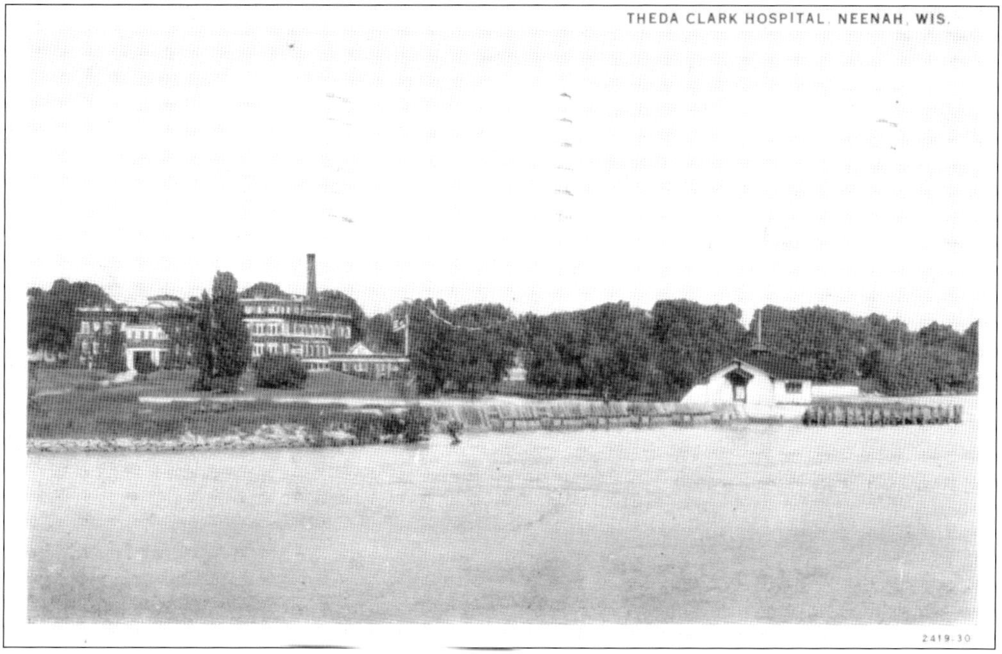

Theda's estate amounted to $96,000. Her family decided that a hospital would be a worthy memorial to her and also serve the community of Neenah. Her brother, Charles B. "Bill" Clark, carried out her wishes, adding to her bequest out of his own funds an additional $30,000. In 1909, the Theda Clark Memorial Hospital was dedicated in her memory. The hospital had a capacity of 25 beds. In 1910, a nursing school was opened at Theda Clark that lasted until 1938. In that time, 127 nurses were trained and graduated from the facility. This 1948 addition to the hospital increased total beds throughout the facility to 164.

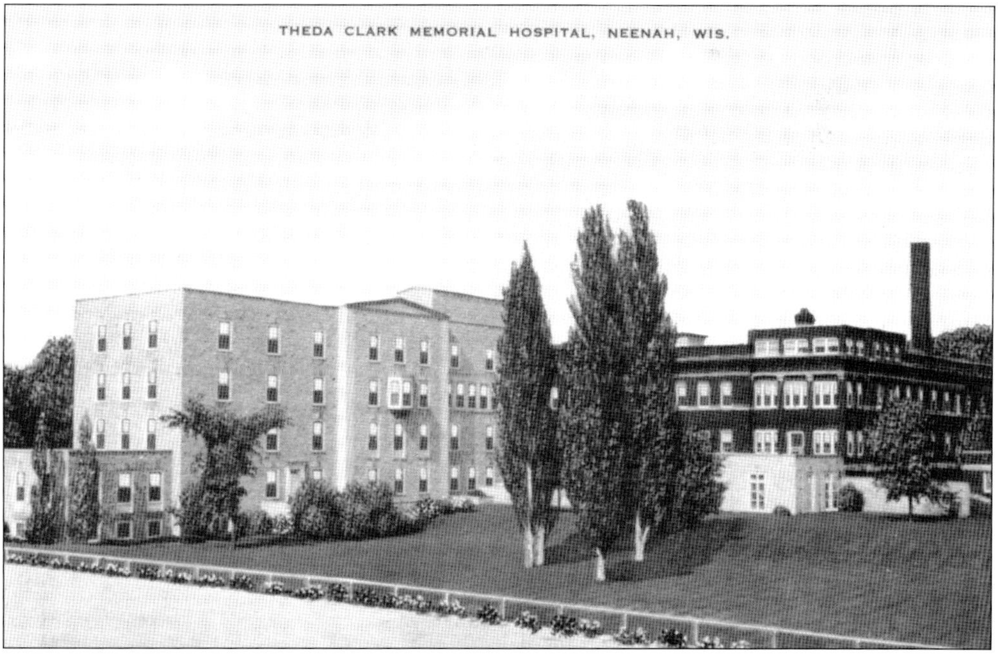

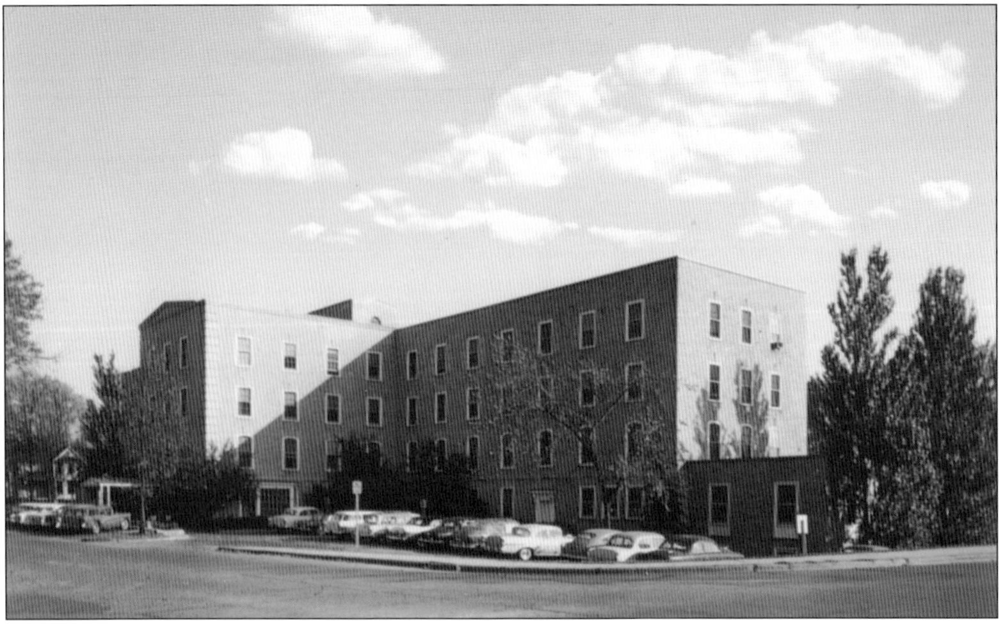

Expanding the hospital was necessary again in the early 1960s, as the scope of its coverage far exceeded the metropolitan area of Neenah proper. A $3.85-million expansion completed in 1963 added a new x-ray wing, a therapy wing, and a six-story hospital bed wing and demolished the original structure that dated to 1909. The main entrance on Lincoln Street became the emergency room entrance, while the new main entrance was relocated to the east side of the new building on Second Street. Bed capacity increased to an immediate 244 with the potential for 312 with the eventual use of the two top floors of the new six-story wing. Between 1967 and 1969, another six-story wing was added earlier than planned due to growth projections far exceeding the hospital's master plan. This type of growth was not expected until 1975.

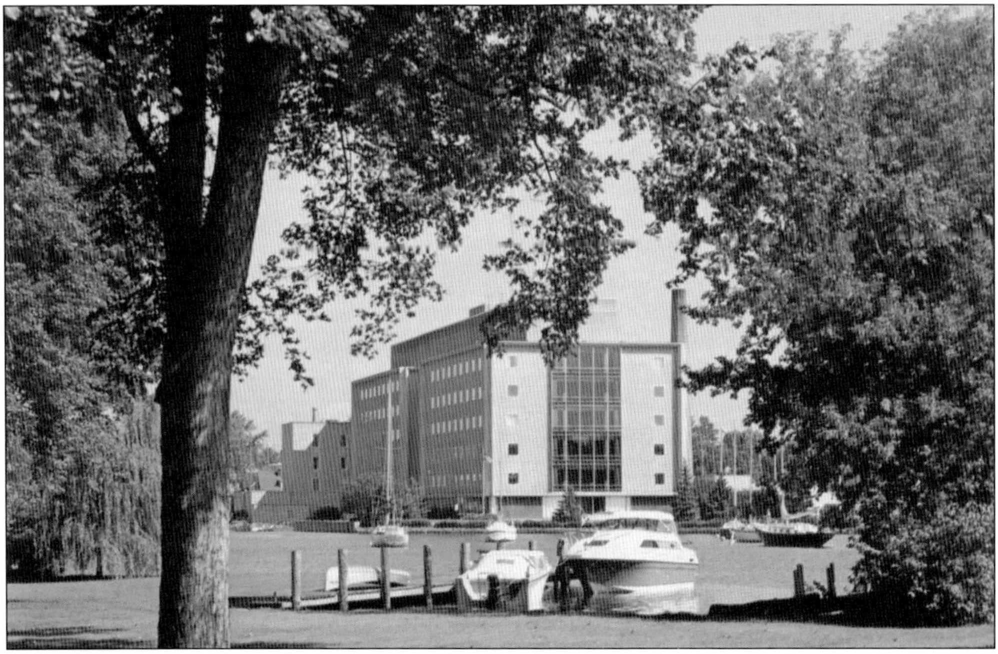

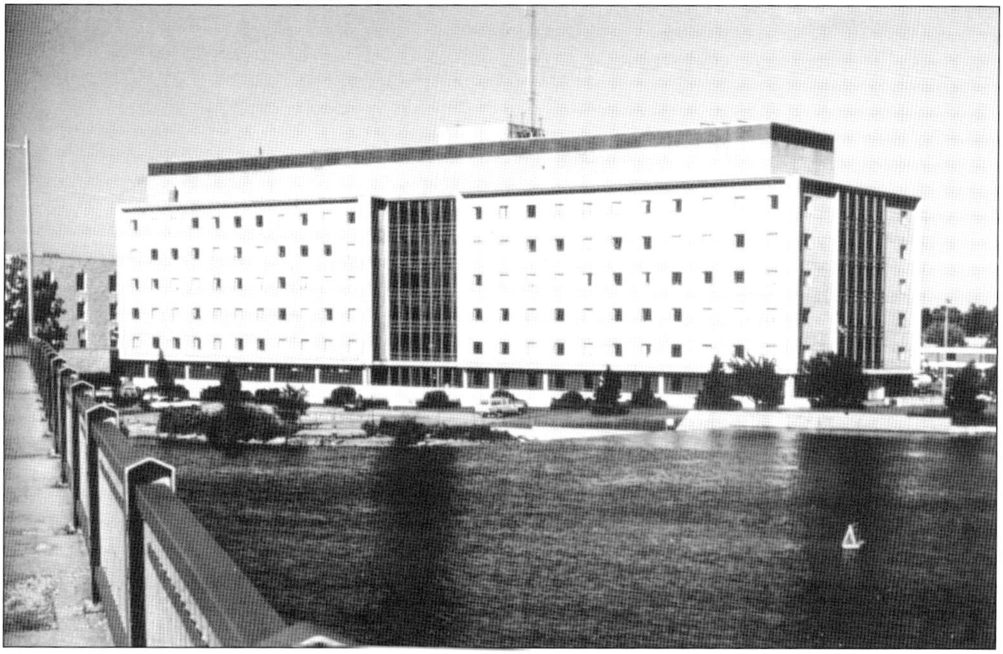

Since the publication of these two postcards, Theda Clark Memorial Hospital has undergone massive changes and far surpassed its original mission to serve the Neenah community. As with many health care organizations, mergers and acquisitions became a necessity over time. In 1987, Theda Clark Medical Center merged with Appleton Medical Center to form Novus Health Group. From that merger came several diverse medical facilities around Northeastern Wisconsin, all under the "ThedaCare" umbrella: Neenah, Appleton, New London, Waupaca, and Shawano, along with physicians' offices and other health care services. Theda Clark Peters would be amazed at how her bequest has helped so many over the past 108 years.

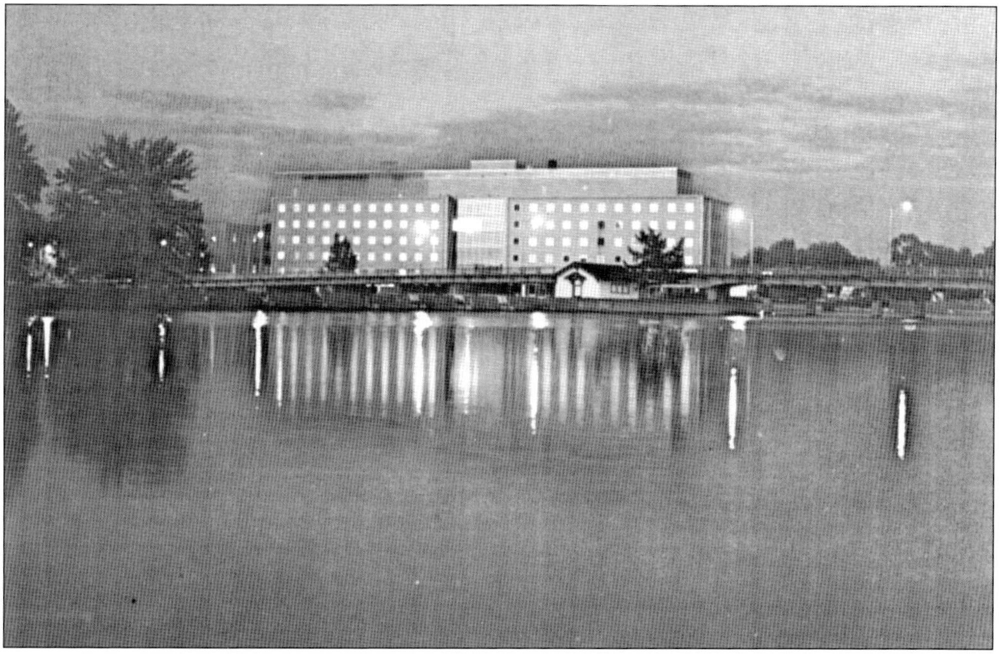

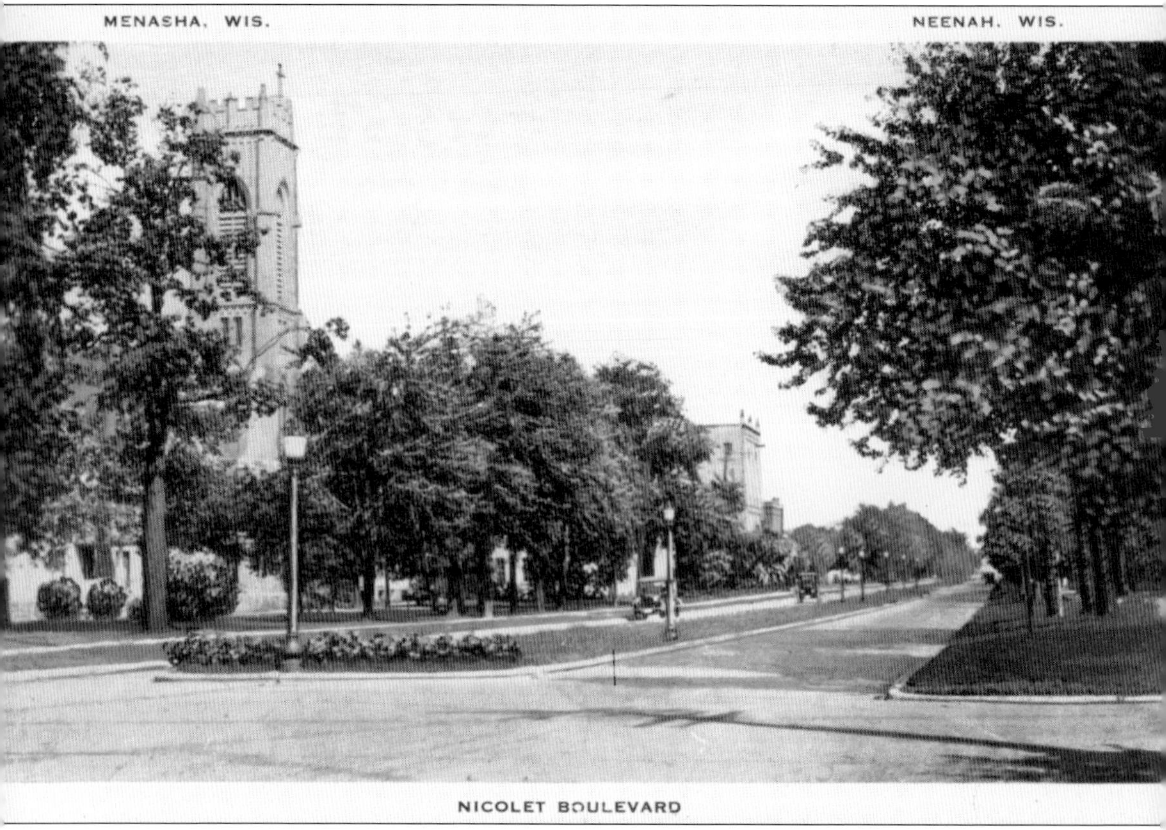

This 1925 postcard shows Nicolet Boulevard, the dividing line between the Twin Cities on Doty Island. Known as simply "the Avenue" on early maps, the street was renamed to honor explorer Jean Nicolet around the time of the Nicolet Monument being dedicated in Menasha's Smith Park in 1906. This postcard shows the demarcation line, with Menasha on the left and Neenah on the right. Visible on the Menasha side are St. Patrick's Catholic Church and, farther down the street, the Walter Brothers Brewery, a fixture in Menasha since 1888. Early 1960 saw the demise of the brewery. It had ceased operations in 1956, though its sister breweries continued operations in Eau Claire, Appleton, and West Bend as well as in Pueblo and Trinidad, Colorado. Unable to match the marketing and sales budgets of the big national breweries, the Walter breweries closed one after another in the 1950s, 1960s, and 1970s. The last one to survive was Walter Brewing in Eau Claire, which lasted until 1989.

Eight

Around Menasha

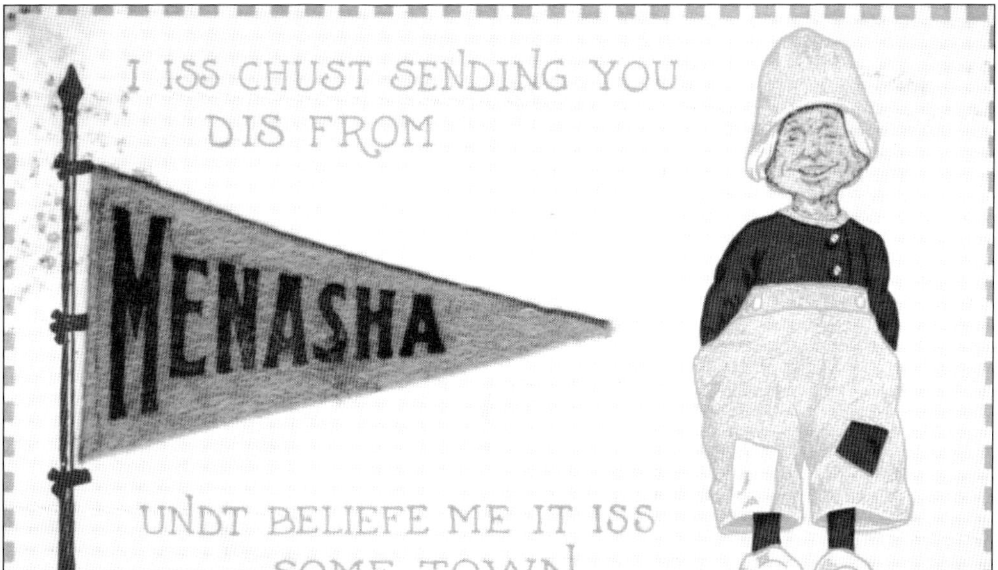

Pennant postcards were stock postcards carried by a publisher that could be imprinted with a town or city name on request. In this case, felt fabric has been cut in a pennant shape and printed with the city name, then glued to the postcard. Often, the pennant would be accompanied by a caricature of an ethnic stereotype with some "witty" saying. These were quite popular in the early 20th century.

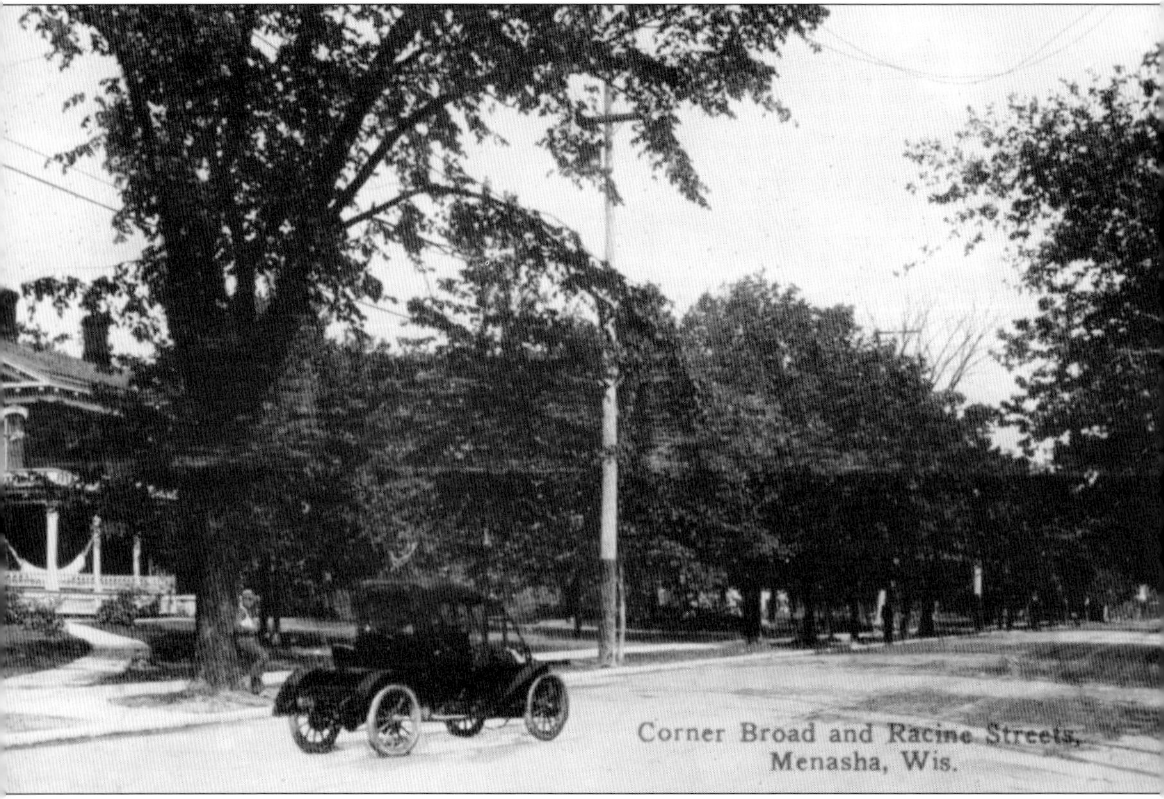

This idyllic postcard of a leisurely automobile ride belies the potential for this stretch of Broad Street. At one time, Menasha had three commercial districts: one at the intersection of Broad and Appleton Streets, one block from this scene; the traditional downtown at the area of Main and Mill Streets; and the area surrounding Main and Tayco Streets. Commercial activities at Broad and Appleton Streets developed as a result of the boat landing and the plank roads that led from that spot as a point of transshipment. With the completion of rail connections in 1861, this area declined in commercial significance, leaving only a few reminders of its former importance. The two taverns and the former grocery remaining at that intersection bear witness to that effort. The US Government Land Office had also been relocated from Green Bay in the 1850s to a location on Broad Street to regulate the sale of public land bought from the Indians.

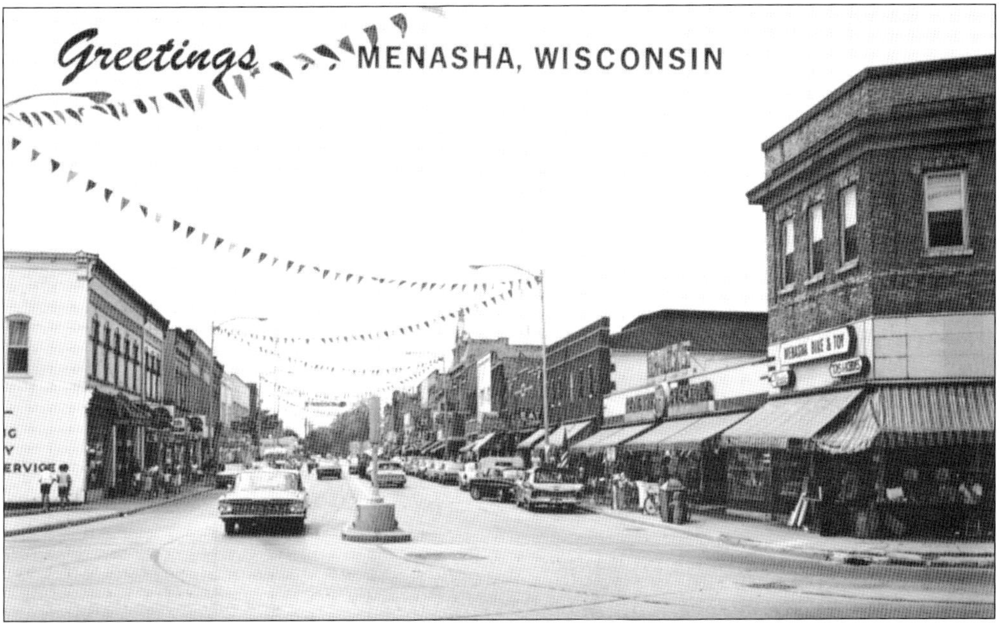

This page features a couple of popular souvenir postcards of the photochrome era. The view above is the traditional "Greetings from" postcard showing a festive downtown view. In this case, Menasha is likely having its popular Prospector Days sidewalk sale, an annual July event that, when partnered with sister city Neenah, gave each civic merchants' association an economic jolt. The postcard below, taken from overhead near Jefferson Park, reveals many landmarks, including the water utility on Broad Street and water tower on Second Street, St. Mary's Church and High School, downtown businesses, the industrial district, and many more. If one knows where to look, it is there.

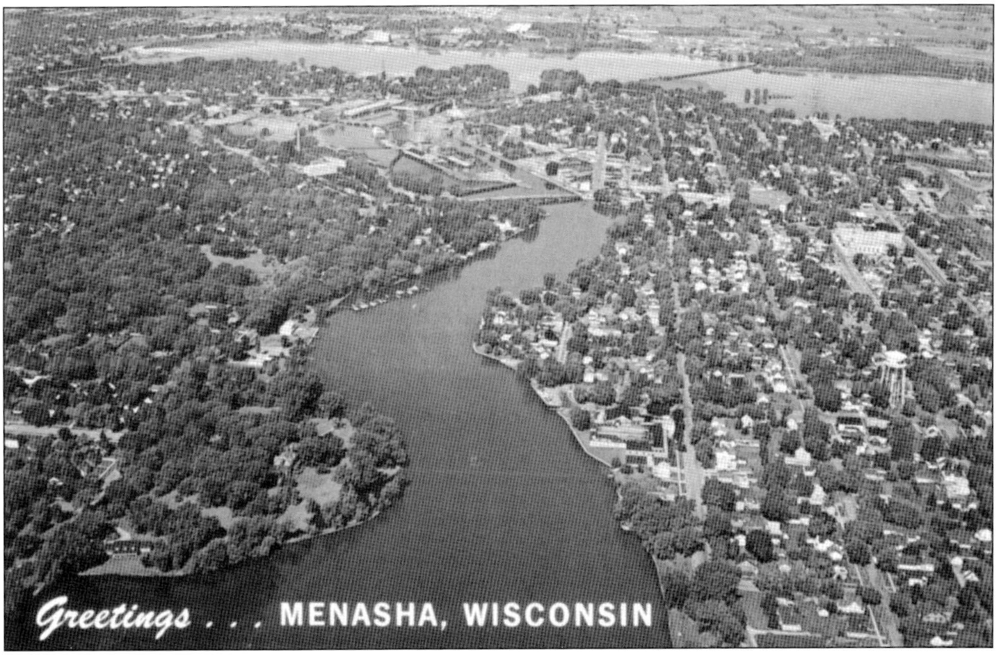

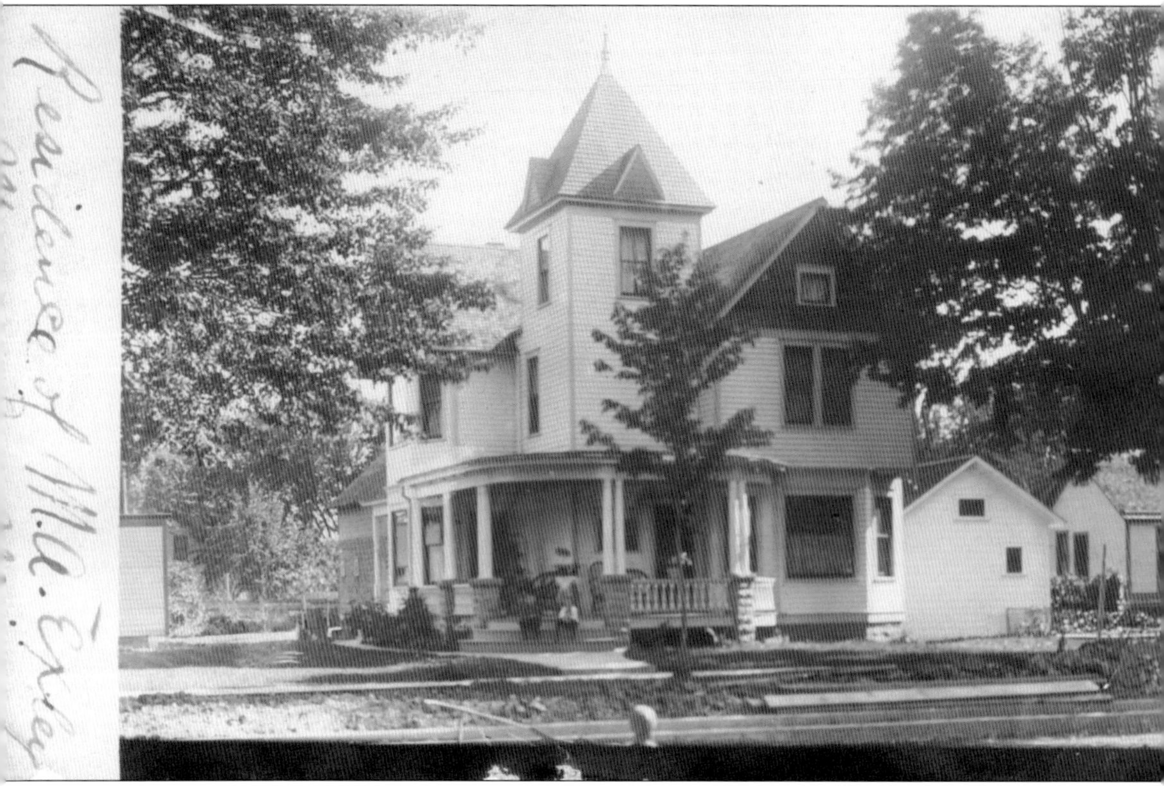

In 1890, Maurice A. Exley came to Menasha from Wausau and with George Rippl opened a meat market on Appleton Street. One year later, the firm built a market on the corner of Broad and Racine Streets. Here they handled a complete assortment of meats and everything else seasonable to be found in a first-class market. Besides retailing, they also did an extensive wholesale business. By the 1920s, George Rippl and Exley had gone their separate ways. Rippl opened his own meat market at 500 Broad Street, and Exley's Market moved to 234 Main Street. He also moved his residence to 309 Broad Street. His home is shown in this postcard. Exley retired from the meat business for good in 1930 and lived until 1937, devoting his leisure time to a farm he owned on Appleton Road.

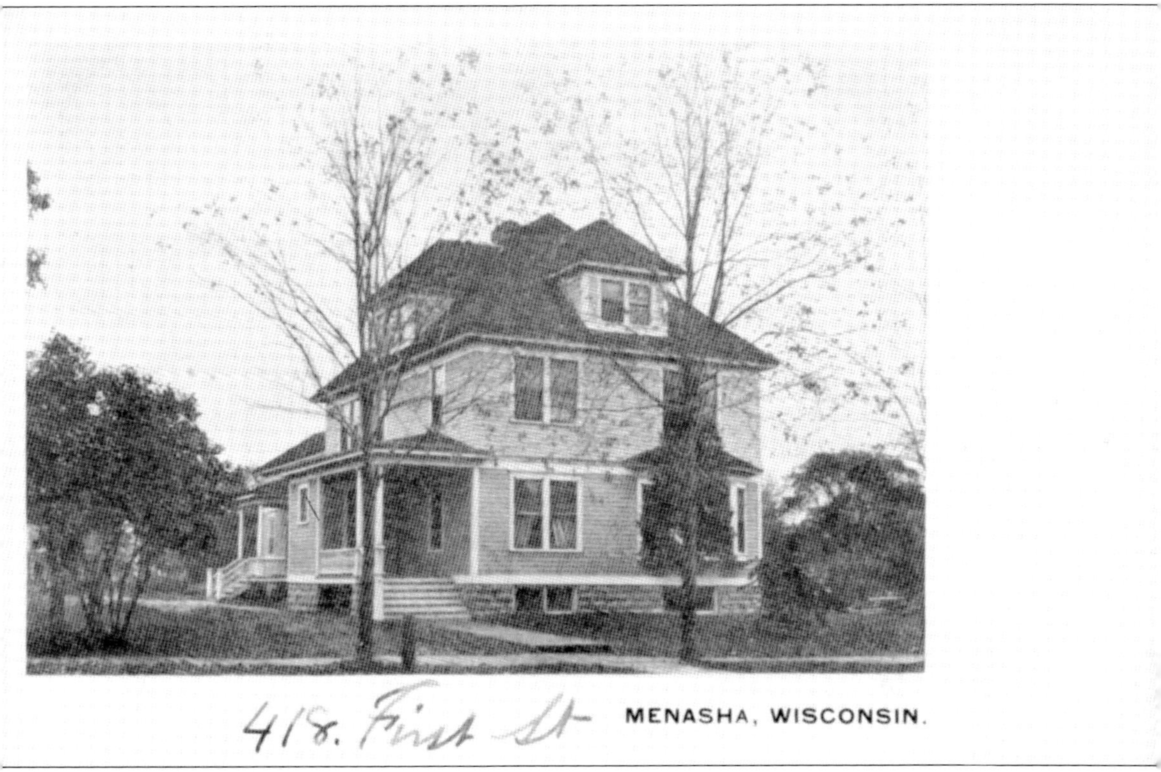

This photographic postcard from 1909 showcases a home at 418 First Street. The home belonged to Joseph C. Underwood, who at the time of his death in 1920 was the second oldest living resident of Menasha at the age of 92. Underwood was a veteran of the Civil War and had come to Menasha 50 years earlier to work in the McKinnon excelsior mill, where he labored for 20 years before retiring. (Excelsior is also known as "wood wool" and is a packaging material for cushioning, a stuffing for plush toys, and a bedding for animals and their cages.) Underwood was a simple man who toiled in a blue-collar job. While he was no politician or notable civic leader, his home is nevertheless immortalized in this postcard. The democratization of photography and the new affordable media allowed for what was once an expensive extravagance.

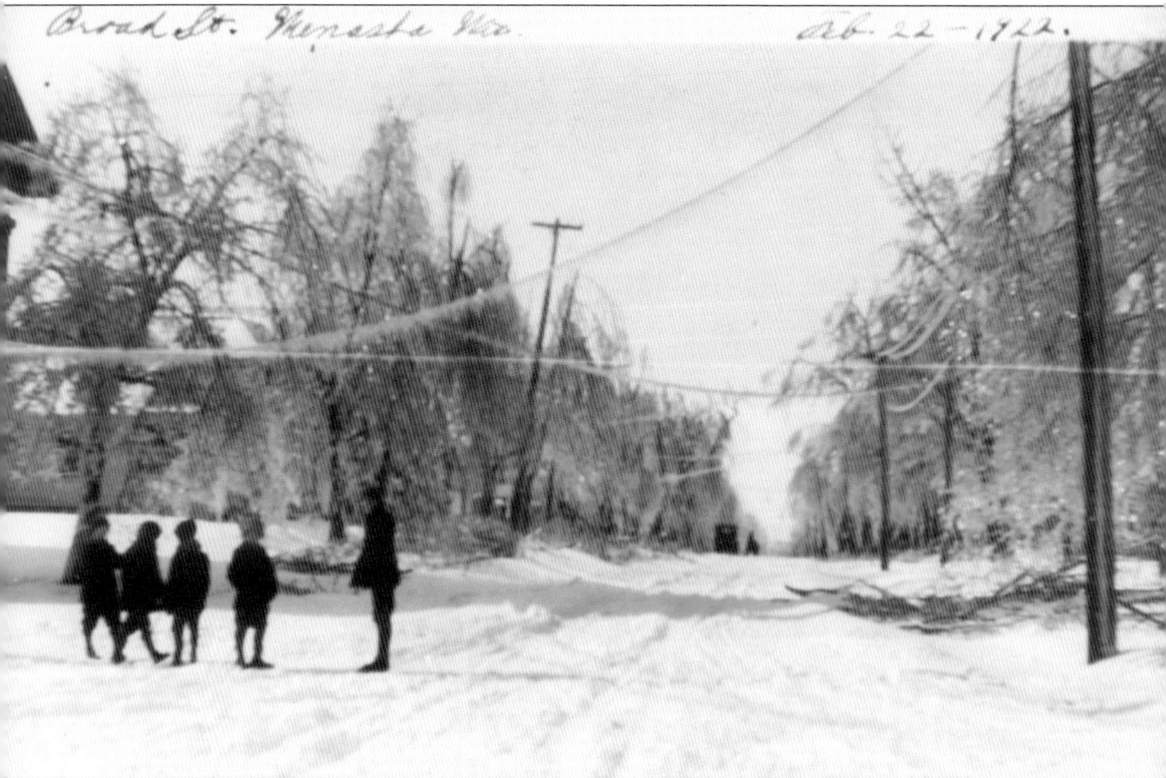

While the new real-photo postcards were most often used to take lasting images of homes, civic buildings, and businesses, occasionally they were used to document news events. Such is the case with this postcard. The February 1922 ice storm that hit the Twin Cities was particularly brutal, downing power lines and causing havoc that lasted for months. Arriving on Washington's Birthday that year, the storm started out as rain but quickly became a freezing sleet that coated everything in sight. While it was recalled in news reports as a particularly beautiful sight to behold, telephone and telegraph service was cut off as lines between Neenah and Oshkosh were snapped by the heavy weight of the ice. Train service was disrupted, not by ice on the tracks but due to the fact that no train orders could be communicated without telephone or telegraph.

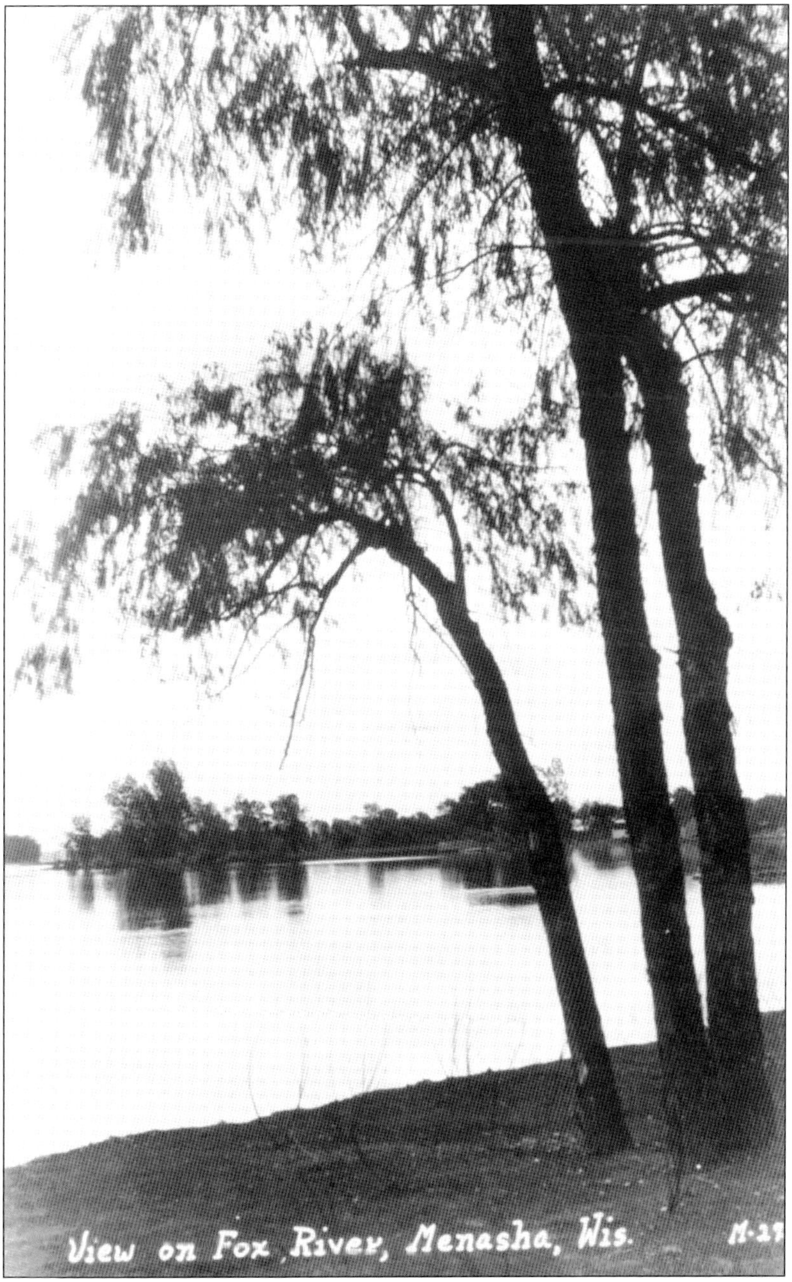

Framed by trees, this look across the Fox River is a dreamy, tranquil view of the lifeblood of Menasha's commerce. Picked as a choice location for settlement by the Menasha founders due to the waterpower the river provided for its mills and factories, the Fox was so named by the French. Explorers Louis Joliet and Jacques Marquette named it Rivière aux Renards ("River of the Foxes") because it went through the territory of the Meskwaki or Fox people, who were called Renards in French. For a time, the river was known as the Neenah, and it was only around 1850 or so that the name Fox became more universally recognized. Until the advent of railroads and improved overland routes, steamboats used to travel the river and into Lake Winnebago, taking passengers to High Cliff, Stockbridge, and even Oshkosh and Fond du Lac.

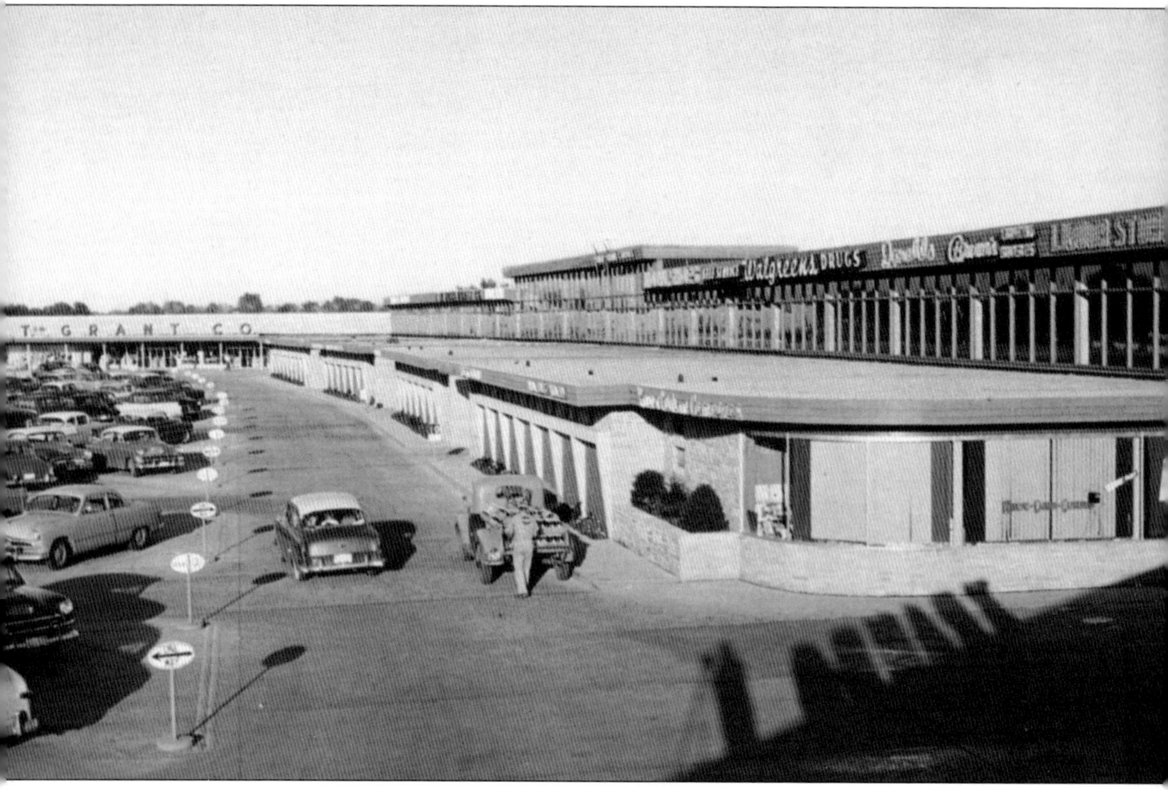

Valley Fair Shopping Center was billed as the first enclosed shopping mall in America. Built in 1954 between Menasha and Appleton on Wisconsin Highway 47, the center boasted 150,000 square feet of space for 33 stores, 5,000 square feet of air-conditioned office space on its second floor, and parking for 2,000 cars. Over the course of the next 40-plus years, the shopping center became a virtual town center for Fox Valley residents, hosting carnivals, farmer's markets, car shows, boat shows, beauty pageants, and other events to garner foot traffic. Until the early 1980s, when a mega shopping mall of over one million square feet was built on US 41 outside Appleton and heralded a long, painful decline, this center held sway on the shopping preferences of the 19 cities, villages, and towns constituting the Fox Valley.

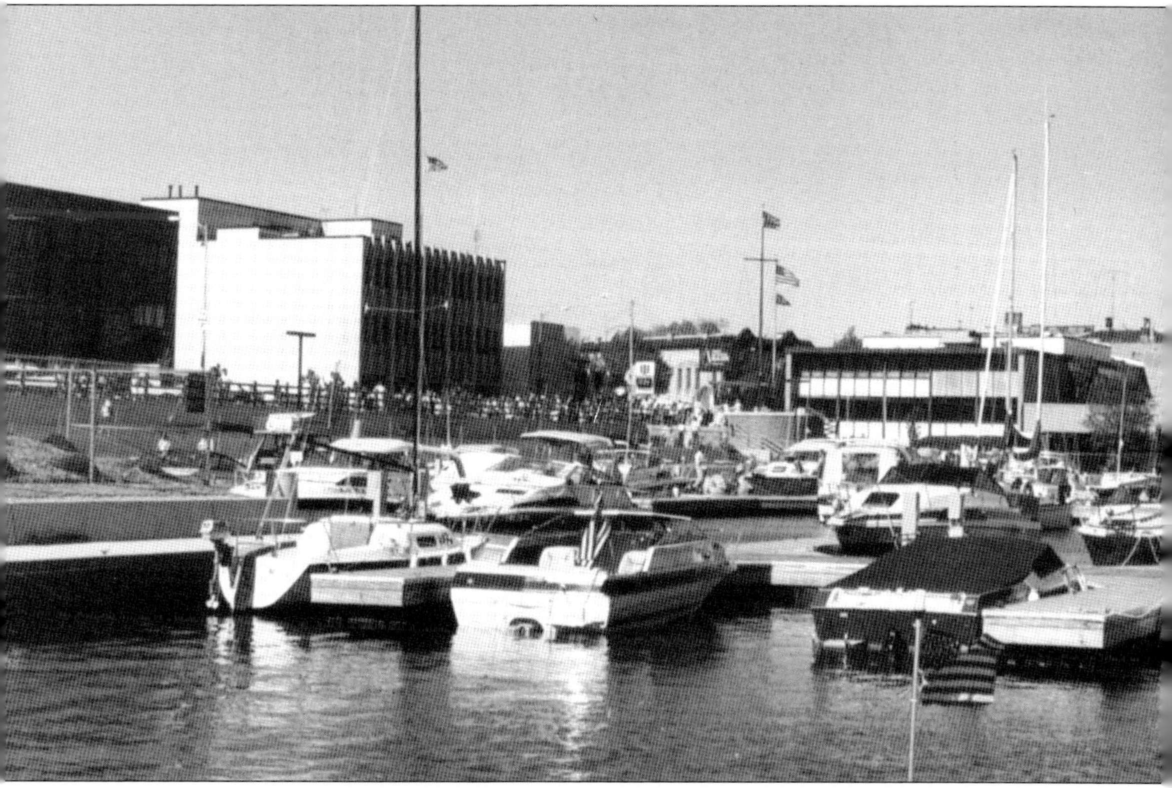

This marina in downtown Menasha opened in May 1987, the culmination of a two-phase, $7-million investment in renovating and revitalizing a stagnating downtown. The 87-slip marina was designed to be open from May 15 to October 15 each summer in conjunction with the traditional navigation season in the area. Upon the marina's completion, the community's focus went across the street to the north side of Main Street, where a three-story office building was to be constructed to house Twin City Savings and Loan. The old Twin City Savings building was then to be converted to the new Menasha City Hall. A sad note with this revitalization was the planned removal of the old city hall, which also originally housed the fire department and dated to 1885. Plans to convert the facility into a restaurant or bar were thwarted with a $400,000 price tag to bring the building up to code. At the time of its demolition in 1988, it was the oldest city hall still standing in the Fox Valley.

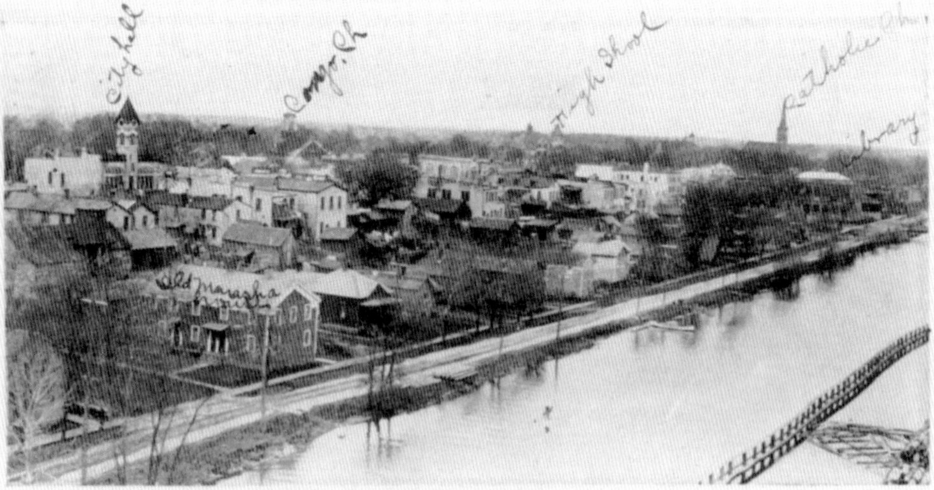

BIRD'S EYE VIEW OF MENASHA, WIS.

This wonderful panorama of Menasha's skyline dates to around 1907. Many civic landmarks have been thoughtfully pointed out by the writer, and one can only wish that the postcard printer had provided a larger photograph instead of the extensive ornate white border. Notice the city hall building, still with its bell tower. Eventually, the tower was deemed unsafe and removed. By 1917, the old city hall had become cramped, and the city purchased the old First National Bank building next to the Hotel Menasha for its offices. Also shown are other landmarks that have been discussed elsewhere in this book, including the Congregationalist church, the second version of Menasha High School, St. Mary's Catholic Church, and the Elisha D. Smith Public Library. One can also detect the Hotel Menasha and the Scott Building at the corner of Main and Milwaukee Streets.

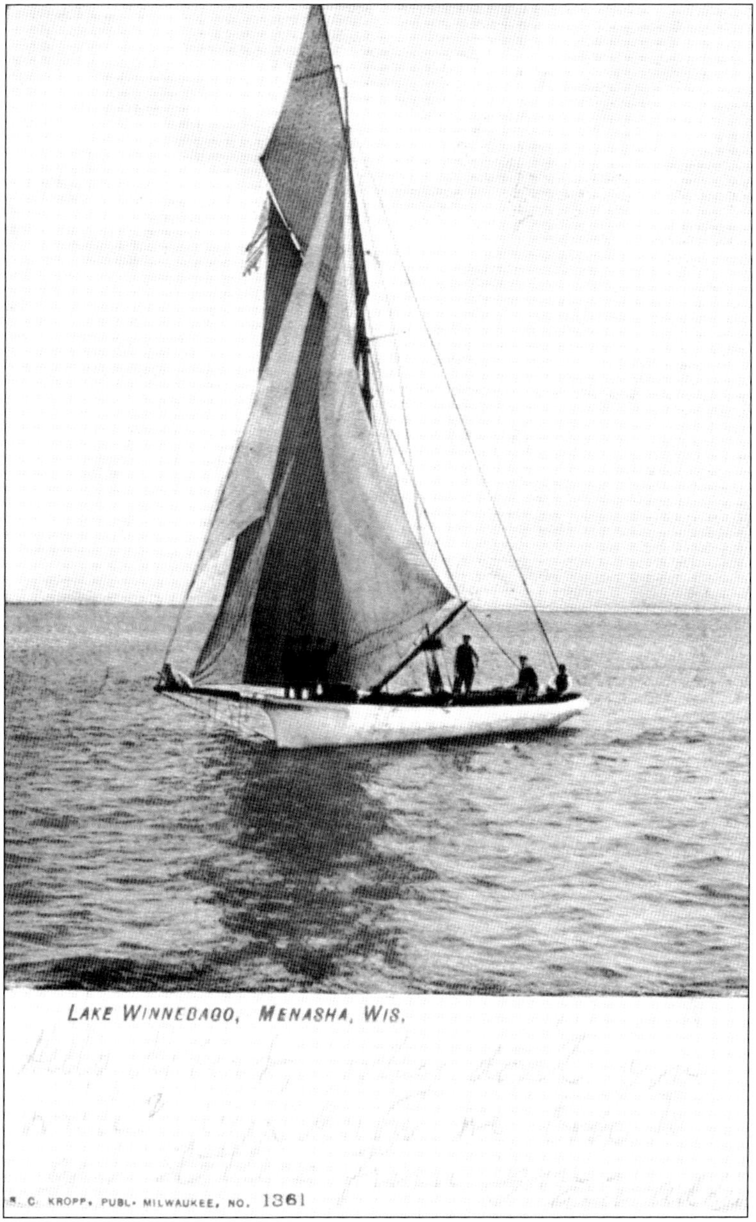

This appears to be another in a series of nondescript postcards that seem to boast of location and little else. Of course, this location, Lake Winnebago, is anything but mundane. And it is an understatement to say that the fortunes of Menasha were largely dictated by its geography and proximity to Lake Winnebago and the confluence of the Fox River. That much is true. This postcard could promote the area's recreation industry from a boating standpoint, but it does little to boast of the lake's propensity for tourism and recreation in the winter months, when ice fishing and spearfishing are common activities. In 1634, the French discovered the Winnebago tribe on the shores of Green Bay, inhabiting the area stretching to Lake Winnebago. Although Ho-Chunk is the people's own name for themselves, their Algonquian neighbors called them Winnebago, which means "people of the filthy water." This term was used by the Algonquians because Lake Winnebago had a strong fish odor in the summer.

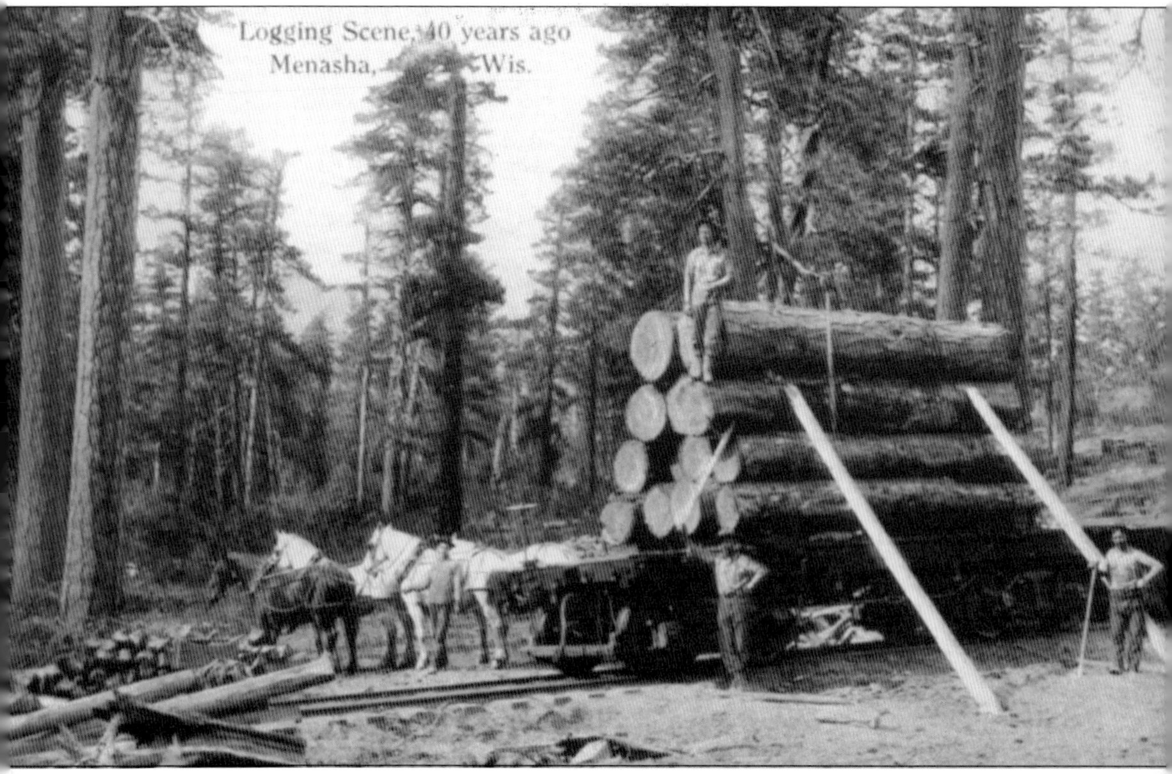

A logging scene from 40 years before on a picture postcard from the 1910s seems a curious choice for this card. Perhaps the printer had obtained rights to this photograph and wanted to use it. If indeed it was from the Menasha area, it was likely the area to the west of town, across Little Lake Butte des Morts, also known as the Hill of the Dead. The name was given by French settlers in reference to a nearby Indian burial mound. The story goes that in 1730, during the Fox Wars, French forces laid siege to the Indian village and massacred most of the inhabitants. The resultant burial ground gave its name to posterity for this lake and location. In recent years, the battle story has come under closer scrutiny. While it is recognized that a burial mound did indeed exist, its creation as the aftermath of an intense battle is now deemed doubtful.

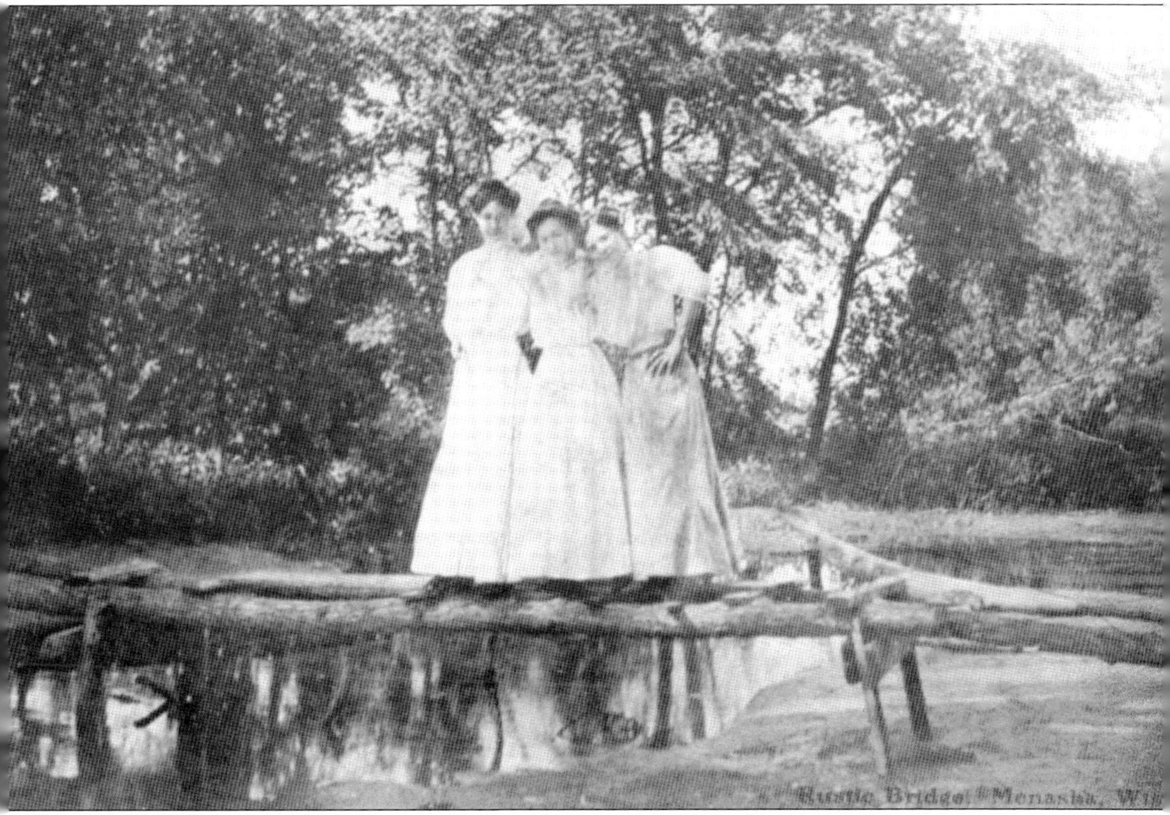

The title "Rustic Bridge" is quite appropriate for this postcard from 1908. It is somewhat reminiscent of the images for Brighton Beach that were featured in chapter one. The rickety pier used to get to the boats seems hardly less precarious than the bridge in this image. But of more interest to the collector is that the surrounding scenery is hand-painted, while the three ladies posing on the rickety bridge remain in black and white. The entire effect gives the look of what today would be termed a Photoshopped image—that the ladies were inserted after the fact. Whether or not this was the creator's intention is unknown, but it is suspected that this was an artistic decision rather than a practical one, in that the ladies' appearance is more defined in black and white than any colorization of the time could provide.

INDEX

Bibliography

Auer, James M. *Centennial Memories: A Brief History of Menasha, Wisconsin.* Menasha, WI: 1953.

Augustin, C.J. Semi-Centennial Souvenir Edition of the *Menasha Press.* Menasha, WI: Menasha Press, 1898.

Cunningham, Gustavus A. *History of Neenah, Illustrated.* Neenah, WI: Neenah Gazette Printing Establishment, 1878.

Glaab, Charles N. *Factories in the Valley: Neenah-Menasha, 1870–1915.* Madison, WI: State Historical Society of Wisconsin, 1969.

Goc, Michael J. Land. *Rich Enough: An Illustrated History of Oshkosh and Winnebago County.* Northridge, CA: Windsor Publications, 1988.

Harney, Richard J. *History of Winnebago County, Wisconsin, and Early History of the Northwest.* London, UK: British Library, Historical Print Editions, 1880, reprinted 2011.

Herziger, Caryl Chandler and Winifred Anderson Pawlowski. *Memories of Doty Island: A Link Between Two Cities.* Neenah, WI: self published, 1999.

Lawson, Publius Virgilius. *History, Winnebago County, Wisconsin: Its Cities, Towns, Resources, People.* Chicago, IL: C.F. Cooper and Company, 1908.

Metz, James. *Prairies, Pines, and People: Winnebago County in a New Perspective.* Oshkosh, WI: Oshkosh Northwestern Company, 1976.

Mitchell, D.C. *Steamboats on the Fox River: A Pictorial History of Navigation in Northeastern Wisconsin.* Oshkosh, WI: Castle-Pierce Press, 1986.

O'Regan, Suzanne Hart. *Ghosts in Sunlight: A Remembrance of Things Past.* Neenah, WI: Neenah Historical Society, 1985.

Smith, Alice. *Millstone and Saw: The Origins of Neenah-Menasha.* Madison, WI: Wisconsin Historical Society, 1967.

Shattuck, S.F., chairman, in collaboration with the Neenah Historical Society. *A History of Neenah.* Neenah, WI: privately published, 1958.

Smith, Mowry Jr. and Giles Clark. *One Third Crew, One Third Boat, One Third Luck: The Menasha Corporation Story, 1849–1974.* Neenah, WI: Menasha Corporation, 1974.